Bumbling into Body Hair:

A Transsexual's Memoir

By Everett Maroon

Booktrope Editions
Seattle WA
2012

Edited by Jennifer D. Munro

Cover Design by Kurtis Hough

ISBN 978-1-935961-33-8

DISCOUNTS OR CUSTOMIZED EDITIONS MAY BE AVAILABLE FOR
EDUCATIONAL AND OTHER GROUPS BASED ON BULK PURCHASE.

For further information please contact info@libertary.com

Library of Congress Control Number: 2012935200

Dedication

For Liam and Tyra

Acknowledgments

Many people have helped this project reach completion and I am sincerely grateful for all of their skills and assistance. These individuals include:

Sarah Martinez for pushing the manuscript in the right direction; Jennifer Munro for her excellent editing work and strangely compatible sense of humor; Ken Shear at Booktrope for being as excited about this project as I am.

I'm proud and honored to have worked with Lea Mesner as a writing coach for several years now. Her sage advice and ability to encourage have been priceless. I also can't thank Robyn Zeiger enough for her counsel and support; people like her make all the difference.

Many thanks go to my close friends who read early versions of the manuscript, helped me recollect specific events, and were willing to read about themselves without wincing, especially Lori Solomon, Barbara Wally, and Michael Driscoll. I'm also thrilled to share this book with my mother, sisters Kathy and Jayne, and brother David, who all had to transition with me and who love me very well.

Finally I have to thank Susanne Beechey, my partner, for her tremendous support, enthusiasm, intelligence, and baked goods, and our son, Emile, who I hope finds an open-minded world as he grows up.

Author's Note:

As a memoir, this book offers my memories and perspective on my experiences. Some names have been changed out of respect to people who were involved. This part of my life story is as true as I could write it, and others are free to disagree. The purpose is to share what I went through and what I've learned and to entertain, and that's what I've done my best to do.

Prologue

As it turns out, cellophane is not capable of erasing a D-cup bosom or acting like a protective wall against the emergence of breasts. Instead of the Hoover Dam on my chest, it appears I am only capable of turning myself into a modern, transparent mummy.

Bras have become a nuisance and I'm not going to spend any more time or money on them than necessary. Mine all look ratty and threadbare, strips of once-white satin that lose their shape the moment I unsecure them. And I have a thing against underwires, having been stabbed by them on so many occasions that I have a callous on my left side. Why only the left side, I'm not sure. Maybe it's the way I point my feet as I walk. Perhaps my left side is more jiggly. But the wireless bras all have the habit of turning into a knotted mess requiring a field manual to reorient for future use. I've accidentally worn them inside-out more often than I'd care to acknowledge.

This is a mistake, I think.

I open up the package of cellophane, hopeful, taking care not to cut myself on the serrated edge. Taking the tube out of the box, I attempt to find the end of the plastic. This is more difficult than it seems, not only because all of the material is transparent and thus nearly invisible to the naked eye, but because it insists on re-clinging to the roll in the three nanoseconds between me peeling it away and trying to get my fingers under the plastic. To start my day off with this on a regular basis is not sustainable, but I presume I'd gain some kind of expertise and it would get easier. Such a skill, however, isn't the kind of thing that one should list on one's **resumé**. "Effective at peeling off cling wrap" just seems creepy.

From their corner of the bedroom, the place where I've made this foray into futility, my two cats watch me in what is either indifference or amusement, refusing to give anything away in their expressions. An infomercial plays on the television in the next room.

I hold down the plastic with one hand and pull the roll around to my back, where I attempt to switch which hand has the end and which is doing the unrolling. This would be simpler if I'd been born a Hindu goddess with six arms. I make one full pass, slicing open a couple of fingers in the process, before tossing the cardboard box altogether. Free from danger, I realize now that my breasts are smashed in completely odd and uncomfortable positions; I look like alien beings are about to burst out of random spots on my chest.

I fiddle a hand under the plastic and attempt to reorient the mounds. Apparently breasts have minds of their own—not a collective mind between them, but two individual sets of intentions and preferences. No sooner do I move my right side to a mashed location that minimizes its bulge than it squirts back to the middle of my chest facing the setting sun. The left side is no more cooperative. I look at the quantity of plastic I've just used in attempting to smooth everything out and acknowledge that if I can't reuse the wrap every day, I will quickly start running up an expensive habit. I don't want breast binding to be like illicit drug use destroying my finances. My skin starts turning bright red from the heat, and my diaphragm is trapped and unhappy, stunting my lungs' expansion ability. Binding doesn't seem to be worth looking like a guilty murderer who also stinks.

I notice the stench of fresh plastic and take stock of my situation. Now that I've wrapped myself in a roll of cellophane, my fingers are bleeding from the razor strip on the box, while sweat oozes out of my temples and armpits. On the floor next to my feet is the disfigured bra I removed to begin this experiment.

Perhaps people learn better when they're in pain. I briefly consider attempting a quick education in quantum physics while my hand still throbs, but getting to a reference book would entail forward momentum. With my torso unable to take in enough air for walking, that seems overly challenging.

This is one of those moments that I just didn't foresee when I lifted my head off the pillow this morning. And it is becoming clear that trying to crush my breasts under eighteen layers of cling wrap won't serve me well. Time to go for Plan B. Before I can come up with a new idea, self-doubt rushes into the void and I tell myself for the umpteenth time that this is all crazy. I might not be a feminine rose, but I'm not a man, either. I peel off the plastic, trying to line up the edges with the rest of the roll in the hopes that I can fit it back into the box and reuse it. Little bits of hair and dust show through the layers, a cheap and messy time capsule of nothing interesting, so I decide that recycling this is yet another poor decision. I don't think I'll ever have a need for wrinkled, sweated-on plastic.

Chapter 1

I couldn't get the images out of my head. I'd woken up from a dream in midsummer, 2003 that seemed to have a mind of its own, and obviously it had decided that inhabiting my thoughts was the way to go. I'd written down as much of it as I could remember, startled by how vivid and real everything had seemed. It went well beyond what my other notable dreams had felt like. It was tangible enough that I woke up with the smells from the narrative caught in my nostrils. I was a camp counselor making breakfast for the PTA in the off season, somewhere in the forest of eastern Pennsylvania. I also scribbled out a picture of my face from the dream. I wasn't just a counselor, I was a male counselor, looking burly and at home in the outdoors, none of which was true in real life. I looked at the drawing, which not only didn't look like my face, but also didn't look human because I wasn't an artist. But I supposed it only had to make sense to me.

Although there were whole industries and 900-number services dedicated to interpreting dream imagery, I felt narcissistic thinking about it this much. And yet here I was, thinking and thinking about it. Better putting it on paper, I thought, than talking about it in a coffee house for people to hear. One clear message from the dream, obviously, was that I had spent too many summers at camp. I did recall that camp mess hall dishwashers are a pain in the ass to figure out, although they are preferable to the alternative, which in my personal experience amounted to sitting in the freezing cold of a clearing, next to the back of the mess, burning my hands off in 130-degree water and some ammonia concoction that peeled off four layers of skin just to get the half-broken plastic dishes clean. Hot hands, cold ass, singed nose hair, and the stench of grease from last night's Breaded Meat Surprise. It was a wonder that hadn't made it into the dream. There could have been some real carnage in a tale about defenseless children at camp and a massive, evil, breaded liver on a rampage.

The dream was about being a man instead of a woman, and not about dishwashers, I got that much. It wasn't any more or less odd than if I were a racing turtle. I wouldn't wake up after dreaming about slowly thumping my way around a racing track and feel the need to give it much thought. So there was no need to go fretting about what this meant for my life. But I spent many spare minutes reflecting on it and "the face," and realized that it was following me around and needed to be released somehow, or it would continue to be my unwanted constant companion.

"So I had this dream the other night," I said one day to my friend, Patricia. Well, she was kind of my girlfriend, kind of my friend with benefits. From time to time we even used the word "partner," but since Patricia was cohabitating with another woman, I thought partner was a bit of an overstatement and had said as much.

"Yeah," she said, prompting me to go on but with disinterest.

"I dreamed I was a camp counselor. A male counselor."

"Uh, huh," she said, intent on her Sudoku puzzle. Five seconds elapsed. She looked up and brushed her dark bangs away from her eyes.

"Wait a minute, are you saying you're transgender now?"

I wasn't ready for her question. I knew she had questions about her own identity, wondering if she should go by a male name or start hormones. I hadn't thought about how someone else would interpret my dream.

"Uh, no. I mean, not necessarily. I mean, I just keep thinking about it."

"Jesus Christ, I knew this was going to happen."

"I'm not following you," I said.

"I just knew this would happen. You're all insistent—'no, no, I'm a butch,' and then wham, it's all, 'I lied! I'm a guy!' You know I have my own gender shit. Why are you doing this to me?"

"It's just a dream. I'm not saying it means anything. I was wondering what you thought about it."

"I'm just saying," she went on, frowning at the puzzle, "that you've told me you're a butch woman. If you want to go back on that and your community, I think that's fucked up."

I didn't ask why she got to split from the butch community with impunity. My dream hadn't even been an actual experience.

"I didn't sign a contract for masculine women. It was just a freaking dream."

And with that, I decided not to talk to her anymore about the transgender thing.

*   *   *

Resigning myself not to discuss the issue did not mean, however, that the issue went away. I looked differently at my face in the mirror. It was a woman's face, clearly, with an angled chin, feminine brow, and full, girly lips. That was the end of it, though. Since 1992 I had sported a short cut, first in an attempt to look like k.d. lang, and later, a simple short-on-the-sides, longer-on-the-top look that I deluded myself into calling my own.

All the staring was obsessive, I knew, but I couldn't stop myself from imagining how my jaw might look more squared, if I had a goatee, or if I had bigger hands. Reality did present itself—knowing how my Lebanese father had looked as an adult, I was probably resigned to a life of unabated hairiness with a nose the size of Alabama. It wasn't just the men in my family who have big schnozzes. My aunt Marie had such big nostrils she could have picked her nose with two fingers at a time. Perhaps it was only a matter of time before I could dock ships in my face.

Big nose, blocky jaw, fuzzy eyebrows, male pattern baldness— this didn't sound like the way towards everlasting beauty. Camp counselor dream aside, what was it I wanted?

It would take a while to answer that question. First I wanted to investigate why anyone else would go through the total chaos of a sex change, turning their world upside down. It would have to wait, though, as life was busy and the big Dyke March in DC was around the corner.

Chapter 2

Within the confines of the District there is a movement to climate-control everything not exposed to the swamp-sour air. And so it was that I sat in my freezing office, after having left my freezing car, which I'd done after venturing out from my freezing house. If asked at the time, I would have wished the tunnels under Capitol Hill were threaded under the entire metro area so I wouldn't have had to venture outside, like, ever. Talk of putting up a biosphere around the city in the summer months was a topic of semi-serious conversation at many a cocktail hour.

I'd agreed to help marshal the annual dyke march. It was held a few hours before every gay pride parade, which many hipster lesbians decreed was over-sponsored, not political enough, and way too male-oriented. Personally, I liked the dancing gay cowboys, but I agreed that the lesbians needed a moment in the sun, which in June in DC, was plentiful if not crushing. I'd marshaled the march before, and the organizers were always looking for people as tall as my five-foot, nine-inch height because it gave the event more of the intimidating presence a dyke march supposedly commanded. It's hard to be out, loud, and proud when everyone with a bullhorn looks like part of the Lollypop Guild. As defined in DC, dyke was an open category — maybe they were a lesbian last year and questioning their gender this year. Maybe they identify as a lesbian and a gay man on alternating days. Maybe they're on a slow transition to Some Other Gender.

But all shades were welcome, unlike in New York, for example, where only people still woman-loving-woman-identified were allowed to march, and everyone else was relegated to cheering from the sidewalk. I had started pondering where I was in all of it. I was a something in a fog of gender. All I had to do, though, was stomp down the streets of DC and shout out things like, "Two, four, six, eight, how do you know your daughter's straight?" Quite the poets, we were. I had my duty to do: yell into a bullhorn toward the end of the line and teach the newest marchers how to eat fire. I did not need to focus on who I was at that moment, I told myself.

To get into the defiant mood of the march I decided to go to my neighborhood's swanky salon for some red highlights. I passed the next three hours in one salon chair after another, sipping a chilled chardonnay. Finally I slipped out from under the hair drying bowl and took a gander in the mirror. I had a gazillion tiny blonde highlights, looking like little cheetah spots all over my head. Reversed cheetah spots, at that.

"Uh—" was all I could manage.

"You look fantastic," exclaimed the woman who was about to charge me ninety dollars.

"You're uh, you're kidding, right?" I put my glasses on and scoured my hair for any hint of red.

A tight-lipped manager walked over, noticing my displeasure. "And how are we doing, madam?" While her tone was friendly enough, her lips didn't crack the latitude of the equator.

"I wanted red highlights."

"Your hair is brown."

"I know what color my hair is," I said, putting down my wine glass and straightening up. Maybe they thought that by intoxicating the clientele, they could get away with fashion murder. "If you couldn't give me red highlights, why did I sit here all afternoon?" The manager looked at the stylist in a non-verbal attempt to ask how she could rectify the situation.

"We're closing in fifteen minutes," she said to the manager, shrugging her shoulders.

"I have somewhere to be tomorrow. I can't go there looking like this." If they put me at the lead of the march, at least I'd be easy to follow.

"Okay, we'll do a quick dye to fill in the lightened areas."

I didn't argue with her. After all, hadn't that been what they were attempting to do all along?

Another half an hour later, I left the salon with some free color-retaining shampoo and conditioner. In the dusk, I couldn't really tell what my hair color was anymore, though I was pretty sure the blonde had been obliterated. How bad could it be?

I got my answer the next morning as I left my apartment to get a bagel. A small man walked up to me, looking lost, which was something of a common occurrence given that the roads in Arlington, Virginia were winding and repetitious—28th Street South, 28th Road South, North 28th Street—it was a better defense against the red-coated British than Pierre L'Enfant's District street design, although less intentionally so. I walked to my car, and he walked up to me.

"Perdón, dónde está la tienda de comestibles?" He was talking to me.

"Um, I'm sorry, I don't speak Spanish." He immediately looked surprised, then disappointed.

"Sorry," he said, walking away, looking for another human with a better shot of knowing what he needed.

I drove up to the bagel store and was confronted with Spanish once again. This time the woman behind the counter noticed I didn't understand her before I responded.

"I'm sorry, ma'am, I thought you were *Latina.*" When I continued to look confused, she added, "It's your hair."

"Say what?"

"You look like Señora Moreno, from *Los Ricos También Lloran.* Sorry."

Not knowing what she was talking about, I stammered through my bagel order and rushed back to the car to check myself out in the vanity mirror. There I finally put it together—they hadn't dyed just the blonde spots, they had dyed all of my hair red, so it had taken on an overall plum shade with brighter red highlights. Back at home, I looked up her reference. So I looked like an old woman on a Telemundo soap opera. That would go over great at the march.

I grabbed a baseball cap on my way out the door. I could get away with wearing it for the next six weeks, sure. Okay, maybe not at work. But it was the only plan I had.

* * *

At least I had my hair dye debacle to thank for wearing a hat that day. As the sun beat down on the city, the stench of urine, car exhaust, and Tidal Basin funk wafted up from the sewers and asphalt of Connecticut Avenue. It gets a little hard to chant about the advantages of gayness when one is suffocating. Tourists saw us and appeared to wonder openly what the fuss was about—300 young to middle-aged, angry-looking, masculine, man-eating lesbians were walking down the street coughing, sweating and chanting. What wasn't to admire?

We rounded the corner, the stream of lesbians chanting ahead of me to the beat of my call. I began to wonder just how long this parade route was, because we were looping around much more than the year before. I couldn't put down my bullhorn and pony up at one of DuPont Circle's taverns to grab a beer. Suddenly a new sensation distracted me—in addition to the heat, the stench, and my fatigued feet—my head was on fire. The vat of chemicals in my hair was activated by my now sweaty scalp. I put my hand to my temple and pulled it back. Yes, the dye was dripping down my face. So now I looked like an angry, masculine, man-eating lesbian who sweat blood. Perfect.

I held the bullhorn in one hand and attempted to wipe my brow with the other before the toxin could reach my eyes. Better the day should be awful than unbearable.

In the midst of shouting, marching, and wiping, I heard someone call out to me. We were toward the end of the parade, which I knew only because marchers had started dropping to the ground like lemmings that couldn't quite reach the sea. I walked up to the DuPont Circle fountain, turning to the voice. It was a young transgender guy—a woman who had transitioned to a man.

"Hey, you," he said, jogging up to me looking perfect, every short hair in place. His clothes didn't look limp or greasy like mine did.

"Aric, how are you?" I greeted him.

"Great. I just wanted to say nice bullhorning. Is that a verb?" He laughed at himself. He was so attractive, with sturdy cheekbones and a chiseled jawline. He looked not only like he was always meant to be male, but that he'd moved the heavens to make it happen.

"It is now."

"So I didn't recognize you for like, half the march. I was wondering, are you GQ?"

GQ. Short form of genderqueer, describing people who didn't identify as male or female but as something that messed with gender itself. There were 2,381 permutations of what that could look like, or so I'd heard.

I worried if I said yes, a Greek chorus would suddenly spring out of the concrete and laugh along with Aric at my ineptitude. My hand wandered to my forehead to make sure I didn't look like a boiled beet. I said the first thing that came to mind.

"Yes, I am Gentlemen's Quarterly." I gave him a big, winning smile.

He shook his head and smiled. "You're so cool. Great to see you! You coming out later tonight?" He leaned in and hugged me as he said this. He must have had our representative amounts of appeal mixed up, because I should have been the one falling over him.

"Coming out, yes, I think so!" *But not the no-more-closeted kind of coming out, Aric,* I thought. *I just don't know if I'll ever have your confidence.*

*   *   *

My legs managed to carry me into my apartment, but after the three-mile march and two flights of stairs, that was about it for the quads and hamstrings brigade, and I flopped down on the couch. There were a lot of images vying for my mind's attention—the march itself, the chants from which I now could not escape, the confused tourists wondering what they were witnessing, and the people at the rally cheering through their sunburns.

My cats sauntered over to me, happy for the Twentieth Century technological miracle of working air conditioning. They continued to avoid getting too close to the smell of dyed hair, hanging out in the corners of the living room. I'd had a good time, sure, but I also had been very preoccupied by how I looked to everyone, and by how clearly female I was, despite what Aric had said. It had cut into my enjoyment of the day, as had my on-again-off-again girlfriend, who had barked orders at me all march long, telling me I was walking too quickly, not chanting loudly enough, and not shepherding weary lesbians to the rally point efficiently enough.

Overall, I was beginning to suspect I should be happier than this.

I needed to know more about this gender stuff, that much was clear. I sat down at my computer and started searching for anything related to sex changes, transitioning, transsexuals, and the like. Porn sites leaped out at me, and it took me a good five minutes to shut down all of the pop-up windows and get back to searching. Discussion boards, email lists, online journal groups—I lurked, reading them without signaling to anyone that I was there. This had the disadvantage of limiting me to whatever discussion was already going on, and I realized that across all of these websites, people were asking and answering the same basic five or six topics about changing gender. Didn't anyone know how to look back three discussions earlier? Ask something new! Ask what I wanted to know about! The discussions were all about:

- How to bind down one's breasts
- How to talk like the opposite gender, which involved the totally unexpected practice of raising or lowering one's voice
- How to walk like a man, which shockingly enough, had nothing to do with the song by Frankie Valli, and
- What happens before, during, and after surgery, which I skipped, assuming it was at least 12,763 steps and three years ahead of where I was.

Plus it seemed that no one agreed on surgery details, anyway.

Although I wasn't in control of the direction of the conversations, the good thing about reading them was that I learned some of the vernacular. Nobody referred to their breasts as such; they were "chesties," "mumps" — short for man-lumps and unrelated to the childhood disease of the same name — or "moobs," short for "man-boobs." It wasn't a vagina, it was a front hole, junk, bonus hole — two for the price of one, kids, get 'em while they last! — or the shocking and nasty, "cockpit." Perhaps I would never experience air travel the same way again.

I understood why there were so many euphemisms instead of clinical names and why they were so often negative. These were the parts that were hard to talk about without a lot of hurt feelings. Even if I could see that there was more to being a man than having an actual penis, my own girl parts were a constant reminder that my brain and body weren't happy with each other. And if nothing else, cockpit sounded worlds more manly than vagina. Maybe I could hate my woman parts enough to only call it by another name, like Voldemort, but I wasn't sure I needed to avoid it in that way.

More surprising than the names was how similar my experience was to what others were describing on the boards. I continued to read in silence, but I knew the day would likely come that I would have to ask my own questions because I hadn't found the answers anywhere else. I knew I couldn't ask Pat, as he was now being called. He'd already told others about my dream—what little of it he had heard—and it had gotten back to me that he and his friends had had a good laugh at my expense. It was territory I was not allowed to tread, apparently. So I had a plan. I would make up an identity online and explore this world without his knowledge. Surely that would be the safe way to go.

* * *

There had been a time when I moved through the world not wondering about grandiose ideas like identity or fulfillment and measuring the difference between myself and others.

Not every eight-year-old girl greatly enjoys dressing up in her father's suit jacket and tie to act out the plot of *Copacabana* with her same-age friend and younger brother. Always, I played Tony. I was not interested in Lola, and frankly, Rico didn't have much of a role, coming in at the end of the song to shoot Tony. I wasn't villain material, anyway. Beth would put on her best dress—a purple and black floral print that looked a lot like the Easter dress my mother had made for me, but, as Beth was Jewish, it must have been for some other occasion. It was great to have Jewish friends—they had Jewish guilt, and I had Catholic shame, and those went really well together, the jam and toast of religion-inspired dysfunction. Plus, she taught me how to play the Dreidel game and I taught her how to dye eggs. We decided eggs won, hands down, in terms of fun, and that playing for pennies was too 1950s for us. I'm not sure why we picked the 1950s except that it had the distinct impression of being "old," meaning our exposure to it was always in black and white, and we had new color televisions at home, making us modern girls who looked down on the things that our parents had enjoyed.

So Beth would load up the two-album set *Best of Barry Manilow* on her parents' stereo and then jump the needle to the start of the song, which now is old school music shuffling. While she did this I would hang out behind the rec room bar getting into character. Being eight, I thought "rec" was actually "wreck," meaning that it was free and clear for us children to leave it looking like a tornado had hit, to use my mother's language. Years later I would see actual tornado footage and be somewhat irritated that Mom had so overstated the messes we'd left behind.

At first I didn't know how to tie the necktie, so I asked my father. If he thought it was a strange request, he didn't show it. But I practiced several hundred times with an old tie of his until I could get it right nearly every time. Beth would start the music and I'd grab a dry dishrag. That's what I thought bartenders did, after all. They wiped the bar, tending it, as it were. Her brother Adam would toddle in partway through the number, at the top of his verse, as Beth was dancing à la Lola, and then we were grappling. It was somewhat humiliating to be bested by a four-year-old during every performance, especially since I was totally holding back from putting my real strength into the struggle, but there was no other way to achieve musical martyrdom. Then Beth would rush over to me, scoop me up, and pretend to cry. I didn't inquire too much into why we performed this song for nobody, over and over again. I just liked being the affable barkeep and pretending to be in love with a pretty girl. And I made sure to get home before my parents did so that I could change back out of my father's clothes and into my own after-school playwear. It was one thing to come home dirty from climbing trees and a game of street hockey, but it was quite another to look like I'd stepped out of *Esquire for Girls*.

For years, after having such fun with the reenactment of this particular tragedy, I would associate tying a half-Windsor with Havana, Cuba.

*   *   *

My office got busy in early autumn, and I didn't have time to think about much beyond work, paying my bills, and feeding my cats. I barreled through the months leading up to the holidays with a complete lack of introspection but a whole lot of stress. I knew that I couldn't continue this way forever, but with the end point of "forever" being so endlessly far away, I wasn't going to consider the consequences of working so hard for so long. On autopilot straight through to the spring, my body was overtaxed, finally devising another plan for me, and suddenly, forever was today.

It started as a weird jolty pain on my left side, slightly above where my elbow would hit my body if I pressed my arm to my side. I thought I'd cut myself, and being prone to accidents, I figured if I wasn't light-headed from blood loss, I was fine. I put my hand to my torso, felt nothing, and carried on, firing off email messages from work. The stabbing persisted. I shut my office door and pulled my shirt out of my pants. A bright red, scaly, and square-shaped patch of rash had taken up residence, looking nothing like my regular skin.

I couldn't recall when I'd done such a thing in the last three days. Scorching myself with a garment steamer, dripping hot grease from a fresh pizza on myself, an unfortunate encounter with lighter fluid—none of those things had occurred recently. I tucked my shirt back in and went to the next office to ask my coworker what she thought it was. We had that level of intimacy, I suppose. She was everyone's unofficial Jewish mother.

"Shingles, definitely," she said to it, as if the spot itself had asked to be identified.

"What? But isn't that what old people get?"

"Well, how old are you?" she asked.

"Not that old! Thirty-four is too young for SHINGLES." I said it like we'd just discovered I had testicular cancer.

"Well, you should go to urgent care and get it checked out. My mother had shingles and she said it felt like someone had put a hot iron on her."

"It's shingles," said the doctor, straightening up. "I'll give you a prescription for Valtrex."

"What's that?" I asked.

"It's an anti-viral. We give them to people with herpes."

"But I don't have herpes."

"Shingles are in the same family." He was not reassuring me here.

"You're saying I have herpes on my chest?"

"No, no, you have shingles. Just get this filled today and keep taking them until the bottle is gone."

I had visions of the pharmacist handing me the pills in a hazmat suit, telling everyone to stand back while he gave me the meds for my social disease.

The pills at first did nothing to make the hot poker mark feel any better. But I took them, failed even by my own psyche that I wasn't getting the benefit of a placebo effect. A few days later, the Angry Red Blob Which Shall Not Be Named had disappeared, almost as suddenly as it had appeared.

*   *   *

During my outbreak, I spent a copious number of hours searching online for anything related to shingles. On the symptoms front I lucked out—there were people out there who looked like they'd had a long-term sexual relationship with a poison ivy plant. So my little hidden area of distress was no big deal. I was struck, however, at the related conditions and causes, which included high stress levels and depression. Fifty hours at work each week, I knew I had stress. I didn't need the National Institutes of Health to tell me that.

As if I needed more evidence, the phone rang. It was my primary care doctor. Dr. Min always made me smile, mostly because she had really crappy short-term memory and because she'd told me she owned more shoes than Imelda Marcos. My first appointment with her years earlier had included the usual medical history inquiry.

"So, what kind of birth control are you using?" she had asked, not looking up from her clipboard.

"I'm not using any birth control." As far as I knew, no pregnancies had resulted from girl-on-girl action.

"Oh, so you're not sexually active?" Why did medical school give people authorization to be rude?

"No, I'm sexually active."

Then she looked up. "But you're not using any birth control?"

"I'm gay," I said, simply.

"Oh," she said, simply. She made some sort of note on the form, which I imagined amounted to *unabashed homosexual* or its equivalent.

Fast forward to my second visit. Granted, this was a year later, my next physical. I didn't expect her to actually remember me in the midst of seeing the 13,854 other patients she needed to counsel to make her malpractice insurance payments.

"Okay, what kind of birth control are you using?"

Really?

"I don't need birth control," I said, sighing. A whole year had passed but I was still annoyed.

"Are you trying to get pregnant?" That clipboard sure got a lot of eye contact from her.

"Nope. Just having sex for fun."

"Uh," she said, wondering why she hadn't noted in my chart last year that I was a crazy person.

"I'm gay. I'm not having sex with men."

"Oh, okay, gotcha."

I twisted my ankle about eight months later; four days after my bad football tackle, I was still having trouble walking, so I made an appointment to see Dr. Min. She had her routine questions for me.

"Birth control? What are you using?" Jesus, this woman needed a much, much better patient history software system.

"Homosexuality. I'm using homosexuality. Works well, I might add."

"Oh." She seemed confused as to why I might answer in this way.

"How about you just write that on the top of my chart there? Do you have a red pen?"

She never asked me again.

Today she was calling with the results from my blood tests, which had been forwarded to her from the urgent care clinic. She wasn't the kind of doctor to call unless there was a problem. Ergo, there was a problem.

"What's up, doc?" I asked.

"You have a weak positive for mono. Have you been sick lately?"

My mind flashed back to me in bed at the end of December, flushed with sweat, too weak to pick up a gallon of milk, and begging for my death from any passersby who could hear me from the street two floors below.

"Yeah, I think so. About three months ago. I thought it was the flu."

"That would be about right. So you had mono, and now you have herpes zoster."

Would these people please stop talking about herpes? She was continuing to talk, despite my sudden bout of anger, saying, "Your immune system is weak right now, and you need to take it easy."

Taking it easy seemed like an impossible task. I was up to my ears at work, I was kind of breaking up, kind of not with Pat, and I was getting ready to move to a new apartment, since my landlord was selling the old one out from under me. I didn't know where to begin on the taking it easy front.

"Okay, is there anything else, doc?"

"No, that's it. I just want you to watch your stress level. Young people like you are not supposed to get shingles."

"So I've been told. Okay, thanks for calling."

Then it hit me that I should probably get a therapist.

Chapter 3

I needed to take control before things totally slip-slid away from me. Someone to talk to who wouldn't give a fig who I thought I was. A therapist sounded like a top priority, so I picked up an always-gratis-because-it-sucks copy of the gay paper and thumbed through the classifieds. I stayed away from reading the back section of the gay paper because many of the ads tended toward the embarrassing overshare. In addition to an unfortunate cat-sitting opportunity for a woman trying to tame a feral animal, there were:

- Ads for modeling—I'm sure a full-figured lesbian-maybe-transsexual was exactly what they had in mind
- Reading books to the blind—I'd find it too irresistible to start making things up
- Suicide-prevention phone line support—too stressful, since I needed jobs with a less disastrous margin of error

I flipped past the help wanted section and found a small ad for a licensed counselor. The ad was straight out of the early Seventies/Ms. Magazine/Women Can Make Money, Too movement, with the silhouette of two women leaning on each other for support. It looked kind of like the flashy reclining woman figure on the backs of many an eighteen-wheeler truck, only it was more lesbian because there were two of them, together, backs touching seductively as only outline figures can. It made me wonder why the truckers didn't go for this logo, since didn't straight men love the idea of two women in bed together?

I paused from my philosophizing and got back to the ad. I stored the number in my cell phone memory, figuring I'd call later. But I was ready for later to morph quickly into sooner.

Wanting to prepare for the moment I met the therapist, I went online again to the now-familiar websites where people talked about transitioning from one sex to the other. I had lurked a lot, mostly not commenting, unless it was about something I'd personally experienced, like taking too hard a gulp of soda and feeling like my esophagus would burst. To leave such illuminations of self on the discussion board I had finally made a handle for myself—the charming name of "fatboi"—a couple of weeks earlier, selecting something with the utmost care one can provide in five minutes.

—*Does anyone have any recommendations for therapists in DC?* I inquired.

Twenty minutes later, I had a list of three people to call. One response in particular caught my eye, but not because of the contact information for the counselor. It interested me because it ended with a question.

—*Hope that helps. So I've seen you around these parts for a little while now. Do you have a name?*

Crap. No, I didn't really have a name, not a boy name, anyway. I didn't have to actually answer this question, right? It was just a series of glowing lights on a screen. Can't a person ask intimate questions online without having developed a long back story to their persona and inventing a name? I stared at the screen, confused. I did not have a name. How could I not have a name?

Really, how could I have one? That would have meant that I had moved out of observing others and jumped into the pool myself. Come to think of it, perhaps I was already splashing around in the deep end.

I didn't know where to begin. Who gets to pick their own name, after all? And then it occurred to me that I knew lots of people who didn't go by their birth names because they couldn't bear Henrietta or Sally or Harold. They just told people to call them something else and, en masse, people did just that. They weren't also telling them to use new pronouns as part of a whole sex change thing, but it was possible for people to buck what their parents had bestowed upon them.

I knew, at least, that I liked three-syllable names more than two-syllable names, but I had to admit that was an arbitrary preference. I knew for certain that I didn't want a name as common as Jenifer. I'd spent so many years snapping my head around when I heard someone say it in public that I had chronic neck tendonitis.

I thought about names that started with vowels, since those seemed, without conducting an actual survey, less common.

Elliot, Adrian, Oliver. I didn't think I was any of those. And I didn't think I'd be taken seriously if I picked the name I thought best described the kind of man I would be: Fred Flintstone. Everett. What about Everett? That might work, I thought. It was long enough, vowelly enough, and I didn't know a single man named Everett.

This was a lot of work for a simple response to a question posed by a stranger, for the right to continue to pretend to be a different person in the online world. Worldly spy I was not.

—*Of course I have a name,* I typed, thinking it was a good way to present attitude but delay saying anything too specific, or actually, saying anything at all.

Less than five minutes later the monitor had another question for me:

—*Well? What is it?*

I was not so good at playing this little game. I typed in my newfound moniker and clicked the submit button. And then tried to pretend the page never existed.

Was I lying? Was I going too far? Was I about to be discovered as some hopeless lesbian with a need for attention and a sense of name style straight from 1906?

Or ... was this a first step toward something?

* * *

We were watching the foot traffic outside Pat's apartment, and Pat was feeling talkative. He'd decided in the previous week to buy a can of chartreuse paint, and what had started out as one accent wall became a bright yellow-green living room. I wasn't sure if he still liked it or had regrets, but I wasn't about to inquire.

"I just don't think anyone takes me seriously," he said, sipping at a diet soda. "All the trannies in DC make fun of me."

He was referring to events from years earlier, before I'd met him. I'd tried to reassure him before but hadn't eased his fears.

"Well, I think you shouldn't worry about them. You just have to do what you need to do. For you. On your terms."

"I knew you'd understand. But I just don't even know how to talk to a doctor so they'll give me hormones."

I didn't know what the resources were in the city.

"What about the GLBT clinic?" By definition, they served gay men, lesbians, bisexuals, and transgender people.

"Are you crazy? I'd have to lie to them, pretend I'm a man trapped in a woman's body. They'll never give me hormones. Jesus, Jenifer. You're so naive."

"Okay, okay. What's your plan, then?"

"I'll just see if I can get my primary doctor to prescribe them."

"Does it work that way?" It wasn't what I'd read online about best practices.

"Well, he could prescribe whatever, he's a doctor."

I held my tongue, figuring I shouldn't argue about such a sensitive topic.

He was talking about feeling alone. I couldn't admit to him I felt the same way.

*   *   *

When the weekend rolled around I rode the subway to a blues music festival in the city. After the debacle of the cling wrap, this time I opted to tape myself down. I wondered what spending time in public as a man would be like, as if simply binding my breasts would make people think I was male. It worked in Blake Edwards movies, so maybe it would work for me. I hoped that nobody I knew would be in attendance but figured I'd be fine since my friends tended to stay away from the drunken downtown festivals unless it was for gay pride.

I amazed myself with the results from athletic tape. It worked so well among my football teammates for keeping swelling down in things like ankles and arms, I figured it would do wonders for my figure. Navy blue, the color of my team's jerseys, it was about an inch and a half wide and was woven to tear off the roll in neat lines. It was certainly the flattest chest I'd produced, and I felt strangely terrific. And it was easy, too, no breastal sneaking away from the site of the flattening. Perhaps this was the way to go. I put on a T-shirt and reveled at myself in the mirror, an uneasy feeling that I shouldn't be this happy. I stuffed that down deep into my chest, too, and I arrived at the festival with an inappropriately large smile, happy to shell out six dollars for water, lemons, sugar, and ice in a jaunty plastic cup that announced to the world: Fresh Lemonade!

It took a couple of hours in the humid sun to feel unbearably hot and sweaty under the tape. I didn't dare try to take it off while I was outside, in part because I didn't think I'd be able to get the tape to stick again to my melting torso, but also because it would probably look creepy to see some random fat man clawing at himself under his shirt. Geez, you can't even take the kids to a drunken music festival in the city anymore, fathers would say. Mothers would hold their children's eyes shut against the perverted sight, like I was Frankenstein's monster come to play with their blind offspring. Instead I just pushed through the—was it pain? I guess at this point it was pain—and partied on. Two concert sets, one yellow chicken on a stick, and two large cups of excited citrus drink later, I landed back at home.

The shirt was off—relief! I felt beautiful, wonderful, crisp air-conditioning hitting my skin, and I was ready to cry tears of joy. Those turned quickly to anguish as I realized the tape had melded with my skin. I had, in less than two seconds, removed a few inches of my skin along with the tape. Blood oozed from the open wound, a perfect rectangle where the skin had been. I yelped in my bathroom. The cats slunk in and watched me dab at myself. This was probably not a good time to ask for dinner, they decided amongst themselves.

I had five more pieces of tape—otherwise known as polygons of pain—to go. My skin under the tape was starting to itch. I had in the past peeled countless pieces of tape off of my fingers and wrists, which I'd habitually wrapped to play football. I supposed those parts of my skin were more durable than the soft fleshy parts on my chest and torso. But clearly I couldn't take them off the same way I just had, unless I wanted to die of unintentional bloodletting. I grabbed the roll of cellophane off the back of the toilet, which had been sitting there since my last disastrous encounter with binding, and ripped off a piece to hold over the exposed wound. I took the hottest shower I could stand and waited for the tape to soften up and release me from its grip.

With perfect timing, the phone rang. I let it go to the answering machine. I could hear, from the other room, Pat's voice.

"Hey," he started, pausing, "I just want you to know I talked to my doctor about starting hormones today, and I think it would be really uncool if you started it, too. I just think it's weird of you to like, copy my identity. Anyway, let's talk."

I thanked him for giving me something else to think about other than my predicament.

I thought back to my day. The point had been to see how people reacted to me if they thought I was male. Trouble was, I wasn't sure how they saw me—I could have looked like a man, or I could have looked like a fat woman with a strange non-endowment up top. I supposed if I'd looked like that, I'd have gotten a lot more in the way of curious staring, but given how hot it was out there, the heat waves off the pavement probably obscured people's perceptions, anyway. And who wanted to notice me in the throng of souvlaki-eating, Fresh Lemonade!-drinking masses? So I wasn't sure my little experiment mattered. But I remembered a bit of the euphoria I'd felt when I'd ventured out. Okay, so maybe it was egocentric to wonder how others saw me, but it had been amazing for me to walk through the world as something other than female.

*   *   *

I was looking at the clearance shoe rack on Connecticut Avenue, which in late summer in DC is more of a grab-and-run-inside and less of a pleasant shopping experience. I was rethinking my decision to wear a tie and cotton sweater vest, but then again, I'd just come from the office. I hadn't owned a skirt since I had bought a couple ten years earlier when insisting to a girlfriend that I wasn't just a predictable butch. And those skirts had been worn precisely once, after which they were subjected to eternal damnation smashed into small balls of fabric in the back of my closet. If I'd walked into work in a skirt or dress I'd probably have to pick people up off the floor. It was no understatement to say that the desire to dress femininely had never existed for me. In fact, my childhood could have been encapsulated as a series of dress-related tantrums:

- The tic-tac-toe-patterned dress my mother made for me for my kindergarten picture, which set me off on a two-hour screaming fit about how ugly it was and how much I hated it and her. I think the photographer stapled me to the chair so I would sit still and he could get 2.27 seconds for one picture. He probably became a landscape photographer after that day.

- The frilly and flowery Easter dress, also constructed by Mom, at the height of Laura Ingalls's fame on *Little House on the Prairie*. I had to wear it to the circus, where I got pulled out of the audience to be the Princess of the Sea and ride around with Bubbles the Clown in the Yellow Submarine. I kid not. A goddamn yellow submarine. Too bad the meaning was lost on me as a nine-year-old. The best part of the ride around the ring was the garb they put me into—not only did I get to cover up a flowered dress, but I was wrapped in about thirty pounds of pink and blue sequins. I will probably not wear that much glitter again in my life.

- The "sun dresses" my mother bought for me in the early eighties, nearly every time she shopped at Bamberger's or JCPenney. Black ones, pastel ones, streaky neon ones that looked like the *Miami Vice* set had thrown up all over the material—I hated all of them but they just kept coming, like the Russian army. I mortally wounded each of them as soon as I could so that they could be decreed unwearable and I could just put on a pair of Levi's.

- The pink prom dress from hell, with a foot-wide bow on the ass. My mom insisted on taking five hours to do my hair and makeup, as if she'd been salivating for the chance to hold me down for this occasion even since I'd been born. I literally screamed for her to get off of my face.

Thinking about so many dresses made sweat climb up my neck. My collar seemed more than capable of soaking it up like a sponge.

I didn't see Aric before I heard him. He was wearing a black tank, board shorts, and flip flops, and he looked like a mustang about to race off to a wilderness preserve.

"Wow, look at you," he said. I anticipated the rest of his sentence before he spoke it, figuring he'd continue with, "I haven't seen anything that sweaty since the last pig roast I attended." Nobody as handsome as him could possibly find me appealing.

"Hey, Aric, how are you?" I asked, pretending interest in the shoe I was holding. Too bad it was a hideous two-toned brown and gray loafer with a tassel. I'd only wanted to know how low it had been marked down because I couldn't imagine anyone paying more than five dollars for something so ugly.

"You really are a gentleman, aren't you," he said, as if my outfit was charming instead of ready to spontaneous ignite from the heat.

"Am I?"

"Don't answer my question with a question."

"Why, does that bother you?" I feigned innocence.

"You just did it again," he said. He accented his frustration by getting a little red in the face, but I saw the faintest of smiles on his lips.

"What am I doing?"

"You're just fucking with me now." Again, a smile. We'd wound up in a cat and mouse game, standing over reject shoes.

"Trust me, honey," I said, laying three fingers on his collarbone, "you would absolutely know if I were fucking with you." I turned on my heel and waved goodbye.

"Wait, can I call you sometime?"

Perfect.

*   *   *

I was reading the posts on my now-favorite website related to people who considered themselves outside of the male-female binary. Thinking about a four-by-four grid of genders was mind-numbing, but I started stressing out about where I fit into the picture. What the hell was I? The choice wasn't vanilla or chocolate anymore. I could be the equivalent of a candy bar explosion mixed in with chocolate sauce, *caramel de leche*, and marshmallow. Throw a few gummy bears and peanuts on top, add whipped cream and a bright red cherry, and there were people out there with much more complex identities than I had.

I felt like I'd missed the boat on the gender stuff. I wasn't even in earshot of the boat's bellowing horns as it pulled away from dock. In fact, the water had settled back into stillness, the sound of crickets taking over from where the noisy propellers had left off.

I grew up a butch, wearing sweater vests when no one else did, button-down Oxford shirts, and a backwards-turned Ascot hat, and wanting so much to be a little prep school boy, packing socks in my pants, too young to wonder why that made me feel so much better inside. But of course there was this girl uniform I had to wear, and complain about it though I might, that's just the way it was and I learned not to question it, or much else for that matter. Whatever feelings I'd had in years past, I was ridiculous if I thought I was a transgender person. I would be a laughing stock with my wispy chin hair and poorly bound boobs. Who would ever really, seriously, see me as a man?

I called the therapist before I could change my mind and left my information on her answering machine.

Chapter 4

All of my reading up on the topic—on websites, in books, and talking to people who'd considered and made or not made the transition—was getting me nowhere. I was intrigued and stuck at the same time. I dismissed the things I had in common with their stories and noted the differences as markers that I was a hundred percent female, even if female meant often getting mistaken for a man.

I didn't feel much along the "Oh my God, this is the wrong body," dysphoria line. My chest never bothered me when I wasn't trying to hit a softball or golf ball, and my voice, which was middle ranged, was fine. The lack of aggressive feelings I presumed all men had was a good thing. But I kept thinking about the beard on my face in the dream, and I had always been frustrated by my lack of muscle mass. And then there was the monthly cycle—I wouldn't have any love lost for that. But what woman would? I wondered what would this body feel like after taking testosterone and having surgery? Would it be any closer to what I wanted it to be? Yes and no. I just wasn't sure. I didn't think I'd be allowed to mess with my original package like this. How much did going through thirty-four years like this matter for the fifty or so that are yet to come, I wondered. I still won't have a johnson. And why, my power-to-the-women training asked me, must it come down to that?

But it had. *After all is said and done*, I thought, *I'll still never be happy with this body.* So what was the point in turning my life upside-down? And couldn't I be a masculine woman and be fine with that? Hadn't my Smurfette poster in my childhood bedroom instructed me that Girls Can Do Anything? She was sliding down a rainbow, after all.

* * *

Other things in life were proceeding as normal. If not "normal," then at least they went on as they had. Work was busy, full of stress and sometimes recognition, even if my boss was a bit clueless. The receptionist, Fatima, loved to greet me in the morning with a critique of my outfit. I'd worn a bow tie this day, and she asked if I was going to sell her a bean pie, à la Louis Farrakhan. She laughed but I smiled only after I passed her.

One day at work one of the other out lesbians (there were seven of us, like some kind of divine council) came up to me in the work room while I was assembling proposals. For all the money our proposals brought in, the executives were stubbornly unwilling to front $200 for a new report binder. It failed to punch rectangular holes and failed at eighty decibels as I sat among ruined pages like so many pieces of confetti. Chad. I was pissed all over again.

"Jenifer," said Wendi, a.k.a. Divine Lesbian Number Four. I stopped the hole punching so I could hear her. "Are you genderqueer?"

I was certainly not ready for this. Couldn't people just leave me be with my suspenders and matching ties? What were they seeing that I wasn't ready to see?

I looked over the rims of my glasses, "GenderQueer. Gentleman's Quarterly," I said, weighing out the words with my hands like I was Bill Cosby on the Electric Company. "Coincidence? I think not." I was glad I'd come up with this little joke before.

That seemed to satisfy her. But it was something to consider. Was I still female, or did I feel like something else inside?

I came home to my answering machine blinking at me impatiently. It was a message from the therapist. I'd forgotten I'd even called her. She said she could see me next week. I could have a free session, and we could see if we thought the arrangement would work.

I called her back before I had the chance to overthink the offer and agreed to meet. And then promptly set about watching television for the next three hours.

* * *

I watched with a wary eye the days tick by on my desk calendar. I wasn't one for daily red "X" marks, which was too much like counting down until my parole hearing. But I saw the big red marks in my mind's eye, and I started getting panicky thinking about sitting down with her. On the one hand I knew I wasn't classically female, on the other I heard Pat's voice in my head, admonishing me for broaching the subject of being some kind of transgender something.

No one could agree on a definition. Were butches, so masculine, already considered trans? Or not, because they were female-identified? Was "transgender" an umbrella category that covered all kinds of identities, or was it a word for people who couldn't seal the deal and make permanent changes to their bodies? And trans-spectrum—were there people who were more trans than others? Was there an authentic transsexual and were there poseurs? In Pat's world, certainly, there were.

Thinking about these questions as pure abstractions was one thing, but considering them while trying to sort out where one fit into the algorithm approached crazy-making. So a simple question of "how do you ID?" was enough to send me into a long journey with my inner Freud. I didn't have an answer.

I pulled into the therapist's driveway very, very early because I didn't want to be late. Not knowing what to do with myself, I backtracked and drove to the Hallmark store around the corner, figuring I could read stupid and funny greeting cards to take the edge off my nervousness. The location must be part of her plan. I looked around to see if there were other clearly anxious people who were there several hours early for their appointments, reading cards with the pissy old lady on the front, but nobody stood out. The cashier must have thought I was a bit of a suspicious character because she started watching me out of the corner of my eye. She needn't have; I'd have sooner wrapped myself in Hallmark paper and ribbons than I'd care to steal a Precious Moments figurine. Although I did have a track record with encasing myself in rolls of cellophane ... but this was different.

I got back in the car with eight minutes left until the appointment, which coincided with the moment I knew I couldn't stomach reading greeting cards anymore. I pulled back into the driveway and saw that the car for the previous client had gone. I walked inside, checking that my shirt was tucked in and my phone ringer turned off. She heard me come into the waiting room, introduced herself as Robyn, not Dr. So-and-so, and told me to come in. I had the urge to run away quickly but didn't, as I was an awfully slow runner and so clumsy that I'd probably run into the door. I walked through her spotless kitchen, thinking that having people in and out of here all day was probably a great motivator for keeping it clean. Or maybe it was the reverse; she'd become a psychologist in order to work out of her home and show off her cleaning prowess.

I walked into the room downstairs and pondered where to sit. A big blue couch, matching loveseat, and oversized chair hogged most of the room's wall space. She had lots of certificates on the wall, all of them appearing genuine. And maybe I didn't care if she was a fakester or not, because by that point, I just needed someone to listen.

I heard her coming down the stairs, so I jumped onto the couch and pretended I'd been there waiting all along. My heaving chest gave me away. So much for not lying to the therapist at my first session.

"So," she began, "it's nice to meet you. Do you have any questions for me, to start with?" She was tall, thin, unassuming, with a noticeable but not irritating Baltimoresque accent.

Did I have any questions, huh? How about, "Am I crazy?" "Why does my life suck?" "Why am I obsessed with this trans crap?" "How can I get out of this awful relationship?" "How much is this going to cost me?" "Are you going to make me beat a pillow with a Wiffle bat?"

I looked at her because making eye contact was a good thing, or so I'd heard.

"No, I don't have any questions."

"Okay, that's okay," she said, reassuring me. "If you ever think of anything, just ask."

I promised I would do so, without any real commitment to the idea.

"So what brings you here today? What would you like to talk about?" She leaned back, showing me we could relax and chat like old friends.

I took that as my cue to talk about anything and everything for the next forty-eight minutes, except the things I really wanted to bring up. Perhaps I just had to see if she could listen to my verbal diarrhea for that long without clawing her face off. So far, she excelled at sitting there and looking interested. She was either totally psychotic or a good therapist.

"So," I said, beginning my concluding statement by talking to the toes of my shoes, "I thought I'd like to talk about my relationship, my stress at work, my sometimes frustration with my mother, and getting over my neuroses. Oh, and I have some gender stuff to talk about."

She knew right then that I was there to transition. And she very intelligently said nothing about it.

Chapter 5

One Sunday morning I scoured the Washington Post for the rental ads. The landlord had called again saying that he was stepping up his attempts to sell the condo I was living in. I, being the tenant, could have first dibs. He was thinking in the ballpark of $220,000. His figure made its way down my ear canals and into my brain, translated as "three bajillion dollars." I told him I'd think about it because I didn't want to him to guess that I was as unable to buy a home more expensive than one that came with a parking brake and vinyl siding.

I wondered if it was time to move into the actual city and out of Virginia, which recently had made its disdain of gay people known with its laws against any same-sex contracts. No wills, no arrangements to care for each other in a health crisis, nothing that could help two unrelated and same-gender people from "approximating" marriage.

I mentioned to Pat that I'd be looking at places in the District, since he had always complained that I lived "far away" and that I was a "boring suburbanite."

"Uh, we need to talk," he said. This was often his refrain right before I was taken to task.

"Oh, about what?" I twirled the phone cord in my hand as I sat on the couch, letting the sun shine on me and the cats. If I'd had a tail I would have flapped it around just like they were.

"So it's cool for you to live in DC, like it's time you got out of that godforsaken state, but I don't want you right on top of me."

"That's not what you said last night," I said with a lilt in my voice.

"Jenifer, really. I'm telling you, I need my space. Why can't you respect that?"

"I respect it, I respect it," I said. "What are you saying?"

"I don't think you should live north of H Street, south of V Street, west of 12th Street, or east of 22nd Street. I just want that area for myself and my partner."

"Pat, that's all of DuPont. You're saying I can't live in DuPont Circle at all?"

"Oh, so now the whole city is yours to live wherever you want?"

"That's pretty much how it works in the United States. I'm sorry that comes as a shock to you."

"Why do you always do this to me? Everything is all about you! You're so selfish!"

Truth be told, everything was too expensive in all of Northwest, and I'd been looking in the other quadrants of the city which were much more affordable and still serviced by the Metro.

"I'm not doing anything to you," I said, trying to calm him down. "I'm just telling you I think I'm going to move out of Virginia and into the city. I don't have anything lined up yet."

"Well," he said, taking it down several decibels, "I do think you should get out of there and into the city. I just need my distance. It's how I protect myself."

I didn't know then that the new apartment I'd find was in a perfect location.

* * *

After I'd seen the therapist a few times, she asked me outright, "Would you rather be liked, or respected?"

What kind of a question is that? I wanted to know. My brain started firing frenetically. *How could anyone not want to be liked? What the hell are you talking about? Why would anyone make that choice? How could you pick respected over liked? What a crazy question! Who thinks up shitty questions like this? What are you really asking me? How could I ever answer such a ridiculous question?*

I realized suddenly that I'd asked all of those things out loud. I looked down at my shoes, always my default instead of making eye contact. If I couldn't be grounded, at least I could look at the floor.

"Liked, Robyn, liked," I said, trying to breathe. "Why would anyone say anything else? Of course I would pick liked." Perhaps speaking more slowly would make me sound more certain.

"Well," she said, looking at me, "I hope that someday you answer by saying 'respected.'"

*   *   *

I hopped in the car with my list of appointments for apartment hunting, looking at everything from English basement apartments to overpriced renovations, damp studios, and one flat with an overuse of cleaner that burned my nostrils.

The last apartment possibility of the day was promising. This was a one-bedroom with a brand new kitchen and a lot of light. It was up three flights of stairs, however, but I told myself I could use the exercise. I made an offer on the place and crossed my fingers that I was done looking around for a place to live. Maybe there were possibilities there. Maybe I could be a different, a better person there.

Maybe I'd just cower in the corner as usual.

*   *   *

"He said what?" My friend Jeffrey was not easily shocked. But my latest admission had caused him to put down his martini so he could take in what he'd heard. We were sitting on the oversized, cushy, vinyl bench in the gay power bar called Halo. Because the bench had thick foam cushions it was hard to balance oneself. Because they were vinyl, they made artificial farting noises wherever human skin came into contact with the seat. So in the summer, while people were trying to look cool in the glow of orange neon lighting, which in itself is difficult, they were also attempting not to move much. It was a line of bobbing and farting, with well-off men pretending they weren't doing either. I often wondered if the owners sat in the back and laughed behind the one-way glass over the bar.

Jeffrey usually opted to stand or sit on the hard stools at the bar. But either of those positions required good balance, which, after three potent drinks, was just a memory for us. A seventy-percent reclined position on the low seating worked better for our level of inebriation.

"He actually said you couldn't live anywhere near DuPont? Who died and made him Gayblade the Princess Protector?"

"Ah, he gave me a ten-block radius I couldn't choose," I corrected him.

"DTMFA, Jenifer. DTMFA!" He took another drag of his cocktail, bookending his sip with disapproving shakes of his head.

DTMFA meant "Dump the motherfucker already," a phrase coined by Dan Savage, a gay advice columnist.

Jeffrey was not and had not been fond of Pat for some time. Jeffrey had noticed early on that the relationship was pained.

He shook his head at me. "I just hope the sex is good. No, great, I hope the sex is great. Is the sex great, woman?" He sliced through the air with his drink as he spoke, not so much for emphasis as the inability to contain his emotions. They were always slipping out in his gestures.

"The sex is great. When we—cough—have sex, that is."

"Oh girl, he is losing his appeal. You need to stop putting up with his tranny ass."

"Okay, now," I started.

"No, really," he said, "he went all Ru Paul on you and you're still with him. He needs to kiss the ground you walk on for that."

I invested my attention in my drink.

At that point a few lobbyist types came in and sat down next to us, making a string of fart sounds on the cushions as they sized up Jeffrey and me. Lobbyists always looked strange in summer casual wear. I, ever the good wing man, knew when to give Jeffrey his space for making a move. I looked at my watch and said I had to run, knowing I'd be lucky to get to the Metro without wiping out on the sidewalk.

The Metro in DC represents a typical cross-section of the city's people on any given day. Hospitality employees, Hill staffers, career bureaucrats, students, older residents—this was the real population of the District, not to be found next to any monument. I sat down on a lightly-populated Metro train and fumbled with my iPod, though all of my friends told me, after a spate of robberies, not to listen to it on the train. I kept the sound level down so I could hear ambient noise and perhaps give my ears a break. I stopped paying attention to which stop I was at, since I knew I was in for a twenty-five-minute ride or so.

The doors opened and closed, the familiar sing-song alert sounding each time. At one stop, a man in a dirty trench coat got on. He had on what had once been nice khaki pants, now discolored and shredded at the bottom, revealing scarred ankles above worn out high-top sneakers. He looked grizzled, had stringy hair and a gray, unkempt beard. After staring at me for many minutes, he suddenly shouted: "Are you a man or a woman? Are you a man or a woman?" There was a brief pause. "Are you a MAN or a WOMAN?"

I watched as everyone on the train looked at him and then me, to see if they themselves could determine my gender. Nobody else seemed to be as angry about it as this guy. I pretended my music was much louder than it was and ignored him. Seeing my stop coming up, I stood up and stood four inches in front of the car doors, as I did usually anyway, screaming crazy man or no screaming crazy man.

The doors opened. I stepped onto the platform. I turned around and looked back toward the car.

"Are you an ASSHOLE or an IDIOT?" I shouted, and the doors closed to people applauding me and laughing at him.

When I got home, I looked around at my possessions, hating that I'd have to box everything up and move. *Packing shouldn't cause so much anxiety*, I thought, but there it was. I needed people I could really talk to. I couldn't even have a conversation with Jeffrey about changing my sex, because I didn't think he'd really understand. There seemed to be a weird line people had drawn between butch and transgender. And was the line really that distinct? Why did it matter to anyone?

I powered up my computer and dove into the trans forum where I was known as Everett. It was such a fake name, as obvious a handle as if I'd named myself Pilbert Dumb Nuts.

—*Just got harassed on the subway*, I typed. I summed up the train ride incident in a few sentences, then erased the post. I thought about what had upset me. Was it that my safety seemed to be at stake because someone couldn't figure out my gender? Had my safety actually been at stake on that train? Or was it because I didn't really know what the answer to his question was anymore?

* * *

The summer was winding down, and Jeffrey and I had made plans to rent a condo on the beach in Delaware for a week. The thought of doing nothing but sitting and reading under an umbrella and listening to the surf made me smile, as if smiling was a sense memory of being at the shore. I had spent considerable time working up a list of items to take with us, thinking of every contingency in which we might need, say, an extra crankshaft for my SUV.

"You are insane," Jeffrey told me as he read the list. We were eating burgers and tater tots at a favorite pub in Mount Pleasant.

"Do you even own a steamer trunk?" he asked.

"No, but don't you think I need one?"

"I'd focus on that lobotomy first."

I rolled my eyes at him. It was powerfully hot outside, and so it was perhaps possible that I had burned off a few necessary brain cells walking from the car to the tavern. But I had made the list while in an air-conditioned space earlier, so I couldn't really use stunning humidity as an excuse.

"Okay, see," he said, now laughing with his finger pointed at one suspect item, "there's no way we need snorkeling gear."

"But we're going to the beach," I said.

"We're not going anywhere our asses would snorkel. And what do you do with this shit after the trip?" I heard him tapping his foot on the floor.

"We'll go to the beach again after this, Jeffrey. Sheesh. Besides, what are you gonna do when we pass a lagoon and we can't go snorkeling because we don't have flippers, goggles, or breathing tubes?" I made perfect sense to me.

"There ain't no lagoons in Delaware, dummy! And there isn't anything to look at unless you want to find used syringes and forty-ounce malt cans."

I harrumphed at him, which was my way of signaling dissent while not opening myself up to defeat. At least he agreed we needed to bring a corkscrew and bottle opener, because Jeffrey would never take a chance on not being able to drink. Priorities were priorities.

* * *

—*You should come up,* read the instant messenger note from one of the people I'd met on the online forum. As the months had gone by I'd evolved from lurking and staring slack-jawed at the screen, to posting a few questions, to someone with a name that others could refer to in their posts. I wasn't an expert on anything, except perhaps, how *not* to bind. Somehow over time I'd gotten to know other blips on the screen and count them as people who knew I was starting to think of myself as transgender.

—*Well, is there a good weekend?* I asked. Samantha and her female-to-male partner, Marcus, lived in Brooklyn, about a four-hour car ride away. Guilt and excitement not being mutually exclusive, it seemed far enough away from DC that I could go there and not see anyone I knew from home.

She suggested a date three weeks away, and I said I'd be there. To meet people as Everett—was that really even possible? Who was I kidding? I wasn't a "real" trans person. Pat was a real trans person. I was just playing around with something because I was bored with my own life. "Real" trans people didn't have a Greek chorus laughing at them in the background every time they thought about their gender identity.

—*We'll email you directions. It'll be so great to meet you!*

Okay, I thought, *maybe this could be a good thing.* Now I had to figure out what to tell people about why I was going out of town, or how I met these people. I wasn't good at the lying thing. I could handle myself at a poker table, sure, but gambling was far afield from, say, going to another city where you'd didn't know anyone and using an assumed name, and oh, assuming the opposite gender role. It didn't really compare with bluffing through a J-7 pocket at a Texas Hold 'Em table. I figured I'd start by avoiding the subject if at all possible. I was fairly certain procrastination and deferment would play to my strengths.

The pretend-it-isn't-there strategy didn't last for long. Later that evening, at dinner with my ex Lori, I had to flub my way through a reason for not being in town.

"There's a movie on the green coming up in a few weeks. Why don't you come with Barbara and me?" Barbara was her new girlfriend, a young lawyer in DC's morass of 50,000 lawyers. Barbara was, to her credit, not a lobbyist.

"Oh, I don't know," I said, looking at my drink, "I'm not sure if I should go."

"What? Why not? You should get out more."

"I just—it's grass. I hate grass stains."

"Okay. What's going on?" She motioned for me to look at her. I couldn't lie if I had to look at her. Damn her for knowing me too well.

"I don't want to be a third wheel." Ah, rule number five of lying—say something that's mostly true.

"Well, you could bring Pat." She must really have wanted me to come along, because she and most of my friends didn't like spending more than ten minutes with him.

"Oh, he and Anna have other plans." I had no idea if this was true, but I was clawing for a way out of this.

"It's Hitchcock they're showing." She baited me, knowing my love of the director.

"Oh? Which?"

"The Thirty-Nine Steps." *Ooh, a good one.*

"Well, I'll let you know, but don't kill me if I don't go." It was much better being kind of honest, at least. I'd known Lori for a decade, since college, and I neither could lie to her nor could I feel okay trying. Deciding between hanging out at the monuments with friends and a surreptitious bag of liquor or driving into the big city to meet people I'd never seen before was starting to look like a no-brainer. Why would I venture to a city as far away as New York for something so uncertain?

The answer came back instantly, seemingly from someone else's brain: *because you have to.*

*   *   *

I was back in the therapist's neighborhood, pondering entering the greeting card store again, but I didn't think I could pull off a fifth or sixth week of browsing cards without buying anything, and it had gotten harder to feign interest because the products didn't turn over that quickly. I couldn't see any cultural advantage to having memorized all of the nasty old lady Shoebox cards, but I also didn't think it made any sense to pretend to look at anything in the Sew and Vac store, unless I wanted to leave with an avocado green Electrolux. So I sat in her driveway and looked through old messages on my phone—my mother, Lori, Jeffrey, Pat, other friends. My universe of people condensed into a two-by-two-inch screen. They were my people but I was so far away from them, alone with my rambling thoughts, unable to share with them. It occurred to me then that there was a giant calendar out there, ticking down the days one by one. I had started to feel, without realizing it, that I was running out of time, quite literally. As I thought this, I didn't know what the sensation meant.

I smiled for Robyn as she let me in, and she pierced through my fake happiness, raising her eyebrow just a tad as I walked past her down the stairs to the counseling office. I think it was by design that she gave clients a moment or two to get comfortable before she came in. I tried to put on my game face in the thirty seconds I had.

"So, how are you doing?" she asked.

"Okay. Busy," I said, which was the truth. Between four new contracts at work, two new employees to manage, and getting ready to move, I was stretched. And those were the stresses I could discuss.

She leaned in on the love seat. I always sat in the same spot, taking one end of the couch so I could be right next to the end table and be able to have a drink or just watch the minute hand on the small clock that stood there. Today was a clock-watching day. But Robyn was having none of it.

"Jenifer, how are you really doing?" She stayed perched forward, waiting to catch my answer as soon as it left my lips.

"I'm tired. I'm just tired."

"Tell me more about that. What's making you feel tired?"

Oh, how therapists speak, I thought. All about feelings and clarification. Why did I pay this woman to make me uncomfortable with my deceptions?

"I feel like nobody knows me." Tick tock. Maybe I could stall long enough so that we'd run out of time.

"Wow. That's a big statement. Why do you feel that way?"

I put my answer into a sigh, as if I could construct a bubble around the sentence and she wouldn't see my words. "Because I think I'm transgender but I'm afraid to tell anyone about it, and I'm exhausted from not telling them."

Oh, shit. I'd gone and said it. I hadn't meant to do that. I could hear the sound of my reality dancing around the room, taunting me like a genie let out of a lamp.

"Well, I was hoping we'd get to talk about this soon!" She smiled and sat back, taking a sip of her Diet Coke. What on earth did she mean?

"What?"

"Tell me what's scaring you."

I sat and thought about her question that had been worded in declarative terms. I forgot about the clock. I thought about people's reactions to me. Perhaps there were people out there who would accept me as I was, like maybe they walked on the planet, but certainly they weren't people who already knew me. I wasn't ready to lose any of them. I wasn't ready to say I could turn my whole world upside-down to become someone so new. I thought a lot of things, and it dawned on me slowly that it was, in fact, five minutes later. And we'd been sitting there with my brain running amok.

"I'm scared I'm not going to be taken seriously. I'm scared my friends won't understand. My mother will get upset or depressed. People will laugh at me. I'll become unlovable."

I noticed tangentially what I was saying, as if I was having an almost out-of-body experience because I was too lazy to leave my body to go watch the scene from the ceiling. Ceiling-corner views were so overrated. But I took stock of what I didn't say: that I wasn't really trans. Why hadn't I said that? Didn't I think that?

Robyn paused, looking at me gently. "Remember when we talked about being liked or respected?"

Oh, that crap again, I thought. And then I recognized her point. *Not too quick on the handoff, are you, Maroon?*

"You're saying I need to tell them even if they'll think I'm nuts or an ass."

"I'm saying maybe that choice is upon you."

We talked slowly for the rest of the session, and she hugged me in her kitchen as I was leaving, like a friend. I got back in the car, thumbing my nose at the Hallmark store and battling insane drivers on the Capitol Beltway. Finally I was back in my neighborhood, and it hit me, I was happy. Honestly happy to have said those things out loud to another human being.

It didn't last.

Chapter 6

I stopped by the cheap haircut place in the strip mall next and punched my first initial into the computer to queue up. That looked strange—an empty J floating in bright green against the black void of the screen. I'd signed my name "J" many times before, but never as a placeholder showing what my full name was, only as shorthand. Lazy was one thing, but obfuscating was different.

I waited for my turn and then went back to meet the hairdresser. It had only been a couple of months since my hair debacle of early summer, and nothing much had changed other than the subtle appearance of brown roots. But this hairdresser seemed confused by me, even though I had gotten the same haircut for years.

"You want a lady cut?" she asked, frowning.

"I just want it short on the sides and in back, longer on top and longest in the middle of the top."

"You want a man's haircut?" She must have been nearsighted, for all of her staring at my follicles.

"I just want the haircut I want," I said. I smiled, afraid I looked frustrated at her. Nobody should piss off a woman with sharp scissors.

"Okay, okay," she said, waving her arms in exasperation and muttering in Arabic about what a crazy lesbian she had in her chair, or so I imagined, having never been taught Arabic by anyone on my Lebanese side of the family.

Ten minutes later I was done, and I tipped her five dollars even though she tsk-tsk'd her way through what was clearly the ordeal of her day. *Maybe I should double down and go over to the Men's Warehouse fifty yards away,* I thought. And then pull out a magic, glittering penis the size of Florida and urinate all over the tux rentals.

Heat burned my cheeks. *Tick tock,* said the clock in my mind.

* * *

Over the phone, Samantha was talking about meeting up in the city and the fun things we could do. I had to pay special attention when talking with her or Marcus because they used the Everett name generously, as if some fairy transmother was paying them per utterage, or like they were training a new dog. Everett, sit down, Everett, good dog, Everett, Everett, here, boy.

It sounded like a fantastic getaway, yet it also sounded terrifying. I hung up and looked through my mail and realized I was shifting gears back again to using Jenifer. How long could I keep this schizophrenia up?

I'd decided, meanwhile, that a neoprene rib protector was a pretty good way to bind, although it was decidedly a heat-keeper and increaser. Not a great option for August, which was when DC annually and officially became a circle of hell. So maybe it was something I could wear in New York on my visit. The thought made me a little giddy. Clearly, I was crazy.

Sanity in the balance or not, I went online, using the recommendations I'd read on a few forums, to buy a fake penis, commonly called a packer or "packy," packy being the strangely more affectionate term. For one did, after all, want some affection for one's manhood, even if said manhood was just a blob of silicone. All of the websites dedicated to selling such products promised they would pass the "pat" test, which of course made me wonder how scientifically such tests had been conducted. Was there a row of men sporting said packies in some kind of penis lineup? Were there criteria for realistic pat sensations? Was there a quality control patting brigade? And didn't patting penises tend to result in a distinct change in uh, texture? Perhaps I was too clinical. I changed my criteria to price, plunking down twelve dollars for an "average" sized one. I didn't want a small packer, certainly, not at five-feet, nine-inches tall, but I didn't feel quite so ostentatious as to get the "large" size. How was one supposed to judge these things from online photos, anyway?

I also fretted about the color. Did it really matter if it was "cream," "mocha," or "chocolate?" It could be bright orange, after all, if it was going to stay in my pants. Was I supposed to examine my inner thighs along with a color swatch? Would some unsuspecting partner say in bed, "Dude, you don't have a real penis, but I love that you matched the color so well?" And why were they using confectionary as a metaphor for race, exactly? I picked the middle color, figuring better to split the difference and trying to respect my mid-tone skin color. I wanted to laugh at myself for spending money on such a thing, but I also wondered if I really wouldn't like it in some sort of visceral, almost nasty way.

* * *

Pat's email indicated he was angry. And he loved me. And I was pissing him off—this time because I'd changed our plans to go out later in the week. Why didn't I respect his schedule? He had another partner, remember.

My cell phone rang with a text from Jeffrey.

Want to get a burger before bowling? I texted back in under something like three seconds that I was ready for meat and tater tots. I was already in the car before he signaled back that he could meet me at a pub near his house in twenty minutes. And I could spend the evening throwing bowling balls and laughing with my Evil Bitches teammates. It was nice to be in a gay bowling league, because the teams had other snarky names like "Dolls with Balls" and "Always in the Gutter."

There was something about walking into the alley with thirty pounds of bowling balls and one's own shoes to make me tingly with excitement. Each week the night was filled with promise that I usually would later curse as I threw one bad shot after another. But we won and lost together, finding little superstitions to use in the midst of games, like petting my bowling towel before each shot. Or more precisely, we would pet the stomach of Patrick the Starfish, who was embroidered on a towel I'd found on sale at Target and decreed should be the Benevolent Bowling Towel. This was wholly unrelated to the names given to my breasts during bowling one night, which were Becky and Bertha. Gay men certainly had quite a fascination with women's breasts. I didn't push them as to why, because they usually started stammering like pre-teens in sex ed class.

Becky, Bertha, and I had a pretty good night—being too full from dinner aside—and we won our three games. As was my routine, I went to the women's room to wash my hands so I wouldn't get grease from the lane all over the steering wheel. There was a woman in there, putting on lipstick, who didn't seem to be from the league.

"Hey," she said in an accusatory way. And then she made a sharp intake of breath and went back to her makeup application as if no sound had just emanated from her.

"What?" I asked, making eleven assumptions about what her deal was.

"Nothing." She looked straight ahead. I finished washing, walked out, and joined my teammates for the ride home.

Jeffrey must have thought he saw something amiss. "What's up?" he asked.

"The straights were taking over the bathroom," I said.

"Motherfuckers."

"Yeah, motherfuckers!"

Tim, our third teammate, hadn't been listening, but now was interested. "Who's a motherfucker?"

"George Bush is a motherfucker, that's who," I said, not wanting to talk about it.

"Well, duh," Tim said, quickly burying himself back in his latest science fiction novel. Tim had been a past president of the gay sci fi club in DC, so I supposed he was just keeping up on each word printed in the genre.

I dropped Tim off first and then Jeffrey. The glow from winning all of our games that week faded as I reflected on the woman in the restroom. She'd thought I was in the wrong place. What had she seen that I hadn't? There was her reaction and the crazy man on the train. Was it because I had short hair? That I was tall and large? Obviously genderqueer? The way I washed my hands? I didn't think I had to be a shrinking violet to prevent those kinds of moments, did I?

I didn't think I could do that.

*   *   *

The moment I opened the door to the beach condo, I knew I'd made a good choice. A glass-top dining table with green iron chairs and vinyl, flower-patterned cushions took up the space next to the front door. The galley kitchen had a blender, a toaster oven, and a coffee maker—the only appliances a typical beach house used by many people over the course of a summer would need. We looked into the living room and saw a sectional sofa happily drowning in a sea of throw pillows. Checking the bedrooms and bathrooms, Jeffrey and I started to sound a little overly gleeful. I threw open the terrace sliding door and heard the surf crashing five stories below. I slid onto a reclining chair, not caring about closing the screen door.

"Sweet pagan goddess, this place is fantastic," squealed Jeffrey.

"Mmmmm," was my response. I had no words for the sense of relief and relaxation.

"This is going to be a great week," he said, tempting fate. I turned to him, holding my hand over my face to block the sun.

"Wanna go to the beach?" I asked.

"Please. Do I want to go to the beach," he said, walking to his bedroom to change.

I escaped from my reality that week, distracted by swimming, reading, clambakes, and my friends. I didn't want to go back home and face the whole push-pull, high-stress environment of the city, much less deal with my gender issues. Here I was simply Jenifer, as if I had never even thought about not being Jenifer. My friends had accepted me for who I'd told them I was, and that was easy.

Saturday rolled around and I packed my things back up, getting ready for the drive.

"Let's do this next summer," said Jeffrey.

"Let's do this every summer," I said.

"Okay, sure."

By the next summer, Jeffrey and I would barely be friends.

*   *   *

The frantic cats sniffed the boxes and furniture, all clustered in the middle of each room. I was already a sweaty mess at barely past 8:30 in the morning. I pulled out the cat carrier and they scattered.

I figured I'd go for the chubby tabby first, especially since he didn't have any claws. I found him huddled in the corner of the closet, doing his best to fuse into the wall. He had put out a strange, sour, "get away" odor, and as I approached, making cat cooing noises, he started hissing.

"Please, big guy, it's okay," I said gently. I reached out and he slapped me, crouching back down again, as if he could curl in on himself and become feline anti-matter. I scooped him up and held him, kissing the top of his head and feeling awful for not being able to explain that he was just moving to a new place, and he'd like this apartment, too. I went over to the crate with him and he began making a low moaning noise. I worried that one of my five neighbors—sweet, older ladies—would call the ASPCA on me for cat abuse, but he quit growling and flexed his hind legs out in opposite directions to keep himself from getting stuffed inside. I could see, in the early morning light, orange hair floating all over the room from his struggles. From the corner of my eye I spotted the little gray cat assessing the situation, not so much so he could intercede on the tabby's behalf, but to watch and learn.

Meanwhile, getting Sebastian in the crate was like trying to fold cellophane into origami swans, and he kept springing out in new directions, defying the dimensions of the crate door. Finally I got him in by pushing on him. Ass-first he went, and I slammed the door into place as he thrashed out at me. The little one saw that I had at last completed my task, and he bolted for the guest room. This one had claws and was more squirmy, but he also was used to taking comfort in the fat rolls of his big brother, so he was halfhearted at defending himself. Even so I felt claws merge with my epidermis. At last I got him into the crate. The two cats mewed and cried. My heart was in my chest because I'd made them so sad.

"We're moving, we're moving," I said, like a mantra, hoping my voice would soothe them a little.

The movers knocked on the door and the looks on their faces told me I must have looked like a sight with my freshly bleeding wounds, the quiet cascade of cat hair falling gently all around me as I held onto a box that was moving of its own accord. I was grateful they didn't turn around and run.

"You like cats?" the foreman asked. Wow, brilliant. Clearly, I like cats. Everyone who likes cats enjoys the thrill from time to time of stuffing them into small boxes.

They took a look around all of the rooms, assessing what to load up first. The foreman frowned again. "This couch isn't going to fit out the door."

"Nope, it sure won't," I said, agreeing. I was still panting from the exertion.

"So we're leaving the couch?"

"No, we're taking it." I'd meant to be more helpful, but my energy was sapped already.

"Uh, so how is it going out?" I could tell I was not earning any confidence points with him.

"Well, it will fit out the balcony door, and we can rope it up and send it down over the railing."

Now he grinned from ear to ear. "All right! I like you! You're a crazy lady!"

"You have no idea," I said.

I needed to start a new chapter in my life. Apparently that chapter would begin with the cats pooping on themselves during the ride to DC.

* * *

Six hours later, we had moved everything down two flights and up three. The movers were not happy that neither building housed an elevator, and they fought back by perspiring on everything I owned. I'd let the cats out and they were now exploring, ignoring me lest I think I could pack them into crates any old time with impunity.

Pat had come over to help me unpack. This month we were back on better terms with each other. He congratulated me on my successful move and gave me a quick hug.

"Wow, you stink," he announced.

"I do indeed. Would you like to help me open boxes?"

"That's why I'm here, love," he said, flitting around the rooms to size up what was where. "I'm glad they got the couch in here."

"It was the easiest part of the move, actually," I said, thinking over the day. "Much easier than taking the front door off its hinges and then realizing the pins didn't want to go back in because the heat had made them warp."

"Oh, shit, that sucks." He looked at the many boxes of books. "Honey, do you really need all of these?"

"I suppose I think I do, or I wouldn't have brought them all here."

"Well, at least you can afford movers and don't ask your friends to move your crap. I am so sick of that shit!"

"Really?" I picked through a box of china in the galley kitchen, "how many people have you moved this year?"

"Okay, so maybe it was back in college, but I am done with that," he exclaimed, emphasizing "done" by waving his hands in the air like he was calling an incomplete pass. Except Pat had no idea what an incomplete pass was, much less how to signal one.

He walked into the back room where I'd put the bed together. Nothing else was set up yet. I had a habit of getting the bed together first so that I could flop on it as soon as my muscles gave out.

"It's really hot in here," he said from the other room.

"Open a window," I said, still focusing on kitchenware.

"Why don't you set up one of these air conditioners?" Since it was late September, this would have been a ridiculous suggestion in much of the country, but for DC, it could be two more months of strange autumn-defying heat.

I sighed and walked up to the unit in the living room. Why didn't he set it up? I grunted as I picked it up, propped it up in the window, plugged it in, and turned it on.

"That's better," Pat said as he walked in the room. "I'll unpack in here."

"Okay. I'll go set up the other one." I walked back to the bedroom and saw that the cats had spread themselves out on the bed, using the cotton sheets as a cooling agent. They were cleaning their paws and looking content.

I heaved up the air conditioner in the window and thought that it should be more centered on the windowsill. So I attempted to lift it, but before I knew it, it had slipped out of my hands and fallen through the open window. Screaming, I grabbed at the cord that was rapidly disappearing from the room and caught the last two inches before the plug. In the half-second of my reaction time, I'd propped my feet up against the baseboard and leaned back so that I wouldn't follow the unit out into the night. I thanked years of video game experience and felt somewhat vindicated that all that wasted time had done me good.

"Pat! Pat! I need you!" My arms were shaking from the strain as the unit continued to bounce against the brick wall of the building.

"What the hell?" He burst in. "Holy crap, Jenifer! What happened?"

"Isn't it obvious?" I laughed despite myself.

"Okay, at least you're laughing. But you're bleeding!"

I looked at the wall and saw red streaks that looked like a sloppy paint job performed by an extremely short painting crew.

"I don't feel anything," I said, figuring my body had shut off my pain receptors for a good reason. I tried to control my shaking. "Should I just let it go?"

"I don't know, let me look," said Pat. He stuck his head out the window. "Oh, it just gets better."

"What? Why?" I leaned in a little, letting the conditioner down another eight inches or so. I wondered quickly if the neighbors downstairs, had they looked outside, would have seen a dangling piece of eighty-pound equipment a few inches from their window.

I saw the problem. Parked thirty feet directly below was a shiny, brand new, red Mustang. I had to get the unit back in through the window.

"Well, okay, then. Hmm."

Pat patted me gently on the shoulder. "Uh, what are you going to do?"

"I guess I'm gonna haul it back up," I said, and no sooner had I finished speaking than I'd choked down on the cord and hauled it in about a foot. I had ceased caring how tired my arms were or how much they were shaking. Handful by handful, I yanked the conditioner closer, hoping the cord wouldn't separate from the housing. "I wonder if the Underwriters Laboratories run this particular test."

"Oh my god, Jen, just focus on getting it in here!"

We could see the top of the unit now.

"It's crowning," I shouted.

It got stuck under the sill overhang. Pat reached out and wiggled it loose, and finally we hauled it in and I could sit down. I'd cut my hands in a few places, but the blood had clotted over already.

"I don't think I'll be picking up anything heavy for a while."

"That's a good idea, hon," Pat said. "Do you have any antibiotic? When was your last tetanus shot?"

"Last year. I'm a klutz, remember?"

"You sure are. You need to buy some stock in health insurance companies. At least the one you're using."

We found the first aid supplies and made our way to the couch to rest. Unpacking was done for the day. The cats were busy playing hide and seek in the semi-empty boxes, and Pat was in a talkative mood.

"So I'm going to shower now and get ready for bed," he said.

"Okay."

"I have to wash off the testosterone so it doesn't get on you."

"Okay."

"Though I bet you'd like that."

"Don't start."

"Fine. But I won't be surprised when you go digging through your trash tomorrow looking for my gel packet, scraping whatever you can get out of it."

I walked over to a box in the living room and took books out of it, looking for a semblance of order.

Chapter 7

I was brushing my teeth at the sink when it first occurred to me that I could just exit, stage left, and leave all of it behind. What was there for me, anyway? I'd failed at my marriage to Lori, even if we were still friends. I was in the midst of a terrible dating situation. I had a good but stressful and mostly thankless job, and I would probably be mired in middle management forever. I looked ahead and couldn't see anything more than my routine. I would miss my feline companions, but I was sure someone would take care of them for me. And so it was that I started plotting my own death. Every calendar and clock was now a marker that my time was running out.

I finished dressing and went to work, envious of the men I saw driving to their offices, decked out in nice suits, looking happy or at least reasonably satisfied with the world. I could wear a suit, sure. But it wasn't the same.

Arnold, one of the senior VPs and co-founders of the company, was at the front door when I walked in. Women in the office had lots of stories about him—that he'd lost his entire family in Austria in the Holocaust, that he made staff cry with mean comments, that he'd gotten the company sued for sexual harassment. He was extremely short and sensitive about it, in that he would notice if one of us didn't make enough eye contact with him. We had an alert system for him. If he was in the office, female employees would pass the word around that it was a "one drawer" or "two drawer" day.

One drawer meant that when he came around the desk to talk to someone, having the top drawer pulled out would be a way of keeping some distance from him. But a two-drawer day was sometimes employed if he was needier and feeling like he could just close the top drawer and invade one's personal space, so we would pull out the larger filing cabinet drawer on the bottom and pretend that we needed it open. Women were nothing if not excellent filers, after all. At least in Arnold's world.

He also reacted differently to people based on, it seemed, whether they greeted him with his first or last name. And here was a tradeoff. People who kept it formal and used only his surname were subject to less frequent outrageous behavior, but they also went automatically and immediately into the Old Humorless Bitch file, which was not an auspicious place to be. For those employing use of his first name, well, they were good people, and he would have your back. When he wasn't aiming for a little frotteurism or voyeurism, that is. I called him Arnold. Anything not to be talked down to, which, granted, would have been difficult for him, given that I was at least eight inches taller than he, but which seemed not to dissuade him when speaking with the OHB crowd.

On this day, he greeted me at the reception desk, "Good morning, Jenifer." He gave me a mini-bow, giving me the impression that he could have passed for Tiny Tim if he'd wanted to. Or an Austrian version of the Lollypop Guild.

"Good morning," I replied, attempting to continue walking.

"Jenifer," he said, making me slow down out of common courtesy, "you know what you need?"

"What, Arnold?" I bit back a sarcastic response.

"Just a little makeup. You have such a lovely face, you should bring out your cheekbones more."

"I'll keep that in mind," I said, and this time I marched down the hall.

*   *   *

Work had been enough to occupy me during the day, but at home, I was uneasy with my own thoughts. Why couldn't I just get this gender/sex crap out of my head? What was wrong with me?

Not adding anything positive to my outlook was an email from Pat.

> —I think we need to take a break. Don't take this the wrong way. I just need some time as I try to figure out what's going on with me. I don't think you're good for me right now. Maybe we can try

> again in a couple of months. Anna thinks it's a
> good idea, too. But that doesn't mean I don't want
> to keep in touch.

I considered throwing my laptop across the room. I liked the laptop too much to do that. Not that taking a break was a bad thing. I was more upset about feeling discarded. It was like loving a ping pong ball during a table tennis tournament.

I poured cereal into a bowl and called it dinner, the cats stalking the sudden appearance of milk in the room. Fending them off, I ate and thought. Maybe a bath would be good for my mood.

I was wrong. Sitting in the tub, I hatched a plan, somehow against my own will, to kill myself. I didn't want to take pills—pills were the typical way women committed suicide. I didn't want to confirm for anyone that I wasn't trans enough in my own death, as irrational as that sounded. I was against handguns, which were impossible to own in the District anyway, so I was limiting my choices if I couldn't die by medication or shooting. Did I want to kick it or not?

I did. And I didn't. But my life seemed like it was coming to a close all on its own. *Tick tock.*

Bludgeoning wasn't remotely possible without some clever device, and I figured I didn't have enough patience for the whole Goldberg contraption thing.

Slashing seemed the best, quickest, and pain-most-tolerable choice. I figured if I cut my dominant arm first, I would still have the strength to cut my weaker side next. And if I were in a warm tub, like now, well sure, that would work.

As a plan, it seemed angry.

I guess I'm angry.

I needed help.

* * *

I pussyfooted around for a few weeks, trying not to think about ending my life, but life seemed increasingly pointless and unavoidable. I wondered if I could ignore my tub, but since I washed everyday and needed the toilet multiple times a day, I had to keep encountering my own unwanted fantasy. At a Robyn session, I came clean about my latest insanity.

"I think I need medication," I said, staring at my usual spot on the floor. Apparently it was the spot that needed the most attention. I think it was an old tea stain on the carpet that made it look more pathetic than the rest of the rug.

"I don't think I can do this on my own. I guess I'm a failure."

"I think you're brave," she said, looking me in the eye. "It's pretty courageous to say you need help."

"I don't feel brave. I feel like time is slipping away."

She looked at me with a serious expression.

"Here's the number of a friend of mine. She's a psychiatrist. I'll call her office and tell them to expect your call." She scribbled on her notepad and then said, casually, "How much time do you think you have?"

She was smooth, that Robyn.

"I don't know, really."

"Well, enough that you can get home, get up in the morning, and call them?"

"Yes. I can do that."

"You want to do that?"

I thought about my answer for a moment.

"Yes, I want to do that."

"Okay. Then let's talk some more about you. How are you feeling about your gender identity this week?"

"I want to just do it already."

Did I just say that?

"You do? That's wonderful!"

Who is she talking to?

She was still talking. I tuned back in. "So is there a new name you've taken? You don't have to tell me if you're not ready yet."

"Everett."

Shut up! You sound like a lunatic! I was ready for her to laugh at how stupid I sounded.

"I love Everett—it really suits you! Everett Maroon. I like it!"

"Really?"

"Really. Do you have a middle name yet?"

"Daniel. It was what my parents wanted to name me originally, before I actually popped out."

"Everett Daniel," she said, like she was trying on a pair of shoes. "I think you did a great job on the name. Any nicknames?"

She was taking a census. "Um, Ev, I guess. Maybe not Evy."

"Okay," she grinned at me. "I wouldn't call you Evy anyway."

I gave her a little smile. "Good!"

"Okay, so tomorrow, you're going to get up and call this number. Right?"

"Yes, Robyn, I promise. I want to feel better than this."

"I want you to feel better than this, Ev."

Ev. She never called me Jenifer again. It was like she'd started using my real name.

*   *   *

I emailed in late to work, thankful that I could thus avoid calling in to work and trying to explain that they shouldn't worry, I'm just trying to keep from killing myself. Then I patiently waited for the clock to approach 9:00 a.m. to place the call. "Hello. My name is—"

"Can you hold please?" The voice was crisp, terse.

"Um— "

"Thank you." And then I was subject to the musical stylings of MC Hammer, the artist who had his own form of time.

Two minutes later the receptionist came back on the line. "Now then, how can I help you?"

It was as if I had called to set up a spa appointment to pay people seventy dollars to put cucumber slices on my eyelids.

"I'm trying to make an appointment to see Dr. Berman." This was Robyn's friend who had experience with GLBT people.

"Okey dokey, sure," she clipped. "How is January 17th?"

January 17th was a perfectly fine day, in my honest opinion. I had nothing against January 17th, even if it was only a few days before the day voted the most depressing of any given year, according to some doctor in England who eked out his fifteen minutes of fame talking about his calculations. But in terms of seeing a psychiatrist, January 17th, two months away, was horrible for me.

"Um, I can't wait that long," I managed.

"Well, that's the soonest—"

I cut her off. "Look, who can I see this week?"

"Well, that's not a lot of time from now."

"No, typically 'this week' isn't far from 'now.' I won't make it past this week."

"Oh." She sounded disappointed.

She asked for my insurance carrier. It did not endear me to her to think that her response was in any way dependent on my answer.

"How about Dr. Menchen?"

Once we were off from the target of Dr. Berman, I didn't really give a shit who else I saw. Robyn was my therapist, after all. This was just for the meds.

"That's fine."

"Okay. Can you come in tomorrow at 4:30?"

I told her I'd be there, hung up, and tried to breathe. As they did when I was stressed out, Sebastian and Ulysses came wandering up to me, on the pretense that they were starving and wasting away. I held them and cried a little, mostly out of relief and somewhat out of fear of the future. *If there is a future.*

* * *

The rest of my day went easier, with that hurdle having been trampled to the ground. I had something to hang on to, even if I hadn't let go of feeling like a total mess.

Pat called to say hello. So much for wanting space.

"So how's your place?" he asked. I tried not to think about the three flights I had to walk up in the heat, the air conditioner that had grown wings, or the image of me dead, floating in the bathtub in my own watered-down blood.

"It's fine. The cats seem to like it, even though it's not as big as my last apartment."

"That's good. They're good buddies for you."

"Yeah, they are," I said, wishing I'd had a phone with a cord so I could twirl something around my fingers.

"Want to do dinner tomorrow?" he asked. "It'll have to be early, I think, I'm busy later." I wondered if he'd forgotten about his "taking a break" email.

"Well," I said, thinking that I rarely, if ever, turned him down, "I can't, actually."

"Oh? What are you up to?"

"I am going to see a psychiatrist." I wondered why I'd said that, but I let it hang in the air to see what he did with it.

"A psychiatrist? You already have a therapist."

"I know. But I think I need medication. I uh, I need something more."

"Why, Jenifer? What are you saying?"

I pet Sebastian absentmindedly, without anything else to fiddle with. The cat didn't seem to mind.

"I'm saying I've been thinking about hurting myself." Sure. I'd been thinking of hurting myself, that much was true. That I was thinking of hurting myself to the degree that I would die, well, Pat could put that together for himself.

"Oh, so the second you get a little depressed the medical world comes running to your aid?" He had started shouting. "I've been depressed for years and nobody's done shit for me! How nice that you can get the help you need so fucking quickly!"

Silence on the line. I looked at the phone as evidence that I actually was having this conversation.

"What would you prefer, Pat, that I go and kill myself so you don't have to be angry that I made an appointment to get some anti-depressants? Is that really what you're saying?"

"No, no of course not. It's just—" he was stammering. "Of course if you're depressed you should get help. I just don't see what you're depressed about."

"So we've gone from I'm-pissed-it's-not-all-about-me to invalidating my feelings? Is that it?"

"No," Pat said, as I hung up on him. *Let's extend the break period a little,* I thought.

* * *

I had big hopes for the psychiatrist. He would be charming and nice, and because I was shelling out 250 dollars for a thirty-minute session, he would be extremely efficient. In reality, everything in his office was milky tan. Blonde wood furniture, tan carpet, beige walls, dark frames surrounding tan-looking pictures and cream diplomas. Tan, tan, tan. I was concerned about his own mental health.

He was short, obviously spent quality time in a gym, and balding, but he was covered in hair everywhere else. This made him not unlike an Ewok. An Ewok in a beige galaxy far, far away from home.

"So, how can I help you? What is going on for you?" He stayed behind his desk and offered me a chair to the side of it. This was perhaps his attempt to not have a desk entirely between us. I figured he thought he was a real hippie, speaking to the people.

"Well, I've been depressed," I began.

"I see. Why do you think you are depressed?" At this point he crossed one leg over the other, and I saw he was wearing freshly shined black shoes. With tan pants. I rushed to quiet the uninvited image of him coming home to a tan house in a tan sports car and being greeted by a tan wife with black hair. I wanted to giggle. He didn't notice my mental story-making and went about scribbling notes onto a sheet of paper squared up on the clipboard.

"Well, work has been hard, and I'm having relationship problems, and I'm transgender." I loved tacking it on to the end like that. I was just testing if he was listening. It seemed safer than saying I was an alien from the planet Xarpathican.

"You think you're a transsexual?" More scribbling.

Since he wasn't looking at me, I stared at his shoes. Though freshly polished, they were worn on the heel and toe. I wondered what kind of gait could produce that wear pattern. Suddenly I felt the need to watch him walk.

"Um, I am a transsexual, yes," I said, trying not to be stubborn.

He finally looked up after writing more with his beige pen. That must have been it. The office was a tribute to his favorite writing instrument.

"Well, that's just not very common," he said, swinging his legs under the desk and hiding the evidence that he took fourth place in the last Annual East Coast Silly Walk Race.

I was not amused. This masculine, unhappy lesbian walks into a psychiatrist's office, and he's shocked to hear they're transgender?

"Uncommon though it may be, there are still plenty of people who are, and I am one of them." I had never had to really fight to be called this, even in my many arguments with Pat about it. Was I sure about what I was saying?

"So how depressed are we talking?" he asked, switching gears.

"Um, very?" I thought of the pain scale pediatricians use for their young patients and wished I had it in my pocket to show him. Let me point to the extremely sad face.

"How very is very?"

"I've been thinking that my time is running out. I've had to stop myself from hurting myself. I've been thinking about killing myself."

"Oh, I see." Scribble, scribble. I imagined tan ink coming out of the pen.

"How would you do it?"

"Do what? Kill myself?" *Seriously?*

"Yes."

I told him. He looked at me for the second time in fifteen minutes. "And how long since you first started thinking this?"

I pondered for a moment. "About three weeks since I figured out how, about three months since I first started seriously considering suicide."

His next question terrified me. "Would you like to go to an in-patient center?"

"No. I would definitely not like to go to an in-patient center. I would like to try some antidepressants first and see if that helps." I was proud that I sounded so reasonable. At least, I thought I sounded reasonable. Maybe I was completely psychotic, just thinking I was stringing sensible words together when really I was saying, "Antler's automobiles spilling potassium at ox math."

"Okay. And tell me, how are you sleeping?"

"I'm not sleeping much."

"Okay. And how many hours would you say you sleep a night?"

I had to think about it. The insomnia had been with me for a while, since earlier in the previous summer, since ... since my dream, really.

"I suppose I get about three hours of sleep a night."

He started writing really hard on his clipboard. It was as if he had sounded a silent alarm on his emergency system, the TAUPE level being the equivalent of the shit hitting the fan.

"Okay, then. I am going to write you a prescription for some Lexapro and some Ambien. I also want you to buy a blue lamp for your bedroom. Blue helps people sleep better. The antidepressant won't make you feel differently for a couple of weeks.

"Now with these Ambien," he continued, despite the fact that I didn't have a sheet with a clipboard for any note-taking, "take one about twenty minutes before you want to fall asleep. Just try it once. If the next day you're feeling nervous or shaky, or confused, don't take another one. Not everyone can handle the Ambien."

I promised him I would follow his orders. I was to see him again in a month. I drove to my neighborhood, went to my local pharmacy, and filled the scripts. And that night, I took my pretty pills and crossed my fingers that I would start feeling better. Maybe if I got some quality sleep I could buy a blue light the next day.

*   *   *

The doc had been right about at least one thing. That sleeping pill knocked me out precisely twenty minutes after I swallowed it. I woke up from the best sleep I'd had in months, the cats snuggled up against me, purring contentedly. I kissed them and jumped out of bed, happy to start my day.

I had practiced my don't-look-at-the-tub strategy, and I still needed it today, but I noted I wasn't as upset to see it as I had been recently. I had a new well of energy in me, and even if the Lexapro wasn't going to kick in for another two weeks, I had a plan and I was working my plan.

I made a cup of coffee, poured it into my travel mug, hopped in my SUV, and sped off for work. *Oh, the day! The gorgeous day! How nice it is to sleep,* I thought, as I changed the radio to an eighties station from my usual NPR. *Fuck NPR!*

Thirty minutes later, I pulled into the parking lot. The engine idling, I wondered where the green metal parking garage door was that I walked through every day to get to my office. *But parking lots don't have parking garage doors,* another part of my brain insisted to me. I agreed with that logic. Which meant something else was wrong.

Then it dawned on me. I had driven to Target in Alexandra, Virginia, an entirely different state from where I worked.

I wondered if that would qualify as "confusion," because I really wanted another full eight hours of sleep from more Ambien. I put the car in gear, cursed at myself, and drove to work, checking every few miles or so that I was still pointed in the right direction.

Once I made it to work, however, I was on a mission. I barreled through my tasks, editing reports, writing proposals, and getting through my voicemail backlog. I was moving so quickly I nearly kicked up a dust storm. It seemed like the lunch hour was upon me before I'd even settled in.

I sat down at my computer with my overpriced but pretty grilled sandwich from across the street, and I found the online game I played most days when I ate at my desk. It was one of those games the player always loses, eventually succumbing to the increasing speed and difficulty of the game. I typically bombed out around level twenty, which was considered expert. The game was perfect for lunch because it took about fifteen minutes to get through the levels. I hit the start button and clicked away, sorting brightly colored shapes into holes of the same shape, enjoying the simple music and thinking I was getting better at this game than I'd realized. *Click, plop, click, plop,* went the pieces. Maybe they had made the game easier. Many minutes later, my hand was getting tired. I looked down at my fingers on the trackball and was somewhat horrified to see that they were a blur, and animated, it seemed, with a mind of their own. I looked back at the screen, and read the screen:

Level 33

Astonished and frightened, I turned off the monitor, the sounds changing from happy chirping to warning, angry beeps signaling I was failing at my task. A big part of me wanted to jump back in, light the screen back up, and save the game.

"Go, go go!" my stoned self yelled at me.

"This is wrong," my not as stoned self yelled back.

I got up, quite unsteady, and felt my pulse race.

Okay. Okay. No more Ambien. That shit is dangerous.

Chapter 8

The antidepressants took effect little by little. My anxiety started to feel controllable, and then minor, and then under my personal threshold of worrisome. Likewise my depression started to ease, and I went from having to keep myself from carrying out my suicide plan, to thinking my plan was just a back-burner option, to thinking it was only for use as a last resort, to thinking blood, yecch, I wouldn't do that anyway. Getting through each day had been hard, but each day was easier than the last.

At some point that I couldn't identify, I started thinking that being a transsexual was less bad than being dead. I was happy for the shift, even if I didn't know when it had started. I was okay. Maybe okay, anyway.

I drove into Robyn's neighborhood and was delighted to see that a Starbucks was under construction at the strip mall by her house. I might have been the only person in America happy to see yet another chain coffee shop. No more fake-browsing greeting cards. I could have a caffeinated beverage and avoid the cashier's silent hostility.

If Robyn was less than pleased with how my appointments with the shrink had gone, she made no comment about it. I thought I could tell that she thought he was an arrogant ass.

"How are you feeling?"

I considered my response, in part because I wanted to get it right, and in part because I had such a hard time these days knowing what emotions I was having at all. "I'm good, I think. I'm starting to feel positive about the future."

She smiled and sat back on the loveseat. She had a warm smile that usually bookended our sessions instead of popping up in the middle like a rodent in a whack-a-mole game.

"So Ev," she said, and I started thinking about what a nice refuge this was, this space where we pretended I was some guy named Everett. I'd heard Samantha and Marcus use it, and Robyn, and some online acquaintances, but that was it. Everett's universe, I supposed, was very small. Jenifer, the still-real me, was the nervous nilly, too afraid to let go.

"Are you there?" she asked, and I had to admit I hadn't been listening. I told her where my mind had gone.

She pushed her curly brown hair out of her face and looked at me.

"So do you see yourself transitioning? What are you thinking about for your future?"

My future. My future, that was still a no-show in the drunken beer fest of Past and Present and To Come.

"I want to start hormones. Low-dose. I want to see how it goes, take it one day at a time, and see where I am in six months." I said it like I'd really thought it through before the words farted out of my mouth.

"I think that's great. Taking it slow sounds like a cautious, do-able plan. I know a doctor you can work with."

"Really?" *Could this actually happen?*

"Do you know what you want to say to everyone?"

"No." *See, this couldn't actually happen.*

"Well, that's okay. Maybe we could talk about that."

I considered the people I knew. Lori. Jeffrey. My family. My coworkers. Oh, there were so many people. I wasn't just thinking about reinventing my world, I was actually reinventing my world.

Pat. *Oh crap, Pat.* We were just getting back on track after our fight. He was not going to take this well.

* * *

I saw a small package under the mailboxes in the lobby of my building and realized it was my gift to myself. I had been waiting for weeks for this, because apparently mocha was a very popular choice in the fake penis market.

In the privacy of my living room, I tore open the package and pulled out my new little friend.

It wasn't too big or too small, it was just right. Now I just needed to avoid having a big bad wolf burst in and steal my new penis for his lunch. It did seem a few shades darker than my own skin, but I still thought it better than the pasty white of the "vanilla" option. Who wanted to look like they had an icicle in their pants?

It clung to my hands as I examined it, the tacky surface a side effect of the packy's "anatomically correct" texture. I couldn't remember a time when I'd touched a non-erect male member, but I'm sure there was a testing crew back at the fake penis factory.

I unzipped my jeans and looked at my crotch. Where was this even supposed to go? Looking at the north pole or down to the equator? I duck-walked to my computer as my pants crumpled under me. Online, I searched for pictures of penises. None of the photos—and there were many, most regrettably shot in less than clean bathrooms—looked like my lump of soft silicone. Once I realized I only needed to find pictures of men in underwear, I had my answer for how to orient my new friend.

The form of the packer ended abruptly behind the fake scrotum, as if only the front of the nuts mattered. Or perhaps there was a parallel universe out there where the back half of the balls had been jettisoned by accident, and now they were just floating in space for eternity, longing for reunification. Cupping the never-to-be-whole sack in my palm, I put the packer in my white briefs, having switched to men's underwear the previous summer. It was nice not seeing flowers on my crotch anymore. The tip of the packer pointed toward my left knee cap.

It felt strange, as if I had suddenly sprouted a limb that was numb to all sensation. It also felt oddly empowering. I strutted around the apartment, quite unlike Tom Cruise in *Risky Business*, and only for about sixteen seconds before my self-consciousness overtook my enthusiasm.

I went to pull the thing out of my shorts and grimaced as I took a few strands of hair with it. This is why people put cornstarch on these things, isn't it? I put it on the top of the radiator in the bathroom and went about making supper for myself. Good thing I lived alone if I was going to leave my penis lying around.

* * *

I had my next appointment with the shrink, and true to form, he had on a tan button-down shirt and brown tie. I really wanted to know how he'd arrived at this blander-than-milk color palette. *Maybe I should tell him I have a fake penis in his color scheme.*

"So how are you feeling?" he asked, and although it was the same question Robyn always asked me, with him I wanted to reply with something sarcastic.

"With my hands," I said, before I could stop myself.

"Nice," he said, smiling at his clipboard. Why was he smiling at the clipboard? The clipboard didn't give him a witty answer, I did! I sighed and guessed that I now had to actually answer his question.

"I think I'm doing better. I don't stay up all night worrying about anything anymore. I'm sleeping more, but I can't handle the Ambien."

"Okay," he said, the tiniest bit of lilt in his voice. He scribbled down a note on his paper. I had the distinct impression that he had no idea what any of his patients' issues were unless he had his notes in front of him.

"So I spoke with your therapist, Dr. Zeiger," he said. He straightened up in his chair. "She seems to believe your claim that you have gender identity disorder."

My claim? Where is he going with this?

"Well, good."

"She seems to think you are ready to start a course of hormone treatment."

It sounded as if I was about to try getting rid of a horrible toe fungus. My ovaries were poisonous mushrooms in his world. Maybe this meant I could attack assholes on the street with my transsexual spores. "Are you a man or a woman?" they would shout, and SSSSWhack! I would hit them with a barrage of sex-changing fungi.

"I am ready. I'm more than ready."

"You know some of the effects are irreversible."

I knew what he meant. Once vocal cords thicken, they stay that way. Hair follicles triggered to grow keep producing hair even after testosterone levels fall, so even older men don't lose their chest hair. Conversely, any head hair I lost from hormones would stay lost. And most definitely if I cut anything away from my body with surgery, it would be gone forever. But I wanted him to give me credit for doing my research.

"Good. I'm counting on it being irreversible."

"Look," he said, actually leaning in and looking at me, "I am a little concerned because until very recently, you were in a major depressive episode. And I still haven't determined if you are maybe bipolar with some hypomania."

"The closest I've come to mania, doctor, is after I took that poison Ambien pill. I think I really need to do this. My depression is because I'm walking around female." I sounded steady and calm. At least, *I* thought I sounded steady and calm.

"Dr. Zeiger intimated to me that you want to start slowly. Can you tell me why?"

"Because it sounds like the more prudent course."

"Well, I have to agree with you."

How nice. The National Institutes of Health psychiatrist agreed with me. As if I had intelligence all on my own. "But I really think you need close monitoring."

"Well, I see Robyn every week." *Please tell me he doesn't want me to see him more often.*

"Well, I would like to see you more often myself," he said.

I looked at him and his tan attempts to cover up all the colors of the world, and told him I couldn't afford to see him more often than I already was, which he countered with a, "Well, I can lower the rate for you." He would be a part of my life, at least for the near future.

I hoped the endocrinologist Robyn referred me to see was less frustrating than the shrink.

*   *   *

I had resolved to pull myself together. None of my coworkers knew about my depression, I hadn't mentioned anything to my family, and after Pat's response, I didn't dare bring it up with any of my friends.

I looked forward, however, to heading up to the city to meet Marcus and Samantha to hang out with new people who only knew me as Everett. Two plus months after their invitation and a couple of cancellations later, I was ready to explore another city. It would be one big masquerade, I told myself. I worried I would forget who the me inside really was anymore, but at least I would be eating decent bagels while I faked my way through New York.

I threw a few changes of clothes into my bag, heaped the cats' food dish with kibble, and put out four bowls of water for them. That should last them two and a half days, I thought. They looked at me, perplexed, for a few seconds and then dove into the food pile, not believing there was a bottom to the container.

Then I was on the highway, pushing through Maryland and Delaware and into New Jersey, my home state, full of memories of my childhood and high school. Was I really serious about all of this? Was I really ready? And why must I annoy myself by asking continuously if I was ready?

With each passing mile, I giggled a little more. I could do this. I wasn't faking it. I was already so masculine—wasn't I really talking about just pushing myself over another couple inches on the gender spectrum?

I rounded the corner onto Marcus and Samantha's street in Park Slope, thankful I hadn't missed any of the 17,285 turnoffs between DC and here. I grabbed my bags, locked the car, and knocked on their door. I could still probably run and chicken out of this.

But the door opened and a smiling woman embraced me. She wasn't much shorter than me, with long brown hair and a clean, slightly fruity smell. She had a round, little girl's face, and a mouth that seemed a little pouty even when she smiled.

"Everett! It's so good to meet you! How was your trip?"

Marcus walked up to me next, a big bear of a man with a love of baseball bordering on fanatical. He had agreed to like me even though he was a devoted Mets fan, while I was a born and bred Yankee fan. His sleepy eyes belied his quick intelligence.

It was like seeing old friends. Maybe this trip was a good idea, after all.

I reconsidered that level of confidence later, while they were introducing me to their group of friends. Everyone was cooler and younger than me, one of the things Pat had sometimes pointed out when we were out in a group. And I didn't know the rules of engagement; I pissed off one person named Booker by using a female pronoun. I apologized and asked Booker if I should have used a male pronoun.

"No," Booker said to me sharply, lining up a shot on the ubiquitous pool table found in gay bars across the country.

"Uh, okay," I said, confused. "What should I use, then?"

Booker made the shot and stood up, frowning at me, clearly exasperated. "You should just have asked. I like different pronouns on different days."

As if that was the obvious answer. I slinked over to another corner of the room and tried to mingle with someone else.

Everyone had thought through their gender identity to higher orders of magnitude than I had considered. And here I'd thought I was the over-analyzer. One person wanted people to use "they" and "their" for their pronouns, even if there was only one of them. Another wanted to create a new pronoun called "per." Several people were genderqueer, and were either differently oriented at different times, or were another gender outside male and female altogether. I had read as much in theory books and online, but interacting with them was much more challenging. I was a kindergartener trying to pass a calculus test.

My chest started itching under my binder because my embarrassment was raising my body temperature. To add to my persistent sense of failure, my packer had started drifting toward starboard. I was the transgender reject of the group. This was how Pat talked about feeling. Maybe everyone went through this. I had a pang of sympathy for him.

I wandered back to where Samantha was and relaxed for a minute. She didn't seem to be assessing me and my authenticity or my trans-manners. She asked if I was ready to go, and I was happy to oblige her.

We left the small tavern and found our way to an all-night restaurant, and I thanked the city for having a twenty-four-hour eatery, since I was used to DC rolling up the sidewalks around midnight. A while after ordering we each were presented with a small fiefdom of food.

I told them I'd pissed one person off that night.

"Oh, yeah, you know, we ask how people identify when we meet them," Marcus said, enjoying a quality piece of challah French toast.

"I will have to remember that," I said. "I've never met any genderqueer people except Pat."

I caught the disapproving look between them at the mention of his name, but it was subtle and over in mere moments.

"Well," Samantha said from her seat at the table, behind a massive plate of bagels, cream cheese, tomatoes, onions, and capers, "don't worry about it. As you get to know more people and they get to know you, you won't feel so nervous."

I let myself be reassured, digging into an eggs Benedict the size of 54th Street. Maybe eating myself through my anxiety would work better today than it had on oh, any day before. It was worth a shot, anyway.

* * *

With loving messages and an evening of Paula Poundstone's humor at a venue in Virginia, Pat and I had repaired the hurt feelings from a few weeks earlier. Now we sat on my couch, the cats lapping up all of the affection we could bestow on them.

I'd just shown Pat a photo of a Hello Kitty taxi in Japan, knowing he had a thing for the cartoon.

"See, this is why I need to visit Japan. Those are my people."

"Because of Hello Kitty?"

"It's a cat with no mouth and a ubiquitous presence. Any country that would support that is my kind of place."

I laughed, then changed the topic of conversation. "Pat, I need to thank you for finding Ulysses and bringing him into our lives."

Ulysses, for his part, looked satisfied in his new role as caressed kitten. Pat had brought the flyer about the new litter of kittens to me. We'd gone to a large house in a rich section of Northwest where the homeowners were looking to place each kitten, and I'd fallen in love with Uly in one flat second.

"Aw, well, I realized that Sebastian was lonely," he said.

"Yes, it was Sebastian that was lonely after my breakup with Lori."

"Of course. Anyone could see that. I'm glad you're happier these days."

I appreciated that but then fretted to myself. I was happier about things that I was hiding from Pat. I braced myself for another wave of guilt.

Chapter 9

The endocrinologist's office was very pretty, with flowered wallpaper and lots of pictures of babies looking ecstatic to be alive. I gave my name to the receptionist and then looked through the stack of magazines for something other than *Parenting* or *Woman's Day*. I would have paid decent money for a copy of *Newsweek*.

A very long time later, I was called back to the doctor's actual office. In addition to his diplomas and board certifications hanging on the wall were several "Best Doctor" awards from *Washingtonian* magazine and other ratings guides. He also had some fright-inducing crystal awards that ironically looked like reproductive organs on the attack. The awards were for his expertise as an OB/GYN, which was his main specialization, endocrinology being his secondary focus. I was glad the awards were on the other side of the room.

He introduced himself to me and said that he was a big fan of Robyn's, and as she was a big fan of mine, he knew he'd like me immediately. I was unsure whether to find that sweet or daunting.

He spoke with the pacing of a box turtle at rest.

"So," he said, drawing out the vowel sound as if he were paid based on how long it took him to say each word, "Robyn tells me you would like to begin testosterone therapy."

"Testosterone therapy" took seven seconds for him to precisely enunciate. Perhaps he was this careful about everything, which would be to my benefit.

"Yes, I would," I replied hastily, trying to make up for lost time. If he met with all of his patients in his office, was he hours behind by the third patient? I wanted to keep him on schedule.

His pacing was so deliberate I wondered if he was trying to restrain himself from beating me to death with a crystalline uterus award. He asked about my plan, which had somehow skyrocketed from being a loose combination of thoughts to some master architecture rivaling the complexity of the Manhattan Project. I told him what I wanted: a slow start on hormones, ramping up after half a year to a full dose, top surgery to excise my breasts, and maybe bottom surgery, but I hadn't looked at those options yet. He nodded his head.

"Okay," he said, as I found myself starting to acclimate to his pace, "I would like to work with you on that. If you would like to work with me on that."

If I thought I was going to get hormones that minute, I was mistaken. I hid that I was crestfallen. He told me to come see him in four weeks.

Buying a gun in Virginia came with no waiting period whatsoever, but getting testosterone—T—was going to take another month. I shook his hand and found my car in the parking lot. I called Marcus and Samantha to talk about how excited I was. Because apparently, I was thrilled.

*   *   *

Pat, meanwhile, was psyched about his changes from T.

"I just feel so different, like I'm coming into my own body now," he said over dinner. "I know you don't understand."

"I think that's great," I said. I poked at my unappetizing mix of entrees that I'd accumulated from the dubious selections at the Old Country Buffet. It was one of his favorite places to eat.

"I just am starting to stress out because I don't really know how to shave. My facial hair is coming in fast."

"Oh, it's not that hard, you just shave down your cheeks," I began, thinking about what my father had told me when I'd asked him. I'd sat next to him in the bathroom in first grade or so, enjoying the smell of the shaving cream and the quiet noise of the stubble giving way.

"Jesus Christ, Jenifer, maybe you can't help me with everything!" He slammed his fork down on the table, making the china rattle, and a few customers looked over at us. "Maybe I don't need some damn lesbian telling me how to shave my face! Maybe I want a real man to give me advice, not you!"

I fought back a frown and tears. I lost the frown battle, and the corners of my mouth flexed downward against my will.

"Oh my god, are you crying? I'm just saying, stop being a know-it-all. I get to do some things on my own, you know."

"Fine," I managed, gripping the word with my teeth. "I don't give a shit how you're going to shave."

"You know, you're really not supportive," he said.

"Pat," I said, "I have been a hundred percent supportive of you since you told me you had 'gender shit.' I told you I believed you about your gender when you said everyone else wrote you off as crazy. I took a week off of work so I could stay with you during the day as you recuperated from a surgery. I've tried to be understanding as you've gone back and forth about what to do, and after two years of me listening to you, you now tell me I'm not supportive? Are you kidding?"

"Okay, fine, you're supportive," he said. "Sheesh. Chill out."

Surprised at myself, I said I was ready to go. I dropped him off at his apartment in silence, holding my thoughts in a small box in the pit of my stomach. When he got out of the car and I was a few blocks away, I considered screaming.

* * *

—I have exciting news, Samantha typed to me.

—Oh, what's that? The possibilities were limitless, and I didn't feel like guessing.

—One of our really good friends is moving to DC! You're going to love him!

—Oh yeah? I typed, starting to feel unsure of where this conversation was going.

—His name is Niles. He's a book junkie like you. If it's okay I'll give him your contact info.

—Okay! Sounds good.

I was getting used to feeling my blood pressure increase, mostly in my fingers and toes. I had my online world and a small piece of the New York City world, and those were both safely away from my enclave in DC. I wasn't ready for anything to merge. Everett and Jenifer were like oil and water, not to be in the same place, at least not without vigorous shaking.

And now this total stranger would know how to reach me. The me, me. Not the virtual me.

* * *

I had seen in an email that there was a new activist group starting up in the District, centered on civil rights for transgender and gender variant people.

"Are you going to go?" Pat asked me, sitting on my couch and petting Sebastian, who appreciated the affection by purring loudly. He'd come over for lunch on H Street, and we'd walked back to my apartment afterward.

"Well, I don't know. I don't know these people. Are you going to go?" I wasn't sure how much energy I had for activists in the midst of everything else.

"I think I'll check it out. I think you should go." His voice had dropped, and many of his words were squeaking out of him. I found it charming.

"You do?"

"Yeah. You know, you can bring that old school butch perspective to the group."

Oh, man. Really? Now I was old school?

"I came out in 1990, Pat."

"Yeah, exactly. That was a long time ago now. You know, you don't have to be trans to go."

"Some people consider butch to be transgender, you know."

"What are you, reading little books on being trans? Butch is butch and a perfectly fine identity. Stop trying to play in the club."

I looked at him and suddenly he seemed nervous. "I'm tired of your shit, Pat. Stop dismissing me."

He sighed. "I'm just saying, it's okay for there to be different communities. We don't all need to take on the same labels."

"You're not talking about labels. You're talking about your territory. I'm sick of you telling me what I can call myself because everything is about you. Sick of it."

"Well, why don't I just leave then? Anna never gives me this shit." He stood up, and Sebastian opened his eyes to see why the caressing had stopped.

"Anna is too exhausted to deal with you anymore."

"That's it," he said, and although he intended to storm out dramatically, he had to stop, put on his shoes, and tie them up. It softened the blow, much to his dislike.

"Good night," I said, wondering why I said it.

I was annoyed that he would piss off my neighbors by slamming my door behind him.

* * *

Lori had met me for breakfast down by the Capitol. Living in DC for so long, neither of us thought anything of eating bagels next to elected officials, but we did think most of their aides and assistants were tools. Slick and polished, all with the requisite U.S. flag pin, which I often pointed out was a violation of the Flag Code, they cut in line, were disrespectful to the employees at the deli we haunted, and never tipped.

"Let me ask you," she said between bites, "why are you still with him? He just gets nastier and nastier."

"His grandmother just died. I think it's his way of dealing."

"Oh, you think so?" She had brown or hazel eyes depending on the day. Today's eyes were a light coffee color. "My father died when I was nineteen. Did I take it out on anyone? No. Maybe he's just an asshole."

"Yeah, maybe. But I care about him."

"Dump him. Meet someone else. You can care about them."

"I don't know. He's going through a lot right now." I had a lot of excuses for him.

"Why, because he started T? So now he gets another reason for his assholic behavior?" She licked cream cheese off her fingers and washed it down with a cream soda. "Damn, I got *dreck* on me. It's all his fault."

"Well, it is a major hormone shift, but no, it doesn't justify his behavior."

"You're sure understanding. I just think it's always something with him."

I nodded and ate my bagel. I pondered if I would turn into a jerk once I switched to T and shut down my ovaries. I thought about telling Lori but took another bite so my mouth would be full until my bravery passed.

"We need to find you a nice girl," she said. "You are a lesbian, after all."

"I really can't have my ex finding me a new partner, okay?" I smiled reflexively.

"Okay, fine. I'll agree to that until I meet someone I think you should date."

"At least you're clear about your conditions."

"At least you're listening."

"It's easier to listen to you because we're not together anymore," I said, chewing.

"I know! What is up with that? Isn't that weird?" She paused and looked at me. "Can I try a bite of your bagel?"

"You got the same thing."

"Yeah, but yours is an egg bagel. Mine's just plain."

I sighed and gave it to her. Some things hadn't changed between us.

*   *   *

Robyn was thrilled when I asked her to write a letter to the endocrinologist that I was cleared to start hormone therapy. It would reassure him that I wasn't a steroid-seeking bodybuilder or Tour de France cyclist, that I wasn't likely to sue him over any of the side effects of a woman on T, and that I was a real, red-blooded transsexual who needed androgens to fulfill my therapy. I wasn't wild about the standards of care that mental health professionals required to get letters like this, but I understood that physicians needed some protection. Until the world changed someday this was the process for hormones and surgery.

"Of course I'll write you a letter. Did he say he needed a letter?" She was a very organized woman, with a thick binder that held the checks she'd received that day, her schedule, people's phone numbers, and extra note paper. It was very Twentieth Century, but it worked for her, and it was reassuring to me, somehow, who had tried for years to have a workable, efficient folder system, but who would give up every few months, realizing it was out of date and inconvenient to keep current. And then I'd see some newer, prettier planner in a store, and the cycle would begin again.

"How about if you email me a letter template or something, and then I can go from there?"

"Oh sure," I said, grinning but quickly worrying about where I would find such a letter. Maybe Marcus knew of one, or maybe I could copy from his. He was still the only female-to-male transsexual I knew in person. Other than Pat, whom of course I couldn't talk to about this.

We agreed I'd get a letter to her in the next couple of days so that I could bring it to the doctor on my next visit. And then I'd get my hormones! I was giddy.

I jumped into the car and dialed Marcus in New York.

"Heya, fella," he said in his relaxed way. His Long Island accent was familiar to me and reassuring.

"I'm getting my letter to start T! I'm getting my letter! I'm thrilled!" I tried to calm down as I nearly ran over a squirrel. Collateral damage.

"Wow, that's great! I've never heard you so excited!"

"I know! I can't remember being this excited!"

"That's awesome!"

"Okay," I said, "I'm going to stop shouting now!"

"Okay," he said, "me too!"

I asked him where I could find a model letter, and he said he'd email a couple to me. I thanked him, squealed a little more, and hung up. As I battled inane drivers on the Beltway, I decided I needed to have a personal manifesto.

I am living life for myself first. I will have no regrets. I will not be responsible for my family, my friends, my lovers, the universe, or anyone who is not me. I will always try to do my best and be satisfied with that.

I knew I was a dork, and I was okay with that. For the rest of the drive home, I felt like the weight of the world was off my shoulders.

One week later, at my next appointment with Robyn, I had my therapist's letter to start hormones. It was like a golden ticket from the Willy Wonka Chocolate Factory.

* * *

I had to pee, badly, but I was in a seminar at some oversized hotel in urban Northern Virginia. The panel finished up, and I headed out, not caring enough about the Q&A session. In the lobby I made my way to the restroom. Three feet from the door a woman put her hand on my arm.

"That's the women's room," she barked at me.

"I can read," I said. My voice cleared up her confusion, and she flushed, embarrassed.

* * *

I met Marcus and Samantha at the IHOP in Virginia. They'd driven down with their friend Niles and his girlfriend Syd, who pulled into the parking lot in an enormous U-Haul truck. Though Niles seemed too small to be driving the truck, he swung it around well and maneuvered it into a spot on the side of the building.

Niles and Syd were friendly and low-key, not like the other people I'd met in Brooklyn that one night out at the bar. And Syd seemed strangely familiar, but I couldn't place her.

We sat down in a cramped booth, and I started feeling nervous that I was on my turf, but not as Jenifer, not as a woman. I could feel myself getting sweaty under my neoprene binder. Niles and Marcus were binding, too, but they looked supremely comfortable. Once again I was failing to measure up. Pat was right, I had no business in this community.

I noticed they were talking to me. Syd was talking to me.

"Now I remember! We wound up looking at the same apartment together."

She remembered me, too. So she knew my "girl name." It was a cardinal rule not to use the old name. It was ten thousand times worse than getting the pronoun wrong. But in the milliseconds that passed between her recognition and telling me about it, she made the calculation to dismiss what she'd learned in favor of maintaining what she knew now. I appreciated her for that. Perhaps she'd tell Niles the moment they were alone, "Oh my goodness, it's a fake transsexual named Jenifer," but I doubted it.

"Well, that's my apartment, now," I said, waving my hand as if we were standing in the living room and I was showing it off. "Where did you decide to move?"

"About a block away," she said. "It's not as nice but it was much cheaper, and we didn't care for three flights of stairs."

"Oh, hell, you made the right decision on that one."

"Wow, so now you have a friend in the neighborhood, Niles," Samantha said, grinning like a matchmaker who got paid by the date.

"A trans friend in the neighborhood," Marcus said, making a yuk-yuk motion with his elbow.

He meant me. I attempted to take this in.

"So Niles hasn't started T yet, either, Everett," Marcus continued.

"That's right," said Niles. "I'm starting soon." He smiled, looking like a kid happy to start kindergarten.

"Yeah, cool," I said. I changed the subject. I was going to start hormones, yes, but I wasn't ready to talk about it with people I didn't know.

I wasn't sure if I was happy or terrified that they were living one block from me.

* * *

I ordered another packer because I'd left the last one on top of the radiator in the bathroom, and as the heat had come on in the fall, it had half-melted before I'd found it. Such a sad, grilled penis. At least I wasn't actually attached to it, though I wouldn't have been able to leave it on a radiator if that were the case.

The tick tock had stopped altogether. I was grateful for that. I was still counting down, but the clock was looking forward to my doctor's appointment to get my T. I didn't have a plan for telling anyone, and I wondered if there would even be any change for awhile if I were on a low dose.

I put my pathetic packer in my pants, but didn't bind myself, and headed to the activist meeting. This would let me have my own private trans moment in my pants but not appear like I was questioning up top, or so I thought.

I wondered if I'd always be an underground transsexual.

The meeting room was a fishbowl in the middle of a national GLBT organization's offices. The District was full of office space for this group or that, so we would have been perfectly content meeting at the National Association of Counties building or the U.S. Apple Association office. The conference room was much sleeker, probably, than the one at the U.S. Apple Association. Gay people know how to design a hip office.

Pat came in and kissed me on the cheek to say hello, then mingled with people he knew. I looked around and counted one familiar face that wasn't Pat. Why did I think I could count myself among them?

The pre-meeting banter died down and the meeting organizers asked everyone to go around the table and give their name and pronoun preference. *Too bad I didn't come to this before the New York trip,* I thought.

Trans. Transgender. Genderqueer. FTX, meaning female transitioning to something unknown. MTF. Trans woman. Some used "man" or "woman," saying trans as a prefix wasn't something they felt inside—for them, they were real men and women already. There were so many people who had figured it out, at least to the point that they had particular names for themselves, names that made sense to them. Some of them had transitioned a long time ago, some were just starting, like Pat. I was older than many of the people in the room, and I kicked myself for hitting my mid-thirties without having the kind of insight they did in their twenties.

Our new group had no name, no agreed upon agenda. As it happened, those were the first agenda items. We debated every possible extension of what such a political coalition could or should do for people in the city; we argued over every permutation of trans as a prefix to something else. We drew parameters around who those people were. By the end of the meeting I was so exhausted from the discussion, I no longer worried about my relationship to the trans community or the other bodies in the room, or who wore their track jacket best of all. I was focused on the conversation and everything that needed doing. It had been a struggle, but hopefully we were setting the stage for good work in the future.

The meeting finally wrapped up, all of us exhausted with our indebtedness to being politically correct. I put my notebook and pen in my bag, and Pat came up to me.

"Gonna go home now?" he asked, looking at me shyly.

"Yup. I've got work tomorrow." We started down the hall to the glittering, very gay elevator. It was late.

"My tall, dark, and handsome honey with his big job." Pat used male pronouns for me often because he said it was how he thought old school butches spoke. I never pointed out to him that I knew a lot of "old school" butches, and I'd only heard one or two of them call another butch "he." Probably neither of us was right.

"Yup. I have an early meeting." I pretended to have a sudden interest in my briefcase's front pocket.

"Well, I'm glad you could come. Thank goodness it wasn't a closed meeting."

"Closed?"

"You know, trans people only. Then you couldn't have come."

I sighed, closing the bag and slinging it over my shoulder. "You just always need to point out how trans you are, don't you," I said, lowering my voice.

"Well, no one else does it," Pat said.

"Everyone in that room called you "Pat" and "he" tonight. I think it's time you gave up the whole victim thing."

He looked like he was deciding whether to continue or give up the argument. Saved by the elevator, I stepped inside. I sighed once the doors were closed. I ignored his two calls to my cell phone as I drove home to the other side of the city, out of his self-declared territory.

* * *

The doctor visit wasn't turning out as I'd planned. I'd thought when I gave him Robyn's letter, some nurse would magically appear and stick me with a syringe full of hormones. I hadn't actually thought past the point of the letter. I was going to have to wait, again. So much for my golden ticket.

I'd already been waiting for months, but I nodded my head in agreement with his plan, which was to call in a prescription at a compounding pharmacy in Wisconsin, and then they would mail a testosterone cream to me. A cream. Like skin lotion. This wasn't the foil packet stuff that Pat was using. I could become a boy and have soft skin, all at the same time. How novel.

I gave him my work address because I didn't trust my apartment building lobby to secure my package, given that they were just left under the mailboxes for anyone to pick up and take. Binders and fake penises were one thing, but I had to draw the line somewhere.

The good doctor judged that it would take about two weeks for me to receive the hormone. And then I would come back a month later to see what my T level was.

Two weeks. I would have to distract myself with something else until then.

Chapter 10

A new binder came in the mail. Once again I pounded up the stairs with delight, then popped open the box to find an extremely small swatch of itchy fabric. Really? This was it?

This was my latest Major Binding Attempt, evidence that I still hadn't found a successful approach to minimizing the girls' appearance. I held the material up between both hands, looking for a tag. Sure enough, it was an XL. Would it stretch enough for me to put it on?

Seeing no zippers or Velcro, I attempted to pull it over my head like a sweater. I was thwarted on several levels, because the hole was smaller than my head, the sides of the fabric were only eighteen inches apart from each other, and the thing had no elastic capacity whatsoever.

I was determined to make it work. With my hands over my head, I worked it down my arms, sliding it to my elbows and shimmying it to the top of my head. This had the decided effect of making me look like I was doing a bellydance-meets-Riverdance, only with more discomfort and far less grace. I hopped up and down, as if there were a way to thrust myself into the thing, or at least work with gravity, so that I was moving up as the material was falling down. Stretched out as it now was, falling as an action was not occurring.

The cats were aware that I had genuinely lost my mind. I was a jumping, cursing, sweaty ball of motion, but I could not get the binder onto my body. Perhaps if there were a binding service that would sew these things onto people, I could have made it work. But as it was, I was stuck with the neoprene rib protector. I was starting to fret that I would never get my boobs flat enough. Or if so, that said flatness would suddenly be compromised during the simple act of bending over to tie my shoes, when the binder would spring open with gusto, releasing Becky and Bertha, like bachelor party strippers bursting out of an oversized Styrofoam cake.

So I had wasted another forty dollars, but I figured research and development always cost big bucks and was worth it in the end. There had to be some way, barring surgery, to minimize their appearance. Maybe I wanted surgery, but I was far away from knowing how to go about it or how to pay for it.

The packy, on the other hand, was fighting the good fight, despite its run-in with the hot radiator. I also noticed that there was a large tear at the base, above one of the cyberskin half-testicles. *Great. I already don't have a penis and now I'm going to castrate myself.* It was like wearing a metaphor.

I turned to my online acquaintances for advice.

—**So uh, does anyone know how to repair a tearing packer?**

—**Ouch**, came the reply. Smartasses, all of them.

—**You have to use a non-silicone based glue.**

Okay, I could handle that. And hopefully I wouldn't glue the thing to my hand, thus necessitating a rather embarrassing visit to the ER. I made a mental note to pick up some glue from the hardware store that weekend.

* * *

Jeffrey and I had made plans to go to an art show opening at one of the galleries that had sprung up on the previously decrepit 14th Street corridor. Free art, whether it was at the Smithsonian or at one of the many small commercial galleries in town, was one of the pluses of living in the city. We thought we'd take in the show, have some complimentary wine, and then get dinner.

My excitement turned to worry when Niles remarked to me that he and Syd would be at the same show. I pictured my worlds colliding. *I have to tell Jeffrey I'm going to come out as Everett. No. I have to tell Niles not to call me Everett in front of Jeffrey. No. Yes.*

After my internal puppet show of feuding voices was over, I settled on mentioning to Niles and Syd that Jeffrey, my best friend, didn't know I was transgender. They already knew that I hadn't told Pat, but they understood why. But I was starting to feel guilty for not leveling with Jeffrey.

He didn't have a lot of positive things to say about trans men, but this wasn't surprising because his only interactions with them were

Pat and Aiden, Jeffrey's former roommate who abandoned the apartment once he'd started transitioning. I couldn't figure out a way to broach the subject with him, however. And I was beginning to think that I liked having Jeffrey not know about me, because it was a way to feel anchored in the world when I still felt so tenuous as Everett. I knew how to be Jenifer, even if I'd pushed hard against the limits of who women could be. But I had no clear idea what kind of man I was.

I found Niles and Syd on the U Street sidewalk, walking up to the gallery. Awkwardly, I told them that Jeffrey would be calling me Jenifer, and they said they were cool with that, though I could tell they thought it was a strange comment. I gulped down the guilt in my throat, thanked them, and then spied Jeffrey walking toward us.

I introduced everyone to each other, and we headed inside, looking at a series of black and white drawings with little pops of color in each. They were supposed to be frustrating to look at, but I failed to find the source of irritation. It wasn't nearly as difficult as say, looking at those awful 3-D posters with the hidden images of whales or tree frogs. I frowned, looking for the things that were supposed to make me uncomfortable.

"This art fails," Jeffrey announced to me.

"You think?" I stared at one of the pictures, a girl crying with green tears streaming down her cheeks.

"And this wine sucks. Let's get out of here."

"Okay," I agreed, trying to find a place to set my glass. There was a minimal entrance, which boasted white walls, a white concrete floor, and a couple of white chairs. One couldn't have the furniture compete with the art, after all. I stashed it on the corner of a curator's desk, trying to be as discreet as possible.

We said our goodbyes to Niles and Syd, and I realized I had probably overreacted to the whole colliding universes thing, but I was playing it safe. I reflected as we walked to the restaurant that I was behaving the same way for two different sets of expectations on gender. How I stood, how I talked. It was just me, but to Jeffrey I was female, and to Niles and Syd, I was male. Maybe being a man would be easier in time.

At dinner, Jeffrey asked how I knew Niles and Syd.

"I met them through some friends of mine in Brooklyn," I said.

"Since when do you have friends in Brooklyn?" he asked, perusing the menu. I couldn't read his expression, since it was buried behind laminated paper.

"Since, I don't know. A while. Remember I went up there a couple months ago?"

"Oh, yeah, sure. You didn't say much about your trip, I guess."

"It was cold. They have good food in New York. The gay bars are all filled with young kids."

"God, I hate that shit," he said, his face still obscured by the menu. "I only go to bars with middle-aged men in them."

"Plenty of that in DC, my friend," I said.

"Thank the baby Jesus," Jeffrey replied.

*   *   *

I started seeing someone else in the mirror—I was still me, but I didn't have to imagine as hard anymore.

I looked at my reflection, hoping the T would arrive early, somehow, and thinking, *let me just keep my sanity through this process.*

Process. It was a word I wasn't used to in my personal aspirations. Was there going to be an actual process, or was I just going to become Mr. Hyde? Would people start reading in the *Post* about half-eaten baby goats in the zoo?

Maybe I'm not ready, I thought. *Maybe I can't do this.* I figured I could just toss out the tub of cream when it showed up and tell Robyn and the good doctor that I wasn't really trans after all, I was just trying to steal my boyfriend's identity. Life was moving faster than I was ready for.

And then I thought about all of the people in the trans activist meeting I'd been to. They'd made the leap of faith. I could do this, too.

I smiled before I realized I'd done it. I was really okay, and I was going to be okay.

Bring it on.

*   *   *

I had won the Outstanding Employee of the Year award at work a couple of months earlier, in December, and while I was thrilled about it and happy to hang the plaque on my wall, my boss seemed to be punishing me for it. He increased my workload by dumping his own projects on me, so in the midst of handling reports, proposals, and other assorted tasks, I was now doing research and analysis on Web technology, then writing it up and sending it to him. One day he'd walked into my office and shut the door behind him.

"What's up?" I asked, pausing from working. My hands hovered over the keyboard in mid-type.

"You think you're so special, don't you?"

"What?" I wracked my brain for some event he could be referencing.

"You're not as great as you think you are. Don't you ever make an agreement with a client in my absence again." With that, he left my office.

It wasn't the first time he'd laid into me, but perhaps it was the most unclear. After comments like that I would just sit at my desk, mouth hanging open in case a venomous insect happened by. And then he would disappear, having guilted me into doing some task for him.

One day a company vice president hopped into the elevator with me as I rode down to the lobby to get a soda.

"Your boss is really great," she said to me, looking at a little animation running on a screen in the corner of the elevator. This had been someone's recent awful idea of modernizing the office building, but shortly after they were installed some higher-up building manager pulled the plug on the project, but not the actual power cord. Thus we were treated, on a daily basis, to weather forecasts from last November. Which by definition made them not forecasts, but archives of some random meteorologist's guess at what the weather was at one point going to be. But the happy rain cloud and thermometer greeted us in the elevators anyway, suggesting we bundle up for an autumn chill. And there was still half a foot of snow on the ground outside.

"Why do you say that?" I asked. Maybe there was some insight about him I hadn't noticed.

"I just loved his report on folksonomies," she said, referring to the report I'd given him two days before about how Web users create their own content. "Really interesting stuff. You stick with him, you'll learn a lot."

"Thanks," I said.

Work couldn't serve as my refuge from the stress of my personal life, and I supposed it never should have to begin with. I wondered idly if he'd be this awful to me if I were a man.

* * *

Maybe it was that I could feel my own anger again, or that I was past the threshold of ignoring a cumulative frustration, but I felt different inside, enough that I couldn't find words to describe the new sensation. It was like being more opaque, more substantial, and perhaps a bit more sure of myself. I let the feelings swim inside me, not having to name them before they found words they liked of their own accord.

I was looking forward to getting my package, supposedly the next day. More accurately, I was excited beyond belief. I wrote a long letter to Pat that talked about everything I'd wanted to say for months, and put it in an envelope, stamped, ready to be mailed. Maybe I couldn't say things face-to-face, but I could certainly still stuff my thoughts into an envelope and send it away and then pretend I'd never done it. It turned into a lead weight, however, glued by a super strong gravitational force to the foyer table. Out of the corner of my eye from the living room, it glowered.

I was in the final stages of waiting. I had done so much waiting, I would have been a professional queue-stander if only there were competitions for such things. So at packing, I was passable, at binding I was mediocre, but at waiting for things in the mail, I was a king. I had been assured by the pharmacy in Wisconsin that they had finished compounding my cream and had sent it out in the mail.

Finding a therapist, needing a shrink, seeing a medical doctor, there were a lot of people and bills to deal with just to get good at waiting. But I had a goal, a clearly delineated place I wanted to be, and a means of breaking the tape at the finish line. I kept this to myself, except for when I posted little tidbits on one online forum or another. I longed for the day when I could come clean to my friends, if only I could find a way to tell them. And I knew that at some point, the testosterone would do my talking for me, so I had to speak up before then.

Chapter 11

My office phone rang. Fatima, the receptionist, was calling me to say I had a package up front.

"Be right there," I said, trying not to jump over my desk to get to the door.

Up at reception, Fatima was clearly interested in my present. "Women's Pharmacy International, huh?" she said, raising an eyebrow at me. "What's in the bag there, Maroon?"

"None of your beeswax," I replied.

"Mm hmm! And you think that's a good answer?" She put her hands on her hips.

"It might not be a good answer, but it's the one you're going to get."

"Ooh! Look at Jenifer ride the sassy train," she called out as I walked back to my office. I liked that Fatima.

None of the doors in the office were affixed with locks, except the human resources office. Many of the staff assumed it was because Arnold wouldn't want anyone to be able to stifle his ability to enter any of the rooms. So even if I had drawn my shades, there was always the chance that he would knock and open the door.

I sat down at my desk, looking at the package. On the return address label was a pretty in pink logo from the Women's Pharmacy, replete with a 1972-era women's symbol. Well, it was kind of undercover, wasn't it? They typically made this cream for post-menopausal women who needed a boost to their libidos. I was going to be taking a lot more than that. I opened the pouch and rifled through a thick pile of warnings and disclaimers about the side effects of using too much of the cream. The side effects were exactly what I wanted. Finding the tub at last, I set it on my desk.

Wow. It's right in front of me. Just a little tub of cream, like hand cream or something. It was very unassuming.

Now I had to get back to work, and it was only 11:27 a.m. How was I going to get through the rest of my day?

I suppressed an urge to smear it on the table, strip, and roll in it. Just one gram every other day, said the doctor. The pouch came with a little measuring spoon. I put the tub and spoon and papers back in the pouch, and I shoved the whole mess in my briefcase, since certainly that's what briefcases were for, to hold people's hormone cream.

Hello, Everett. Why are you keeping me in the dark over here? I kept seeing the pink logo out of the corner of my eye. *Yes, that's right, I called you Everett. And soon everyone else will, too. Come over here and sink your fingers into me.*

Maybe I needed to up my dosage of the Lexapro. The cream was talking to me. I had purchased haunted cream.

"Come in," I said to the knock at my door. It was Sandy, my next-door office mate.

"Want to go to lunch with a few of us? We're going to the tapas place."

"Sure," I said, grateful to have a distraction for a while. "When are folks leaving?"

"Right now. You ready?"

"Sure am."

"You're in a good mood today," she commented. "What's going on?"

"Oh, nothing," I said, smiling. "It's just a good day generally."

*   *   *

One week later I felt like a caveman. There weren't any real changes of course, although I had a sore throat and a sudden interest in sex, for which I had no outlets. I worried that the T was making me dumber or fuzzy in the head. It was going to be tough, after years of believing that women were the better sex, to acknowledge that men had their strengths, too, and not just the ability to write their names in the snow with their urine. I was a little sad that all the T in the world wouldn't make me any more able to pee my name on a lawn, especially with a nickname as short as Ev.

The makers of the cream wanted me to rub it on my crotch. *My ...seriously?* I read the instructions three times, sure that I had misinterpreted them. Nope. Put it right on the genitals. And so I had.

I had to restrain the urge to go hog wild and put a few spoonfuls on at once. When it came right down to it, I had no idea how long anything would take to affect me. Time would tell.

I wanted to post an update on my online journal, but there was nothing to say. It would have looked like: *Friday, put the cream on today. Sunday, I put more cream on today. Tuesday, guess what? Yup, more cream.*

So aside from feeling like I was having seasonal allergies and a bout of mid-thirties expected female sexual peak, everything was the same. Except that driving to work I pulled down the vanity mirror at every traffic light, looking for facial hair, probing my pores like I thought I'd discover treasure. So commuting doubled as quality personal exploration time. The other drivers were not amused, as I missed the first five nanoseconds of many a green light, which was a big no-no in a town as self-important as DC.

* * *

It was in the midst of attempting to avoid Pat when he called me.

"Let's go out to dinner," he said.

"Uh, okay," I said, slightly suspicious. "Why?"

"I just think it would be good to connect again. We used to spend so much time together. Let's hit the buffet."

We set a date the day after next and then talked about reality shows. We still agreed on whom we wanted to win and lose on television contests.

So maybe I would tell him in person. Or send the letter before our date. Or after. Clearly, I didn't have much of a plan regarding all of this. But I did have large quantities of guilt.

It was Robyn who wanted me to move past that. She also wanted me to stop calling it "lying" to describe that I wasn't out to everyone.

"Lying is about manipulating people to achieve an end that is basically dysfunctional or fraudulent."

"And that doesn't describe me ... why?" I played with my disposable cup of hot tea that I'd picked up at Starbucks. The store had gone from zero to finished in three months. Amazing execution of technology, wasted on coffee retailing. I wondered if the Hallmark store staff missed me.

"It doesn't describe you, because you're transitioning. You have to start somewhere, come out to people one at a time. You need to give yourself a break. You're doing great, from where I'm sitting." She looked so genuine about it. Clearly, I had pulled the wool over her eyes.

"Brave, huh?" I was starting to burn my hands on the cup, so I put it down. Why on earth did the water need to be so hot? To make the warning worth the cost of printing?

"Pat wants to see me for dinner tomorrow," I said, changing the subject.

"Ah," she said, sitting back. She, like my friends, didn't like him, though she hadn't said as much. "Are you two back together?"

"No, uh, not really. I think I have more distance from the whole situation. I mean, I don't know. We'll see how it goes." *Way to sound really sure of yourself, there, bucko.*

"Well," she said, "we can talk about that next time, after you've seen him. But let's talk about you. You look great!"

I must have looked surprised, because she added a "really," as if it could be a reinforcing punctuation mark.

I continued to doubt her.

"You don't think you're changing at all?" she asked gently.

"I'm not sure. I think I have a few chin hairs, is all."

"Your face is changing, and your voice is different, Ev."

"Really?" I thought she was just trying to make me feel better.

"Really. You know, maybe you should take some pictures. How long has it been now?"

"Three months. See, it's only been three months. That's not enough time for anything much to happen."

"Maybe not much, but you can't deny you're not exactly the same, either."

I sat and thought about it. "You really think my voice is different?"

"Ev, your voice is noticeably different. It's not a woman's voice, anymore."

"Well, now I worry about something else, then."

"And what is that?"

"I worry," I said, sipping my tea, "that I won't ever see me objectively."

"Well, we'll work on that, too, dear."

I thanked Robyn, giving her a big hug on my way out the door. It was a nice thing, this being understood and un-judged.

* * *

Robyn wasn't the only one who heard a difference.

"Do you have a cold?" Sandy asked me at work.

"Just allergies," I replied. "I never had seasonal allergies before I moved to this damn city." This was a completely true statement in its own right, if not exactly a correct answer to her question.

"Tell me about it."

How long was it going to last, this hormone thing, before people started seeing me as different than I used to be? It was one thing to get used to a new hair style on someone, but wasn't I talking about something a bit more extreme than that?

I got up and went out for a short walk to get lunch, wearing my usual ensemble of dress shirt, trousers, and sweater vest. There wasn't a cloud in the narrow strips of sky visible from downtown Bethesda, but suddenly I was wet. It took me a long moment to realize what had happened.

I had someone's spit on my face. I wiped it off on my pants, being devoid of tissues, and turned to the person who was visibly angry with me. In shock, I tried to comprehend what I'd done to warrant this behavior.

He was middle-aged, in a wool hat that was very cute and age-appropriate, but too much for this April heat. He wore the Bethesda-standard, business casual outfit, and wire-framed glasses. He looked like somebody's funny uncle, but he was red in the face, veins popping at his temples and neck, fists clenched at his sides, ten feet away from me on the sidewalk as I was attempting to cross at the corner.

"Who the fuck do you think you are?" he shouted at me, and I thought he must be the most nicely dressed douche I'd ever seen.

"You ain't a man! You can't go walking like no man! You freak! You make me sick!"

I saw my chance to get across the street from him, and even though I was large and slow, I guessed I could outrun him. I sprinted across as strangers stared at him. He made no move to follow me.

An older lady came over to me. "Are you okay, hon?" she asked in the vernacular of a suburban Marylander.

"Yeah, I think so, thanks," I replied, pretending I was, in fact, okay.

"Okay, good. Take care of yourself, miss."

Miss. Man. Freak. Who was I? What was I? I wasn't identifiable to people anymore as male or female. I was at risk because of it, apparently.

Whatever I was, I didn't deserve to be accosted anymore. I had to fight for myself and my right to walk down the street so I could pay through the nose for a gourmet sandwich, just like everybody else.

* * *

We hadn't said much on the ride to the restaurant, if one could call a country buffet a restaurant. As had become typical, I drove.

It was customary in metropolitan DC to pay the host before walking back to the buffet tables to consume anything. I pulled some money out of my wallet and paid for us. We piled food on our plates, a mix of appealing and unappetizing. It was hard to tell which was which in the low lighting.

"So, how are you?" I asked Pat, not looking at him.

"I'm so happy to be starting a new job. Thanks for telling me I should take that internship."

"I didn't say you should, really, just that you should think about what you really want, and where you're going, since you kept saying you weren't happy where you were." Pat had been working in a retirement home, running the art center.

"Right. God, that job really sucked. Except I'll miss all the residents." He corrected himself. "Some of the residents."

"Yes. Especially the one who announces her age every time you see her."

He nodded. We ate for a while and talked about whatever was going on in DC. And then I told Pat I'd started T.

He was quiet for a little while, then he said, "I knew it."

"What?"

"I knew you weren't really a butch. I knew you would pull this shit on me."

"Shit?" Apparently it was all I could manage.

"That's why you pushed me into this."

"I didn't," I began, but he cut me off.

"You did. You made me go on T, to be your guinea pig, and all along it was you who wanted to be on hormones!"

"I didn't make you do anything, Pat. You said you wanted to transition. You said nobody treated you as a man. You said you were so happy I saw you as trans. You told me for a year you wanted to start T."

"Oh my God, what have I done?" he asked the ceiling. "I made a monster. I am so angry at you for lying to me all this time."

"I, I wasn't lying, I was just—"

"You did lie! You said you were just a butch. A lesbian. That's a woman, Jenifer."

People had started staring at us.

"Every time I tried to bring it up to you, you teased me, dismissed me, so I thought we should just focus on you for a while."

"So you could live vicariously through me?"

"Of course not!"

"I think that's what it was," he said, his fried okra falling off his fork.

"You can say it all you like, but that's not what happened." I tried to control my breathing.

"You can say it all you like, but that is what happened," he said, frowning at me. "And you know what?"

"What, Pat?" I wasn't sure I wanted to know the answer.

"Partner is off the table."

"What?" *Am I hearing this right?*

"You heard me. We're not partners."

"Jesus, Mary, and Joseph, we never were partners! What the hell are you talking about?"

"No, you know what? I'm breaking up with you."

"That's fine. I think we should break up, too."

"Oh, so now you can go around telling people you broke up with me?"

"What are you, eleven? Who gives a shit who knows who broke up with—I can't even ask the question!"

"You just better think hard about bad mouthing me in this town," Pat said, leaning in, punctuating his sentence with his cheap fork.

"I hardly think I'll be the one doing the bad-mouthing." I stood up and started walking to the car, not really caring whether he made it out with me or not. Pat followed me out, continuing to shout to me, but I had stopped listening. I hadn't gotten to talk to him about how he felt about his progress, when I'd started T, what kind I was on, or anything of any substance. There was just this fight, and soon, there would be quiet as I drove to my side of the city.

"And another thing," he said as we climbed in the car, "I don't want to see you at the trans men support group. That's my space, so stay out of it. You can have the activist group."

*   *   *

Bowling was unexpectedly difficult. I hadn't considered how my muscle development would affect my skill at bowling. Each week it was as if I were throwing a lighter and lighter rock at the lane.

"Jenifer, your game has gone to shit," announced Jeffrey during warm-ups. "Why are you trying to smash the hell out of the pins?"

"I bet she has some pent-up needs that need attending," Tim suggested, grinning.

Jeffrey and I rolled our eyes at him in something approaching unison.

"Isn't that what that Pat character is for, or has he finally been given the heave ho?"

"We're over," I said.

"Good," said Jeffrey.

"I think," I continued.

"Look, just go easier on your throws, okay?"

I had spent considerable time and money on bowling lessons and equipment, and I had a wonderful fingertip-drilled ball that made very pretty hook shots when I took my time on the lane. But the ball needed time to do its work, so heaving it as hard as possible resulted in a terrible throw every time. I wanted to release it more softly. It was my arm that was having the trouble. This muscle mass stuff was no joke.

"Does her ass look smaller to you, Jeffrey?" Tim asked casually. I loved the sport of bowling for the attention it placed on one's caboose.

"You know, now that you mention it, it does. Maroon, you been working out?"

"Shut up, boys," I said, throwing a strike.

"That's what I'm talking about!" Jeffrey grinned while I walked back to the chairs and took a sip of my soda.

"Now please, tell Becky and Bertha to do that during the game, not just practice," said Jeffrey.

"Contrary to popular opinion, Jeffrey," I said, polishing my ball, "my breasts are not prehensile. So cut it out."

"That's not what Pat told me," Jeffrey said, smiling.

"Obviously I attend these weekly bowling excursions for more than the gamesmanship of it all."

"Of course you do, darling. You do it for our wonderful company." And with that, they stood next to each other, cocking their heads at complementary angles and smiling.

* * *

I had gone through two tubs of T and was just starting my third. My testosterone levels were a little low, so the good doctor had increased the strength of the prescription. This prompted the compounding pharmacy in Wisconsin to call his office and ask if he was sure, because wouldn't that strength have some unintended consequences for the woman taking it? He'd reassured them it would be fine.

I was definitely getting belly hair. I also could tell that my belly was taking on a decidedly beer-driven shape, and my thighs in particular were getting thinner. It was all very subtle but noticeable to someone staring at themselves for hours on end. My self-absorption annoyed me. But I couldn't look away.

My voice seemed to have settled for the moment, somewhere in the medium frog range. I could have smoked two packs a day for ten years to get a similar effect, although of course that would come with other negative consequences for my health. I only had to shave every few days on my chin and upper lip, and I really enjoyed the whole shaving routine. I had muscle cramps in my arms, and I had started getting charley horses in my calves and hamstrings like I'd had when I was a growing child.

The immediate downside was the hot flashes. They would strike with no warning, and suddenly I was red, sweating, and gasping for breath. Too bad that starting hormone therapy did not include the Get Out of Menopause Free card.

I also had greatly increased my capacity to sweat, so now I felt like a wild boar on the run from hunters when I worked out or did anything even mildly strenuous, including walking up the three flights to my apartment.

There was the slightest increase in my sideburn hair, the hair shafts at first darkening, and then getting a little longer. It was a quiet shift, as were all of these changes, but I had to remember that I wasn't an objective party to my own body, and I hadn't been for some time. The cats didn't change their attitude toward me, as I'd heard had happened to some FTMs when they started hormones.

I was still taking it one day at a time, telling myself that I was going to try this for six months and then evaluate if I wanted to keep going.

I stared at myself in my bathroom mirror for long periods, looking at the fine chin hair. I tried counting them, even as I laughed at how stupid that was. Of course, laughing, which caused my jaw to move, interrupted hair counting.

Great. I was a laughing madman. But I was laughing, even if it was at myself.

I had to tear myself away from myself to get to the next Coalition to Amend the DC Human Rights Act, as the activist group was now called. Unwieldy, but it was a name that meant what it said. The number of people attending each meeting had dropped markedly since the first days, but the people who were still going were very dedicated to the cause.

I walked up the stairs to the row house in Adams Morgan where we had started having our meetings. No more swanky, posh nonprofit office for us. We were getting down to business in an underfunded, very needed service organization's office. I loosened my tie as I trudged up in the unseasonably warm June evening. I had put on my binder, which always made me about five degrees hotter. It also fought heavy breathing, which I was noticing I needed to do on the third flight.

I sat down in a chair and got out my small notebook, attempting not to noticeably suck in large quantities of air. I was the first one there.

As people trickled in, I saw that some of the faces were now familiar, and I knew that one of the people in the room was one of the moderators of the online forum I frequented. They still all seemed so hip and cooler than me, but as I got to talking with them, I realized they had the same fears about themselves that I did. How did strangers see them? I wanted to ask them these questions outright, but I couldn't, not yet, anyway. I just went to the meeting as if I'd always had a belly full of hair, and that my hot flashes were the result of a fever brought on by non-contagious Ebola. Surely that was plausible. I figured I should tell them my new name at some point.

We got down to the business of doing work, going over which city council members were interested in our cause, where we were encountering resistance, and how to stay off the media's radar, all to try to increase protections for trans and gender variant people.

I realized that I was not only allowed to help, but that they saw me as one of them, no matter whether I called myself a woman or a man or something else entirely. Perhaps if people had no investment in my identity, they had no reason not to be supportive. They sure acted like they were okay with whatever I called myself.

It was refreshing not to worry. I had done enough worrying. Even still, I wasn't ready to tell them about my other persona. What if Everett would never be the real me?

Chapter 12

Dr. Min was confused.

"You have a very high testosterone level," she said to me on the phone. I could imagine her expression as she said it—probably frowning, squinting at the lab results to make sure she was reading them right.

"That's okay," I said in a sing-song tone to communicate that the world was a joyous and happy place.

"I don't think so," she said. "Your hormone rate is all wrong for a healthy female."

"Look," I told her, "I'm transitioning."

"Okay," she said, and then realizing that she wasn't actually any more clear about what was going on, added, "Wait, what are you doing?"

"I've realized I'm a transsexual, and I'm on testosterone to bring about male secondary sex characteristics." It sounded so reasonable, somehow.

"Oh," she said, dragging out the vowel sound so it was more like a sigh than a word. "So who is this Dr. Travers? He put you on testosterone?"

"Yes. I thought we should share the lab results with you."

She appreciated that and said she had to read up on transsexuals to see what specific needs they had. She was nothing if not thorough.

"You need a hysterectomy, you know."

Add that to the list of sentences I wasn't expecting to hear that day. In any case, I'd gotten conflicting advice regarding such surgery, but I didn't want to tell Dr. Min that I wasn't listening to her recommendation.

"Well, one step at a time," I said, not sure if it was the Lexapro or a sudden bout of madness that made me sound so undeniably cheery.

"Okay. Maybe I'll talk to this Dr. Travers."

"Feel free!"

* * *

My mother knew something was up, in part because mothers always do, having that secret maternal underground database of their children's activities. I tried to stay one step ahead of her, always finding a way to explain something in our every other week phone calls. My voice change, for example. I was relieved every time she bought my stories. I presumed she wanted to believe me, and even if I'd shown up on her door looking like the lumberjack of my long-ago dream, saying I was just in a traveling theater show of *The Legend of Paul Bunyan*, she'd have been all-too happy to nod in agreement that I made the best Paul Bunyan ever. It's not like Sandy Duncan transitioned after playing Peter Pan. She even got that lucrative Wheat Thins endorsement.

In the spring I'd said I had seasonal allergies. In June I was amazed at how I seemed to be allergic to grass. Grass cutting season would take me through late October, I imagined. That was clever of me. I just had to remember to sneeze every so often to really sell it. I could pull that off. Trying to remember to sneeze, however, is about as easy as trying to remember to have one's heart beat on command. There's a reason cardiovascular circulation is automatic. But Mom didn't call me on my lie.

Lori asked if I was feeling okay when she saw me having one of my hot flashes, and I remarked that, hey, it was August, and getting hot was a part of living in DC. I think she chalked it up to my weight, but she cared about my feelings so said nothing.

Jeffrey and his friend Michael noticed that I seemed stronger and asked what gym routine I was using. I shrugged it off. I surprised myself with my newfound ability to come up with ridiculous excuses for my progression, even as I wondered what would be the easiest way to spill the beans to my friends.

The question was really what to tell them. Was I going to stay on T, after all, or just change this much and then stop? If I went off of hormones, I knew that some things would revert back to how they'd been before. My fat would re-redistribute, like doing the cha-cha with my own cellulite. My body hair would stop taking over more real estate on my skin—not a bad idea, considering that I'd recently crossed the new threshold of butt crack hair. Having pondered this question for many long minutes, I could not come up with an evolutionary reason for ass hair on men. All it did was get caught up in the normal business of walking. Surely it wasn't in any way helpful during the humans' long hunting and gathering phase.

*   *   *

I'd spent considerable energy over the past several months handing out postcards to people at any even-tangentially GLBT event I could find in the city. Those of us on the coalition stalked all of the June Pride events, collecting nearly 1,200 signatures calling for the City Council to expand the non-discrimination law. In a last minute rush, we delivered a full set of postcards to each council member at a hearing for the new law.

The chair of the hearing asked how many of the council members wanted to support this measure to add "gender identity or expression" to the bill, and some coalition members cried when every hand went up in the air so that they could cosponsor the bill.

The email about the moment went around like wildfire, filling my inbox as every person chimed in with their congratulations. The next meeting would be thrilling.

Once again I was the early bird, even knowing full well that this was a gang of folks who were late to everything. Other people trickled in until there were five or six people, folks I had met only through this group. We chatted casually about the heat, wondering when the summer was going to cave in and realize it was time for fall. Then an activist named Ruby walked in and sat down on one of the folding chairs.

"Wow," she said, "you look fantastic!" She was talking to me.

"Gee, thanks," I said, sounding more demure than I'd intended.

"I mean, you were beautiful and handsome before, but now, just wow. When did you start hormones?"

I had to think fast. Her words were like little explosions in my heart.

"Um, early spring."

"Well, that's a lot of good changes in six months. Good for you!"

Other people nodded and smiled at me. I took a few seconds to realize what sensation I was experiencing. It was happy.

"What name should we call you?"

"Everett, thanks for asking."

"Everett, I love that name! You do look like an Everett."

"I do?" I felt myself blinking a lot, trying to focus. It seemed too stereotypical to ask someone to pinch me, so I refrained. But it would have been helpful.

"Isn't there a city called Everett?" one woman asked.

"Yes, I guess so," I said, having never before thought of the connection.

A new person walked into the room. We did our usual introductions, and I beamed all over again when I said my name.

"Hi, everyone, I'm Jamie," she said, looking embarrassed. "I'm really excited that I'll be starting hormones next month," she added, in an attempt to explain her appearance. She was six months "behind" me, and I remembered very easily the thrill of starting to take hormones. It felt like taking control of my life.

Folks congratulated her and we got down to the business of the meeting. In my own mind I was a bit distracted by my euphoria. So people who knew me as Jenifer before were still okay with this new name. Maybe I could really bring my worlds together.

I still had my doubts, even if they were fading a little, like a ghost I was beginning to suspect didn't really exist.

* * *

I had passed the six-month mark and was still using the T cream. I didn't want to stop, but I didn't want to give up on the possibility of ever having children, either. I wasn't sure if I should leave my chest as it was until I either had a kid or decided I wasn't going to procreate. If I didn't keep Becky and Bertha around, but had a child, I figured, I could just make do with formula.

I was still on speaking terms with Pat, but our relationship and conversations were more strained than ever. He remarked that it must be nice to have a support group for my transition, meaning the people I'd met online, the people in other cities, and Syd and Niles. I had answered, "Well, that's what I get for being a nice guy. Yay me."

I didn't know how the trans men support group that he'd taken dibs on was going.

Six months had gone by so fast, a big contrast to the nine months leading up to it that had ticked by so slowly. It was good and uncomfortable all at once—good in that I felt more in touch with myself and my body than I ever had, but uncomfortable because of some people's reactions.

One night I'd decided to meet up with Aiden, my ex-coworker, and his boyfriend, Derrick, at a gay bar in Logan Circle. Pat wanted to come along, thinking it would be a fun time out and, since we hadn't seen each other in a while, probably low-stress for us. If asked, I would not have had a good answer for why we still spoke at all.

Aiden and Derrick hugged me when I walked in. They smiled and stood back to look at me.

"Wow, check you out," said Aiden, smiling. "You look fantastic."

"Really? Thanks," I said, suddenly feeling shy.

"And your voice is so low," added Derrick. "You wanna sing us some Barry White?"

"Oh, stop it! I can't sing like Barry White and you know it."

We chatted and caught up. Aiden and Jeffrey had had a falling out so I was glad he still wanted to see me, since Aiden had laid low after pulling a disappearing act on me and Jeffrey. He still seemed a little shaky emotionally, but overall well and reasonably happy. Maybe there was life for him even after all of his mess. Toward the end of the evening, Aiden asked if I would like to join him at a support group for trans men that met in the middle of Maryland. I was unsure until he included the fact that they met at a Friendly's restaurant. If anything would pull me into a support group space, it was the promise of peanut butter sundaes.

Pat and I headed out a little later, walking through a parking lot that would surely become a building soon in DC's construction boom.

He seemed pissed and sighed audibly. I asked what was wrong.

"I just can't believe he would say your voice has changed."

"Okay," I responded, bracing myself. "Why can't you believe it?"

He stopped walking. "Because you sound exactly the same," he said, gesticulating for emphasis. "Why don't I get them telling me my voice is lower? This is just bullshit."

I felt guilty for three seconds. Then I got angry.

"You know what, Pat? I've had it with you."

He blinked. "Oh, you've had it?"

"Yes. You know, nobody has been less supportive of me than you. And I'm tired of feeling guilty. Let's just forget it. Have a nice life."

"Oh, you think that's it?"

"That's it."

"I knew you would do this," he hissed. "I knew you'd just walk away like this."

And I did, in fact, walk away.

Chapter 13

Immersed in one of my periodically busy periods at work, I had thrown myself into my projects, wallowing in deadlines, requirements, and demanding clients. Whales can stay underwater for twenty minutes or more; I was just hoping for five to fix a mini-crisis. Thus it was that I didn't notice one of the company executives standing in my doorway, waiting for me to look up and acknowledge her.

"Well, you started a little drama over at headquarters, my dear," said Mary, smiling and sitting in the chair on the other side of my desk. A small woman, she always dressed impeccably, had a dry wit that I presumed was a byproduct of living in small town Nebraska, and seemed genuinely to like me.

"Oh, dear, what did I do now?" I asked, feigning worry. If it had been truly bad news I figured we'd be in her office, not mine.

"Remember when you emailed HR about how it looked like the company had dropped gender identity and expression from the non-discrimination policy?"

"Sure. After the management training last week." Oh, how we all loved cookie-cutter videos that had nothing to do with our firm's core values. "What, uh, what … has there been a response?"

"Wait for it," Mary said. She grinned like a Cheshire cat. "The head of HR walked into Billy's office, and she asked him, 'What does sexual expression mean?'" Billy was a senior manager at headquarters who was an out and proud black gay man. In fact, of the senior folks in that office, he was the only out and proud gay man.

"Oh my God," I said. "What on earth is *sexual expression*?"

"That's what he asked her."

"Of course he did. It gets better, doesn't it?"

"Define better," she said. "I suppose she inadvertently put together 'sexual orientation' and 'gender identity and expression.'"

"Inadvertently. That's kind," I said.

"I try," Mary replied. "Billy of course looked at her like she had ten heads."

"Please tell me he corrected her."

"He asked her if she meant gender expression, and he explained what that was."

"Well, far be it for us to want the head of human resources to know who's covered by her own non-discrimination clause."

"Jenifer, you ask for so much," Mary said.

"I know, I'm so hard to please. Is she clear now? I never did get a response to my email."

"It's sorted out, yes. She'll be sending out an email to everyone later today."

"Oh, good. I didn't mean to give her a heart attack, thinking people were going to be having sex in the hallways with impunity or anything."

"Yes, that is exactly what she thought," Mary said. "Then she asked Billy, 'But do we have anyone here like that?'"

"No! She did not!" I laughed.

"She did indeed. He told her that she may not know of anyone and he may not know of anyone, but don't we need the policy all the same?"

"Thank goodness Billy has his head on straight, no pun intended."

"Oh, I think pun was intended," she said, standing up. She looked at the papers on my desk. "How's the latest proposal?"

"It will be done in the next hour, I'm guessing."

"Great. Thanks for your work on this."

"Oh, hey, we need to keep the projects coming, right? Don't worry, when I'm all done, I'll sexually express something in the reception area."

"I'm not listening," she said, putting her hands over her ears, and she walked out of my office.

A couple of hours later, I relayed the story to my new boss, an Englishman, who had replaced my old boss, an Englishman. On all other levels they were different. My new supervisor came with a wry sense of humor and a masterful ability to drink anyone else under the table, which I'd found out the hard way at a happy hour a couple of years earlier, before I worked for him directly. His office was ringed with Washington Capitals posters, because even though there wasn't a single hockey league in the UK, he'd said it was the closest Americans had come to decent football, meaning soccer, and meaning a very specific dig at the professional soccer league in the U.S. He had evolved into being an actual hockey fan, however, with season tickets in the middle of the arena, two feet from the rink glass. He could have hopped on the Zamboni machine, should the desire so strike him.

I was handing off the finished proposal to him so it could go in the stack with the others that were pending, when he asked me to relate what was already becoming "the sexual expression" story. At the end of my narration, he laughed and shook his head.

"Yeah, she's an innocent one, isn't she? But I don't think you should transition at this company, Jenifer."

I didn't think he caught me losing my breath. I played haughty with him and, looking over my glasses, said, "Whether I or anyone else chooses to transition at this company, the fact of the matter is that 'gender identity or expression' should be a protected category in this company, and that we forgot to include it during a training video is rather awful. And I suggest we bring some sensitivity trainers in to talk to HR."

"Hey, that's not a bad idea. How much do you suppose they cost?"

I couldn't tell if he was joking with me or not.

"I don't know, Chris," I said. I started the turn on my pivot foot. "But I suppose it's rather less expensive than the lawsuit someone would bring if they declared there was a hostile work environment here."

"Dear God, that's the truth," he said, and he picked up the proposal as if to say, okay, I'm going to do official work now. I kept my poker face until I had made it three feet down the hall.

* * *

Jeffrey and I had a dinner date. We wanted to dine outside while the weather was still warm.

"Look what the cat dragged in," he said as I approached him outside the door to the eatery.

"Please. We know no cat could drag my ass anywhere."

"Okay, good point."

We got our table, and I relaxed into the witty banter that I appreciated from Jeffrey. He had a hard time letting people in emotionally, but on the repartee front he was engaging and spirited. It was his preferred method of communication.

He was happy that the relationship between Pat and me had ended.

"I just think you deserve better." He stirred his martini like most people pet a beloved animal.

"I think I deserve better, too."

"I'm just saying, Jenifer, that Mr. Wannabeaman is itching to become his own art installation someday. He's going to transition to gallery space."

I didn't catch my frown in time before Jeffrey noticed it.

"You're better off, really," he said in an attempt to bolster his argument. "Besides, you're a lesbian. You need a woman, it's in the definition. Look it up."

"Well, darling, not all lesbians agree." He looked dubious. "What if I weren't a lesbian, anyway?"

"Please, if you weren't a dyke, we wouldn't be friends," he said, and he took another sip from his glass. "I don't hang out with the straights."

That made me wonder how he would take the news about Everett.

*　*　*

Aiden called me, inviting me to the suburban Friendly's trans men support group he'd mentioned weeks earlier. I'd agreed, eager to meet other people who'd gone through this whole transition thing but who didn't know Pat.

We pulled into the parking lot after driving for nearly an hour down bland Maryland highways. It was nice to catch up with Aiden. I made sure not to bring up the subject of Jeffrey, knowing that their friendship had ended badly.

Walking inside the restaurant, I didn't see any other people who stuck out as FTM, not that it was particularly easy to tell.

Testosterone did its work very well, thickening faces and vocal cords, changing even skin texture. They showed up in one bunch, five or six strangers that Aiden introduced me to. They were mostly middle-aged, all sporting some kind of facial hair style, running the gamut from mutton chop sideburns, to goatee, to full-on beardedness like I'd had in my dream so long ago.

"So how long have you been on T?" a trans man named Alex asked me. Aiden had whispered to me that Alex was pretty well known in trans circles on the east coast.

"Uh, a little more than six months," I said. A drop in the bucket compared to everyone else at the table.

"So cute, a newbie," another man, Frank, said to me. "You look great," he added.

Alex was peddling an "STP," or stand-to-pee device for five dollars. I'd ruled out such things, given my tendency toward clumsiness. One spill on my jeans or fumble of the device into the bottom of the urinal, and I would be a failure at even the most basic human function. But Alex was a consummate salesman.

"Best one on the market," he said to me. "There are a lot of prettier, more expensive ones out there, but this one works, which is the point. And it's better than using a coffee can lid."

I tried to wrap my brain around how one could use such a thing for such a purpose. It seemed an insult to Folgers. I gave Alex a fiver anyway, turning the plastic-wrapped stick over in my hands. It looked a bit like a medicine spoon, only the spoon part was larger and flatter. I figured it would sit in a junk drawer next to a dozen broken pens and a few spent AA batteries.

"Too bad Melissa's not here," said Frank. "She's a doctor at the clinic in Baltimore, and she could answer a lot of questions for you."

"Oh, that's okay," I said, trying to sound confident yet not arrogant. I wasn't comfortable asking questions in front of a group of strangers.

We talked about "man things," including sports, fishing, and muscle mass, interspersed with tidbits about being transsexual, all in light of knowing everyone at the table had prior experience being female. I didn't realize then what a huge gift that was, but I would later come to appreciate it.

Piling back into the car on the ride home, Aiden asked me what I'd thought.

"Seems like a nice bunch of guys," I admitted. "Very not-DC."

"Yeah, I know, but I love that."

"Well, I can see why. They weren't trying to out-cool each other."

"Refreshing, right?"

"As refreshing as a sundae."

*   *   *

I told Robyn I'd kept pondering over her question to me from last year. Today she was wearing a faded Provincetown souvenir sweatshirt, the iron-on rainbow almost invisible against the once-navy blue fabric.

"Oh, which question is that?"

I suspected she already knew which I'd meant. "If I'd rather be liked or respected."

"Yes, that question. Would you like to talk about it again?"

I paused, not knowing how to begin. "Here's the thing that bothers me," I said. "If my relationships are with people who like me but maybe don't respect me, what happens when I start insisting on their respect?"

She succeeded at not smiling but I sensed it was there, just under the surface of her skin. "What do you think happens?"

I looked at one of the three clocks in the room. None of them ever chimed. "I think … I think they tell me to shove it."

"So?"

I knew where she was going with this, or so I thought.

"So, I could lose people."

"Yes. And what do you think about that?"

"Are you going to ask a question to every comment of mine?"

"I'm just seeing what you really feel about this." She shrugged and sat back, as if my thoughts needed more space in the room. I looked at the familiar couches, the fireplace that was never lit, the water machine, the books about successful strategies for couples, the heating vents in the wall over her head. I hoped the pause would give some part of my brain time to identify my emotions.

"I suppose, if I lose people, I'm only losing people who need me to be a certain way that I can't be anymore."

"So what are you losing, then?" Again with the questions.

"I'm not sure. Maybe a lot, or maybe a lot of heartache."

"Yup," Robyn said.

"If that's the case, then it's all in my hands."

"Bingo."

"Bingo, great," I said. "What do I win?"

"Everything," Robyn said. "Ev, you win everything."

* * *

I had to admit I'd become obsessed with the stand-to-pee device. I looked at it with a mixture of interest and trepidation. I never had been much of a camper. I had no experience with urinating into anything other than a toilet, a diaper, and on rare occasion before age seven, a swimming pool.

Standing in the shower, I examined the thing. My bladder signaled it was ready for our little test run.

And suddenly, I was peeing and standing at the same time. It was a little like walking, patting one's stomach, and chewing gum at the same time. Amusing with no real purpose.

I calculated my increase in manliness at less than zero. But it was novel.

Now I needed to wash the wall of the shower. I wasn't sure I would get to the point where I could try actually aiming at something like a urinal.

This STP was clear plastic and looked nothing like a penis. I knew men supposedly didn't look at each other in the men's room, but how could I be sure? And wouldn't I be fishing around in my pants, trying to get the thing lined up right so I didn't pee all over myself? That might look strange at the very least. This "stand to pee" thing required more research, clearly.

* * *

Jeffrey and I had decided, with our friend Michael, to have Thanksgiving locally instead of heading out to our respective families who were scattered across the continent. I was happy to agree to the plan, mostly because I loved to cook, but also because I didn't want to have to explain everything to my relatives just yet. It was one thing to have reached the point where I wanted to tell them what was going on with me, but I still didn't have a plan. I didn't even know where to begin.

Michael offered his kitchen for the upcoming feast, a few weeks away. "Now that everything is all remodeled, I think you'll like using it." He had a flair in his speech and the tiniest of lisps, so that his words came out as if they were slightly lighter than the air in the room.

"You know of course, dear," I said, as if he were a child, "that the kitchen in my apartment is less than two years old." Our whole building had been redone the year before I'd moved into it.

"Yes, and therefore it is older than my kitchen," he said, clapping his hands together at the end of his sentence as an additional punctuation mark. "Further," he said, looking quite coquettish, "I might add that my kitchen is in my house, which makes it better to me than your kitchen."

"You can't argue with that," Jeffrey added.

I rolled my eyes at them. They were ganging up on me. Jeffrey called Michael the Contessa, and Michael had nicknamed Jeffrey "Diva." And although my breasts had their own nicknames, I, the entire person, did not. Although I didn't even receive a term of affection, I supposed we would in fact be doing Thanksgiving supper at Michael's. I wouldn't have thought twice about it except that Michael almost never cooked and was bound not to have certain critical kitchen tools, such as a roasting or sauté pan.

"You're going to have to stock up," I warned him. "Making the turkey dinner takes a lot of stuff."

"Darling, you give me a list and I will procure everything on it," Michael promised. I had no doubt that he could walk into Williams-Sonoma, hand the list to the first unsuspecting worker in a green apron, and declare that everything on the list, whatever it was, needed to be put in bags for him *tout suite*.

"Any excuse to shop," said Jeffrey. "Good for you. And don't even think about rolling your eyes, girlie girl. We'll liquor you up right good and you'll have a great time."

"She'll be with us," added Michael. "How could she not have a good time?"

They looked at each other and then at me to wait for my reaction. I let the moment get pregnant and then said, "Okay, here's what you need to buy."

Chapter 14

That's it, I thought. I traced my fingers around the bottom of the jar, absorbing the last dregs of T cream.

I knew the day would come when I ran out of my initial supply of hormones, and I wanted to be okay with it. I tossed the jar in the bathroom trash, noticing the bathtub for the first time since I'd stopped thinking about killing myself there. I stepped inside and took my shower with my eyes closed, feeling for the shampoo bottle and soap.

I made it through my daily routine just fine, I told myself. Commute through the city, curse at the other drivers, listen to NPR, get through the phone calls and email and project issues. Manage up and down. Avoid Arnold the groping maniac. Have lunch with a few colleagues. Come home. Change. Meet up with friends for drinks. Come home again. Watch cable television until sleep sets in. On Mondays, go bowling.

Is this all there is? I wondered. *So I'm just going to stop taking T and what? Pretend I never took it in the first place? Half the people I know call me one name while the other half never finds out?*

I hadn't noticed a day or a specific second when Jenifer the name felt like it wasn't real anymore, but I had wandered by that moment at some point, and now it was in the past. Everett as my name didn't feel quite real, either. I was caught in the middle, telling lies no matter what words came out of my mouth. I didn't know what to do, so I figured I'd just wait until a solution came to me. Surely something would pop up and present itself.

I hadn't thought that my sign from the universe would come in the form of an email from an old acquaintance, a director in DC who focused on women's theater. And not just any women's theater, but bleeding heart, women-are-people too, a woman needs a man like a fish needs a bicycle women's theater. Second wave, Ms. Magazine to the core.

I'd love to get together with you, she said in her email. *I have a new project I hope you'd like to do with me. It'll be a surprise! You'll never guess what it is!*

A few days later, she sent me the script. I read the title and knew this would be a truly horrible idea.

Sappho in Love.

She wanted me to do a staged reading as the Ancient Greek, lesbian poet herself. *Lord have mercy.*

I said okay.

*   *   *

Every burner supported a pot or pan, and Michael's brand new kitchen, which had never seen so much as a dime spot of grease, was now covered with utensils and food bits. Jeffrey stalked a pot of collard greens, stewing them with a mouth-watering smoked turkey leg, and Michael had procured an authentic polksa kielbasa from his local Polish butcher, which made me wonder if there were butchers still making their own sausages from the intestines of sheep?

I made sure that the potatoes weren't getting too mushy in the boiling water, that the apple pie baked only as long as needed, and that I was properly basting the turkey, after having rubbed it with my own assortment of spices and fresh herbs tucked under the breast skin. The green beans had broiled with olive oil, thyme, and sliced almonds. I also had a sweet potato casserole to pop in next to the bird—I'd named it Number Fourteen, as it was as close a name I could give it before Jeffrey protested. I still needed to reheat some sweet potato biscuits I'd made at Michael's the night before.

Jeffrey and I had driven up the previous day. We'd walked in and promptly started celebrating the holiday with a few well-mixed drinks. Jeffrey snapped a pumpkin cheesecake into existence, the smell filling the house the way cheap, scented candles only dreamed of doing. To cap off the delightful evening, it had snowed, so we were in quite the holiday mood when the morning rolled around. Slipping into early afternoon, however, my sing-songiness had evaporated as I pushed forward through cooking.

I was worried about my mood and how going off of T might edge me back toward unhappiness. Like breaking up with a secret lover—in this case, a tub of testosterone cream—I was going through a big adjustment but I couldn't tell anyone about it, except my friends online. I couldn't tell if I was genuinely unhappy about stopping the hormones and what that said about me, or if I was suffering through an abrupt shift in my brain chemistry, or both. So I mostly was glad to throw myself into the six-hour project of making the big dinner.

"Look at her go," Michael said, standing at the threshold of the kitchen.

"I know, right? Jenifer's a cooking goddess," Jeffrey said, and he walked past me to grab two small biscuits.

"Oh, get one for me," Michael called out, not daring to get too near the activity. It was as if food preparation were the crucifix to his vampireness.

"Okay, okay, everyone, settle down. Everything's almost ready."

They stood in the doorway, drooling.

I whipped up a gravy for the turkey, deglazing the roasting pan with red wine and adding in flour and butter, all the while watching the temperature so it would hold together.

"Don't you dare stick your finger in here," I warned Michael. "We wouldn't want the Contessa burning her little piggies."

"Oh, see, she's looking out for me," Michael said, smiling.

"I ain't looking out for nothing," I said, still intent on the pan of gravy. "I'm just not running to the ER with you after I spent all day getting this ready."

"Priorities, priorities," said Jeffrey.

We sat down for dinner in Michael's dining room, which the boys had set up for feasting. Michael's neighbor Claude joined us with a bubbling casserole pan of macaroni and cheese. He was French-Canadian, a tall man in a red flannel shirt, with neatly groomed hair going gray at his temples. I liked him.

"So this is the Jenifer about whom I've heard so much?" he asked. I appreciated his perfect grammar.

"The very one," I said. "I hope it's all been good."

"It has, it has," Claude confirmed. "So you're the one who knows Aiden?"

"Well, Jeffrey knows him, too," I said, now wondering if Claude had met Aiden or only heard about him.

"Oh, right, because you were roommates with her," said Claude.

"Him," Jeffrey corrected. "But yes."

"Right," said Claude. "Sorry."

"It's okay," said Michael. "I don't think I'm very good at the pronoun stuff. I mean, if I met someone after they had a sex change, I'd be fine with it, but I don't think I could switch if someone I knew made the change."

"To Number Fourteen," I toasted.

"To Number Fourteen," the men agreed, all of us raising our wine glasses.

* * *

They were kicking me out of their house.

"Go to the party already," Lori said. "You're mopey. Go and have some fun, why don't you?"

"Because I'm mopey," I answered. "I don't know but two of the people at the party. I don't really even know the guy the party's for." Niles and his friend Ethan were throwing a goodbye party for a fellow named Chrystopher, who was moving out of DC. That he had lived in DC for only six months seemed not to have slowed down his ability to make friends, and not just friends, but friends who were grieving enough to host a *bon voyage fête*. I'd lived in the area for three years before I could count two or three friends who weren't coworkers.

"It doesn't matter, just go. That's how you meet people."

Lori and Barbara had moved in together in a cute little up-and-down row house near the DC convention center. I'd helped them move a few weeks earlier, and there were still many unpacked boxes scattered throughout the rooms.

As part of their enthusiasm for this new chapter in their lives, they had adopted two kittens. One of the kittens was curled up in a ball on my thigh. This seemed preferable to me than sitting around in some cramped living room toasting a guy I'd said a couple of dozen words to.

I looked at Barbara. She was the more laid-back of the two, but she had her own brand of matter-of-factness. "What do you think?" I asked her.

"Honestly, I think you should check it out," she said, absent-mindedly twirling her long, curly hair. "You only live a block away. You can leave after an hour and it won't be a big deal."

"Okay, okay, I'll go. But it's a freaking potluck. I don't know what to bring." The kitten kicked in her sleep, then settled down. She was probably chasing rabbits.

"Oh, you'll figure something out," Lori said. "You could just whip up some brownies in that mixer of yours."

I was an avid fan of my new KitchenAid mixer, going as far as to name it Grapey. Grapey was my favorite appliance in my little galley. My mother hadn't approved of me buying a purple kitchen gadget, remarking that I was going to have to look at it for thirty more years, but the color made me smile.

"I'm out of butter, but I do have some fruit in the fridge. I could bring that."

"It's not going to matter," said Lori, and I knew she wasn't going to stop pushing until I was out the door. Even then, I could expect two follow-up phone calls: to make sure I was on my way, and to make sure I was there. I was either going to have to set up an elaborate ruse to sound like I was at an actual party, or I was going to have to physically attend the thing. Honesty seemed easier.

They hugged me on my way out, telling me to have fun and call later to let them know how it went. I realized they were more my family than my friends at that point. That was nice.

* * *

Back at home the fixings were slim. I had one apple, one orange, two bananas, some grapes I had forgotten I'd purchased, and thus couldn't recall how long they'd been in the fridge, and a few blueberries. It was either fruit salad or a half-eaten take-out meatball sandwich from three days earlier.

I chopped up the fruit roughly, not caring too much how it looked, poured in a little orange juice, and covered my glass bowl with some of the cellophane leftover from my binding experiment. Now that I had my tried-and-true method, I could spare the cling wrap for my actual kitchen needs.

I mussed with my hair a little, de-cat haired my outfit using one of seventeen tape rolls I kept stashed around the apartment for just such a purpose, and left for the party. I heard Lori and Barbara in my head, telling me I'd have a great time. Great time, great time. *How about some more reasonable expectations?* I wondered. How about some semi-interesting conversation, and nobody who'll turn to me and say to me drunkenly, "Wow you're so cool, why don't we ever hang out?"

A few minutes later, I walked in the room and sure enough, knew only the host, the host's friend, and the man of honor.

"Ooh, fruit salad," Niles cooed. "So cool to bring that when it's not even summer."

"Oh, you're too kind," I said, thinking it looked particularly pathetic, like something you'd see relegated to a plastic side dish in a hospital cafeteria. "I ran out of time to bake something."

"No worries, we've got plenty of stuff." He offered to fix me a drink. I accepted. His friend Ethan had already begun to break out the Christmas holiday decorations. Lights were in a state of detanglement.

This was one of those spaces where I wasn't clear who knew what about me. Certainly Niles knew I went by Everett but still used Jenifer in public. I didn't know, however, what he may have told Ethan and Chrystopher. I could wear the packy, since it wasn't a bulging, X-rated accessory, but I'd been unsure about whether I should bind or not. In the end, I'd decided to ignore my doubts for a couple of hours and had gone ahead and strapped on my binder.

Twenty minutes into doing the DC small talk thing, another guest arrived, bearing very colorful cookies on what looked like a homemade pottery plate. Not homemade in the sense that it looked like crap, but distinctly not mass-produced or to be found at Crate and Barrel. She was cute and seemed familiar. I couldn't place her. I crossed my fingers she wasn't someone I knew through Pat.

"Ooh, you brought cookies," Niles gushed. "Susanne, you're the best."

"I just finished frosting them," she said, and she set the plate on the table with the rest of the potluck dishes.

They were in fact a plate of Christmas tree-shaped cookies. "I kind of rushed to make them," Susanne apologized. Some bore traditional Christmas colors, while others were frosted with Hannukah colors of blue and white. "They can double as Hannukah bushes," Niles said, picking one up and popping it in his mouth. "Mmm," he mumbled.

Susanne sat down and joined the conversation. Short, curly hair bounced when she laughed, and she kept pushing her wireframes up the bridge of her nose. Putting some of the buffet items on a plate for myself, I made sure to include one of her cookies.

The thing was delicious. Sweet, buttery, and with a hint of salt. I asked Susanne where she got the recipe, and she brightly replied that she had procured it in the third grade from a *Reading Is Fundamental*-type book truck. The author was Betty Crocker. We laughed. I shook my head that Lori and Barbara had been right, I could go out and have fun at a party.

People began talking about their latest crushes and whether they were in relationships or not.

"Yeah," I said, waving my arms in dismissiveness, "I'm post-crush. I mean, I'm too old for crushes." *Holy crap, stop talking,* a voice inside shouted. "I mean, I'm okay with it being just me and my cats for the rest of my life." *Oh my God, do you hear yourself! You just became the crazy cat lady! What the hell?* "So yeah, I mean, I think it's great if other people have crushes, but you know, I'm just not in that space anymore." *And how are they supposed to respond to that, you idiot?*

"Your cats are awesome," Niles said, his nice way to get me off the hook.

"I'm very fortunate," I replied. I hoped that as the seconds passed the embarrassment would fade.

The conversation turned to other things, and after a while, I got up to leave. I had a rule at the time to leave social events early, at least early enough that I would miss any late-party drama and hopefully be missed, thus encouraging future invitations. Having not done a proper study of the effects of my premature departures, I had no idea if this really worked or not. People seemed sad to see me go, or perhaps they were good at pretending to be sad when socially awkward people left the room.

I called Niles the next day in part to assess the damage.

"Oh, no, you were fine," he said, laughing at me. "You made us laugh. And frankly, I'm just so happy that Pat guy is out of the picture."

"You are?" I hadn't realized Niles had formed an opinion. The most he and Pat had spent time together was when Pat and I had brought over cupcakes—decorated to look like breasts—to his and Syd's place after Niles had his chest reconstruction surgery. What better to bring to someone who's just removed his breasts than little cupcakes with nipples, after all?

"Yeah, Syd and I had a couple of conversations like, 'How can we spend time with Everett without seeing Pat?'"

"Wow. What did you come up with?"

He paused, apparently feeling guilty or hesitant. "Well, we just figured that we couldn't hang out with you that much."

"Oh." *So much for living halfway across town from Pat,* I thought.

"But why did you call?" asked Niles, seemingly eager to change the subject.

"Well, uh, I wanted to know about a woman at the party yesterday. Susanne."

"Oh, Susanne," he said, drawing out the second syllable as if there had been other people at the party whose names had started with "soo" that I could also be calling about just now. "What do you want to know?"

"Um, she's not single, right? She's with someone? Like a super successful person who's discovered the cure for cancer?" In my head I saw her skipping through fields of lavender with a gorgeous, androgynous, world-famous scientist and settling in to a gourmet picnic while Vivaldi played in the background.

"No, she's single. Do you like her, Ev?"

"Well, I just thought maybe I should ask her out. She seems like an All-American girl type."

He laughed. I wondered what was so funny. When he got his breath back he explained. "She's Canadian, silly."

"Oh. She is?" Now I was really embarrassed. "Make that 'girl next door' then. You never can tell with those Canadians, anyway."

"Yeah, well, I can't give you her number without talking to her."

I started to sweat, or maybe it was the radiators hissing in my apartment and spraying wet air on me. "No, I know that. I just was wondering if, uh, oh, you know." No need to finish the sentence, really.

"Well, she's on Friendster. You can find her there."

I thanked the technology gurus for social networking sites. "Oh, that's cool. My cat has a profile there."

"I thought you had your own profile, Ev."

I sighed in the phone without meaning to. "I did. Pat said I was using it to steal his friends, so I got rid of it."

"Oh, for God's sake."

"I know, I know. But I kept Ulysses' profile."

"Well, it's been like, what, most of a year? You could probably make a new profile now. You don't owe him anything."

"This is true," I agreed. "Well, I'll send her a message, at any rate."

"Yeah? You're gonna ask Susanne out? He's gonna ask Susanne out," Niles said to Syd. I heard muffled giggling.

"Okay, okay, go have your laugh fest, now. I'm gonna go and find her online."

"It's just exciting! Good luck! I won't say a thing."

We hung up, and I knew that he would have great difficulty not relaying the scene to her. I didn't know he had plans with Susanne later that day.

*   *   *

I drove into a corner of DC that was a tangle of curling roads completely different from the usual neat grid of lettered and numbered streets in the rest of the city. Disoriented, I thought that I might wind up missing the rehearsal altogether, wandering around aimlessly in some neighborhood west of Georgetown. I didn't think there *was* anything west of Georgetown, other than Virginia.

Finally I found the house. I walked up a large hill after parking, script in hand. In the seventy feet between my car and the door, my glasses froze up, so my first few minutes inside were foggy. I was greeted by a colorful gaggle of women of varying ages, ethnicities, sizes, and volumes of laughter, which I knew because I'd entered in mid-guffaw.

Deb, the director, introduced me around the room. These were all professional actors, and here I was, in the midst of them and their energy. They talked about other theater projects they'd worked on together and chatted about their families, playing some quick catch up with each other. It was a refreshing atmosphere in a glass-walled studio that was an oasis against the freezing temperatures outside.

And then it dawned on me, five minutes into watching them engage with each other. Not a single woman in the room seemed unhappy with her gender. They weren't stereotypically feminine, but they all had, it appeared at least, made their way through the world as women, and they'd taken that up in unique ways. One was a round earth mother, with a flowing dress that acted as an extension of her long hair. A woman who could have been Kate Mulgrew's older sister carried a cane that I suspected she could whip out in defense should anyone mess with her on the street, and she had a glint in her eye that sparkled with hard-learned wisdom. Another woman was there in a crisp suit, looking a little like my Vice President, Mary, the perfection of her appearance seeming to mask a personal sadness. The director looked like her usual self, in a sparkly and brightly colored T-shirt with worn jeans and a suit vest.

We went around the room to do introductions, and I nervously announced myself as Jenifer. I looked at these women and realized how much room there was in the category of womanhood. Yet even with all that space, I wasn't happy. I couldn't find my own place as a woman because I wasn't a woman.

I suspected life was going to get pretty tumultuous pretty soon if I kept moving forward with changing my gender. I'd have to go back on T again. I'd pushed my gender presentation as far as it could stretch, and now I needed to reverse course or come out into the open about who I was. It was like intentionally jumping into a pit of lava, as decisions went. Maybe I just needed more time.

I focused on the play and hoped that the next couple of hours wouldn't involve me thinking about my gender. I was tired of all this thinking.

Chapter 15

I stared at the computer screen, unsure how to write this email. Susanne's profile picture on Friendster was a plate of her cookies, so I knew I had the right Susanne, at least. And there in her biography paragraph she noted she was Canadian. *How forthright of her. Not that being from the north country is a problem,* I thought.

I started typing. When I'd composed the message, I sat back and looked at it.

> **Subject: Would you like to continue our conversation ... somewhere in our fair city?** It was nice to meet you at the party the other day. I was wondering if you would like to have dinner with me.

That sounded fine, I thought. I blinked and noticed the picture of my cat. Cursing myself for deleting my account, I added:

> **And now I realize you're getting this from my cat, Ulysses. This is his owner, Everett. If you've read this far, you're a trooper! Feel free to drop me a line, my number is 202-555-1822. And have a nice holiday.**
>
> **E**

For the love of Pete, you're such an incredible dumbass. I clicked on the Send button before I could think better of it. *Well, we'll see if she ever writes back,* I thought nonchalantly, even as I knew I would probably refresh the online inbox 1,382 times before the next day rolled around, as was my habit.

* * *

"Oh, I know who that is," Lori said. "Bar, didn't we meet her at that party a few months ago?"

Barbara twirled her hair and furrowed her brow, thinking. One of the kittens was climbing up the drapes, so I jumped up to save the fabric. I'd come over to their place to watch one of the last few regular season football games. Every week we would get together to watch our favorite teams play on Lori's Don't-Miss-a-Game-But-Pay-Through-the-Nose satellite service, and I would cook up some football theme-inspired snack, like nachos with black beans and blue corn chips, since black and blue is what the players would be after the game.

"Yeah, I think we did meet her. She's nice." Barbara was clearly still accessing her memory banks, trying to assess the potential date.

"And cute," Lori added. "That's the important part. There are all kinds of nice people, but anyone you ask on a date should be attractive."

"Oh, Lori," Barbara and I said.

"Well, so when did you email her?" Lori asked.

"Three days ago or so," I said.

Lori looked shocked. "And you haven't heard back? Why not?"

"I couldn't guess, since, you know, I haven't heard back."

Barbara laughed. "Well, it's only a few days before Christmas. Maybe she's out of town."

"So reasonable," I said, jumping up to rescue the draperies yet again.

"I don't know why he does that," Lori said, eating a mini-burger that was supposed to be in the shape of a football.

"Because he can," I said, sighing.

*   *   *

Robyn was looking at me for an answer. I stared at my footwear, which I figured she knew meant I was having trouble coming up with words to answer her.

"I just don't know," I managed. "I have no idea what comes next."

"Well, that's okay," she said, taking a sip from her soda can. "Let's take a step back. You were on T for eight months. Talk about how that made you feel."

"Great. Ecstatic. Worried people would notice. Confident. Masculine. Horny. Terrified."

"Wonderful," Robyn exclaimed.

"Yeah, wonderful, too," I said. My smile gave my joke away.

"Your sense of humor really comes in handy, doesn't it?"

"Best coping skill ever."

"Okay, okay, so tell me what was terrifying about being on T."

Of course she had to pick a negative one first. *Therapists!* I formed my opinion as I started talking, not realizing what my thoughts were before I spoke them. "Well, it was kind of a recap of puberty, in that my body was changing and I was trying to catch up and deal with it. I look back on being a teenager now, and I think I was really unhappy when I got breasts that other people could notice."

"Oh? Because people noticed them or because they happened without your consent?"

I thought for a few seconds and said, "Both. I really started hating how I looked when I was a junior in high school or so, and that was right when I was starting to fill out and get hips. I stopped enjoying being in my own skin, I think."

"So the T reminded you of that?" She was trying to understand.

"It's just that, yes, it reminded me of how my body shifted the first time, which was a negative experience for me. But I liked the changes I was getting from the T, even if it meant several near-collisions on the way to work."

"What?"

I didn't see the need to share my daily commuting chin inspections with her.

"Never mind, it's not important. I guess I was really happy to be on the T. I was taking a wait-and-see approach, but I've enjoyed the changes."

"So tell me, Ev," she said, and I knew a big question was coming, "then why did you stop?"

I took a few seconds to find the words that would work.

"Concern about coming out. I just didn't know what I was trying to do with the T, anymore. So stopping and giving myself time to think seemed helpful."

"Okay, so that means you've been thinking?"

Damn her for making sense. "I've kind of been thinking," I admitted.

"Oh good," she said, smiling like a cat that is about to trap its prey. "What do you kind of think now?"

"I guess I still don't know. A big part of me really wants to just do it and transition, and another part of me is afraid to turn my whole world upside-down."

"I get it. You're happy with your life and you don't want to lose that."

"What? No, I just. I need to figure out how to tell people. Jeffrey. Lori. My mother and my siblings. All those people at work."

"And what's the worst you think will happen when you tell them?"

I didn't miss that she'd said "when" instead of "if."

"Oh, I don't know, someone bludgeoning me with a bat and then leaving me for dead in the street?"

"Other than that."

"Other than that it won't be worst anymore."

"Okay, Ev, is that your real fear?"

"No."

She studied me for a minute, then sat back and asked, "What's really keeping you from doing this? Do you not want to transition? Do you want me to stop calling you Everett?"

I felt a tear roll down my cheek, like a scout checking on the lay of the land to see if the rest of the troop should follow behind.

"No, I am Everett. I just want to tell people about me before I start T again. I don't want to do it in the closet anymore."

"Does that sound like a good idea to you?"

Knowing there was no right answer, I gave a small smile and said, "Yes."

*   *   *

I'd set up the date at my favorite fire-baked pizzeria, a sleepy restaurant until it was featured in a local foodies blog, and then it was always packed to the seams, bursting with young, drunk patrons from the lobbying district, the non-profit set, and Capitol

Hill. On the day after New Year's, however, the place was empty except for one other table.

Susanne met me at the bar, taking off her winter hat and unwrapping a scarf the length of an adult boa constrictor. It took her thirty seconds to remove all of her outerwear. She'd emailed me from her parents' house in Michigan, saying she was stuck with dialup and had just gotten my message. A quick cheery email exchange, and we'd set up this date.

"Hi, there," she said, smiling.

"Hi, thanks for meeting me," I said, trying to keep my smile out of the goofy nerdy range.

We got a table and were checked on often by the waitress, who didn't have much else to do but who also seemed to find us amusing. Our pizzas arrived, hers a sausage and extra cheese, and mine a mushroom lover's that Michael would have hissed at, given his abhorrence of fungi.

She looked at me and my pizza. "So are you a vegetarian?"

"Oh, no. I just like the mushroom pizza here."

"Thank God," was her response, and I laughed.

We talked about our love of Kitchen Aid mixers, and that we'd each named ours: hers was Bette, and mine, Grapey. We'd also both previously bought mixers for other people's weddings and then wondered why we hadn't purchased one for ourselves.

"I love baking," I said. "I enjoy it so much I want to retire early and start my own bakery someday."

"Shut up," said Susanne, laughing. "That's what I want to do!" Somehow this made sense to me, because she was currently a Ph.D. student in public policy. Who wouldn't want to retire from that and bake cake all day?

"No kidding. That's great."

Things were going so well I decided to take a risk and let her know everything about my gender goings on. As soon as I started talking, I wanted to erase the decision and start over with any other topic of conversation. Hummingbirds. The state of the economy in Guam. Bloomsday parties. Monkey rectums.

"So I've been transitioning, taking it really slowly," I said, feeling exposed. "Many of my friends still only know me as Jenifer, but for more and more people I'm Everett now. So you could call me either, really." *Stop talking!*

The voice in my head was powerless to stop me.

"Well, that sounds like it can be hard at times," she said.

I fought to stay on my seat and not fall onto the floor. "Yes, it can be. I'm taking things at my own pace. It's been interesting, I guess."

"You're not the first person I've met with complicated gender," Susanne said, looking at me. She wasn't backing away. I didn't know what to make of this. Maybe she was a psychopath, collecting people with gender issues in her basement and putting them in little cages so she could have her own private transsexual zoo.

Or maybe it was just okay.

The waitress stopped by our table, looking at us with a sly grin, and giving us boxes for the rest of our pizzas.

We stepped outside and saw that it was raining, and we each opened our umbrellas. With pizza boxes in one hand and the umbrellas in the other, our departing hug was more like a clumpfest. She thanked me for the good conversation and sprinted across the street to get to the Metro before it rained any harder. I smiled, but a little thought bugged me. What if she didn't think that was a date we just had?

*   *   *

Jeffrey and I were out at the upscale bar again, and I was attempting to play wing man for a gentleman who had come in alone and had been drinking for fifteen minutes.

"Which one?" Jeffrey asked, looking at the bar and trying to determine who I'd identified for him.

"Pinstripes, fourth from the end," I said, without using a finger to point, lest Jeffrey break it off my hand and use it as a swizzle stick.

"Oh, nice," he started, and then frowned. "Can't do, sorry."

"What? Why? He meets all your requirements. Well attired, eyes an eye width apart, didn't skimp on the footwear, good manicure."

"Oh my god, you make me sound so shallow!"

I paused. "You're not shallow. You've just figured out good markers for dateability."

"Well, I've already dated him. He's a no-go."

"Oh. Damnit, man, why you have to already be around the block?"

"Watch it, miss," Jeffrey whispered. "Tell me about your date instead. What's the scoop?" He finished his drink and motioned to the bartender for another. I told him about the pizza date with Susanne and realized I was more excited about how it had gone than I'd thought. Except for the end of it, which still had me wondering if I'd done something wrong, I'd had a great evening.

"Well, thank God you did it, at least. That Pat shit was getting old."

"Yeah, I know," I said, finishing my drink, as if the mere act was a metaphor for closure. I motioned to the bartender to make another for me.

"I mean, it might not go anywhere with this woman," Jeffrey warned. "But it's good to get out there and see who else is available."

I agreed. He laughed when I said we had set another date already.

All of my friends made the rounds to check in on The Date. I was a little astonished at their interest and took it as yet another sign that they'd all wanted me to get out of the Pat relationship. I spoke to each of them in turn and heard clapping, excited voices, and, in the case of Lori and Barbara, cheering. Even my work colleagues inquired. Sandy and Fatima gave me big smiles and thumbs up. I appreciated that they were happy for me, even as I was a little embarrassed that I'd clearly been miserable for a while.

* * *

The psychiatrist was staring at his clipboard again, the one that held the scratched notes on my temperament, diagnoses, and problems, or so I supposed.

"So you have stopped the hormone therapy," he said, still on his rampage against English contractions.

"Yes," I said.

"And how is that for you?"

"Um, I'm adjusting. I'm figuring out what to think about it."

"Some of the changes from the testosterone are reversing, yes?"

I looked at him and figured he was an android with no color perception.

"Yes. My facial hair is growing back more slowly after I've shaved, and my muscles are getting softer." I felt a wave of sadness.

"So. Do you think you are not a transsexual?"

"Uh, I do think I'm trans, yes."

"So why have you stopped then?"

I admitted it was a good question. "I need to get my life aligned better, tell people, and then start it again, I think. With a doctor who's managed other cases like mine."

"I see. You seem more clear on your thoughts than you had said."

"The joys of talk therapy," I said.

"Yes," he agreed. Then he leaned forward. "So I need to tell you something."

Here it comes, I thought. *He was once a hairless woman.*

"I am going to be leaving this practice and moving to a new office. Would you like to continue with me over there? It's only a few blocks east of here."

"Oh," I said, trying not to show my disappointment. "Sure. Your new receptionist will call me?" Good grief, I was starting to talk like him.

"Yes. So our next session won't be here."

"Okay," I said. But the office never called, and I never found out where he'd moved.

Chapter 16

All of my people were coming to the *Sappho in Love* reading. Jeffrey, Lori, Barbara, Niles, Susanne, a coworker of mine and her lesbian partner, people who knew me as one or the other gender, and all of them were going to be in the same room. This was all my fault. My asteroids, that I'd been juggling so carefully, would come colliding together, spraying out all kinds of crap in the process. *Perhaps I should up my Lexapro dosage.* I silenced the idea as soon as it squeaked out. I didn't have a shrink anymore. And I only had three refills on my medication and no one to oversee me going off the pills. But I could concern myself with that later. Right now I had to cross my fingers that my friends who knew me as Everett would remember not to use that name in front of the "Jenifer people," since I was listed in the program as Jenifer.

I was dancing with danger. This wasn't like the art show with only three of my friends to moderate and me there the whole time. This was a group of fifteen people I knew, and I was helpless, warming up behind a curtain, out of earshot.

I peeked out and looked at the audience. Fifty people crowded onto folding chairs in the art gallery that was serving as our performance space. The director, Deb, called us together for a breathing exercise. We "mmm'd" and "ah'd" our way together, and once again I was touched by the strength of the women around me. I was going to give up being a mother, a sister, a daughter, a woman some saw as strong in her own right, for a life of uncertainty. Was it worth it, really? Did the Everett People see me as a poser? Were the Jenifer People wondering when I'd realize I wasn't really good at being a Jenifer? None of it mattered in the end. I focused on getting ready to give a performance at least a quarter as proficient as the other people on stage with me.

Deb thanked us again for supporting her, and then gave us all a present, pressed into our palms one by one—a very seventies-era, purple, woman symbol pendant. I put it in my pocket and smiled, because I just wasn't that kind of girl anymore.

The audience applauded us when we were finished, and I was certain my performance fared worst, given the paucity of experience in acting I'd had. Two classes as a teen and four high school musicals later, it was an accomplishment that I knew what the concept of intention was. Even so, people were gracious enough to compliment me. I walked out with the rest of the cast after taking our bows, and my friends there to support me clapped me on the back and told me what they'd liked.

"Everett was hysterical," Niles said in Jeffrey's general direction, I learned later.

"Uh, huh," Jeffrey said.

"I mean, to see him out there with those women, that's funny stuff."

Jeffrey stopped him. "I don't know who you're talking about."

"Oh," stammered Niles. He ran his fingers through his hair. "Sorry."

Jeffrey gave him the consideration of a shrug to show they were all square.

Fortunately for me, I missed this conversation. I was busy talking to my coworker, Gail, and her partner.

"Love the bow tie," Gail said. "You don't wear them around the office anymore."

I didn't wear them because I felt too self-consciously male in them, though it hadn't been an issue once upon a time in my obliviousness. "Well, they're really hard to tie," I said. "I don't seem to get any better at it."

"Well, it looks great on you," she said, patting me on the shoulder.

"Well, thank you," I said, unsure who to start talking to next. I saw that Susanne was standing next to Lori and Barbara, and I remembered that they already knew each other. DC was a smaller town than it seemed to people who typically brushed it off as a big city. But people in the District were only about three degrees of separation apart.

"Nice job," said Barbara, smiling at me.

"Thanks."

"You're not half bad," Lori said, and as someone who'd gone to college as a theater major, I took that as a compliment. "How many times did you rehearse?"

"Twice," I said.

"Wow, that is good, then."

"Well, it was just a staged reading," I admitted, shrugging. "The playwright wanted to see how it read before doing a revision."

Susanne looked around the room. "The playwright's here?"

"Yup," I said, pointing to a woman in the front row who was now talking to Deb.

"Wow," Lori said, staring at her, "she's dressed like Mo from *Dykes to Watch Out For*."

I saw that the playwright was in fact wearing a red and black striped shirt and had short cropped hair. Out of the lesbian context, she could have been mistaken for a small, female version of Freddy Krueger of *Nightmare on Elm Street* movie fame. "Oh, I'd never noticed!"

"Well," said Jeffrey, walking over to us, "she has a cargoload of rewrites to do, judging from the performance. The actors really had to put a lot into the script to make it work." Jeffrey was a former theater major, too.

"You mean they don't always have to do that?" I asked.

"They shouldn't have to bend over backwards like you all did," Lori agreed.

Lest we be overheard, we changed topics, and Susanne and I departed together, off to get some dinner in the neighborhood. As we walked down the stairs from the building, she took my hand and held it. I smiled. And gave a sigh of relief.

* * *

Robyn listened to the whole story patiently.

"So they were all together, and nothing bad happened?"

"I guess not. But it was still unsettling."

"Well," she said, "we've talked about this before. What's your plan for bringing your worlds together?"

I threw up my arms in defeat. "I don't know what I'm doing. I mean, sometimes I act like I've got it all together, but I don't know what my next step is. I think about telling my mother, and I just know she's going to be crushed. I don't want to hurt her."

"So how do you think this will hurt her?"

"She'll think she did something wrong." This was perfectly obvious to me. How could Robyn not see it?

"Was that her response when you told her you were gay?"

"Yes."

"And she got through it?"

"I see where you're going with this. I think the trans thing is different."

"Okay," she said, engaging me and my weak logic. "How so?"

"Well, this is permanent."

"Was being gay something you thought of as temporary?"

"No, of course not. But I also wasn't altering my body in order to be gay. I wasn't making a statement about the human body she'd produced."

"So what do you think her response was about?"

That's a good question. "Uh, what the neighbors and her friends would think. I think she presumed that being gay was bad. And she'd have to explain my behavior to people."

"So you think she'll have a hard time because she'll have to explain this, too?"

"I guess so, yes." I was fidgeting with Robyn's business card on her end table, as if my nervousness could no longer be contained within the confines of my body.

"And why do you care what she tells them?"

Another good question. Robyn could therapize circles around the shrink who'd disappeared. "Because I don't want to disappoint her," I said. I was kidding myself that I could actually pull this off.

* * *

I had a third date with Ms. Smartypants, as I called Susanne, which Lori wanted me to change to Ms. Hotpants. I resisted this suggestion, figuring Susanne wouldn't like it and besides, I'd never seen her in anything approaching such a fashion choice. Susanne stuck precariously closely to an academic's wardrobe of dark tones, comfortable trousers, and loose-fitting shirts.

We met up at the Corcoran Gallery of Art near the White House to see an Andy Warhol exhibit. I'd broken several speeding laws getting to the gallery from my office in Bethesda, but I'd picked up a present for her beforehand, a sugar cookie in the shape of a flower bouquet. I'd heard that Susanne had several allergies and wasn't sure if I could give her actual flowers, or if she'd wind up sneezing out her sinuses thanks to me, so the cookie seemed a better choice. After leaving the car in a legal parking spot, one of six in the city, I saw her standing outside the building.

"This is for you," I said, giving her the shrink-wrapped cookie. "There's a little almond paste in it. I hope that's okay."

"Oh, that's really sweet," she said, smiling as she inspected the ingredients list. "Thanks so much!" She leaned in and kissed my lips. She smelled like rich chocolate.

We wandered past a few dozen Warhol prints and paintings, talking about what we found interesting and pondering the curator's notes on the walls of each exhibit room. They wanted us to get some very specific things out of the collection that we just weren't seeing. And neither Susanne nor I wanted to be told what to think. She held my hand through most of the exhibit. I was no longer worried about our intentions on the "just friends" front.

Leaving the gallery, I asked if she wanted to come to my place to have some cheesecake I'd made. I assumed she'd decline, having already noted that she wanted to take things slowly.

"Okay," she said. "I like cheesecake."

We drove back to my apartment. I asked her if she was okay with my two cats, and she said she'd be good for a bit, sure. Breaking out the cheesecake onto plates and brewing some hot tea, we sat on the couch. She looked around my living room. I still hadn't seen the inside of her apartment, although I'd driven her home after the second date, pleased that she lived only a few blocks away from me. How nice that obeying Pat's territory map worked in my favor after all.

"This is great cheesecake," she said between bites. I noticed she'd also unwrapped her cookie and taken a few bites.

"How's the cookie?"

"It's really good. And very sweet of you." She moved in closer, took my fork out of my hand, and placed it on the plate. "I want to kiss you."

Not being one to resist such an offer from such a sassy woman, I kissed her back. She was lovely. She leaned onto me.

"Hang on, my cell phone," I muttered, trying to fish it out of my front jeans pocket so it would stop being jammed into my thigh.

"How about this," she said, looking directly at me with a crooked, wry smile, "you take out your cell phone and I'll take off my shirt?"

This is wonderful, this dating thing, I thought. *Screw growing old with cats.*

* * *

We tried to keep it at a slow pace, this thing we were doing. We had delayed putting words to it, not calling it dating or a relationship, but several weeks into it we had begun telling people we were seeing each other. It became too difficult to explain without using a socially-accepted term for dating, and besides, we liked each other's company and weren't afraid to call it what it was. I let a whole month go by before I told her I loved her, which she received well even if she didn't repeat it back to me. I preferred that, not wanting her to be a parrot.

Winter came full bore upon the metropolitan area, meaning that a scant couple of inches of snowfall were more than enough to shut down the city. I called Susanne to see if she was staying home from the university, since I had decided to work from home and avoid the crazy drivers who all but lost their minds on snowy roads.

"We could go to the mall," she suggested. I already knew from Jeffrey that people who lived in the city but didn't have a car loved other people's car access to everything, like kids who would never leave my family room because their parents didn't own a TV. I said I had time later in the afternoon. My four-wheel-drive car was more than capable of handling anything a DC winter could throw at it.

Hours later, we were holding hands and strolling around the Pentagon City Mall, a pretentious glut of luxury stores that paled in comparison to the metropolis of consumerism just a few miles away in Virginia, the Tyson's Corner Mall. Two-foot snowdrifts wouldn't be able to keep shoppers away from that place, which had its own zip code.

I had a shopping bag in one hand and Susanne's hand in my other. Then, at a random step, she said, "I love you."

I walked into a bench.

"What?" I rubbed my knee.

"I said I love you, silly," she answered, now laughing at me.

"Oh." *Quite the Shakespeare, jerk,* I thought. "You do? That's great!"

"Come here," Susanne commanded, and I stood up and stopped tending to my bruise.

She kissed me in the middle of the mall, in sight of Williams-Sonoma, Coach, Aveda, and smiling customers.

Chapter 17

I was thrilled to get a promotion at work, less for the duties involved, since I'd been performing them already, than for the acknowledgement that I was a real project manager and for the salary increase. Sadly, the promotion came with an office move, to situate me closer to my new VP. Mary had been made a senior executive so I didn't see her as often anymore. I was going to miss this office, with its southern exposure and view of a park. I was putting all of my files and supplies in boxes when my coworker, Denise, who worked in the wing where I was moving, poked her nose in to see how I was coming along. She was a diminutive thirty-something woman, but her boisterous laugh made up for what she lacked in physiological volume. And she found a lot of things funny.

"I'm so excited you're moving to my tower," she said with a grin.

"I just hate the smell over there." I tried in vain to find a box to pack my tabletop bowling set.

"The smell?"

"They use some kind of orange rind cleaner over there, and it makes me sneeze."

"I've never noticed it," she said, obviously searching for a memory of Sneezy Orange Smell. "Well, it'll be good to have you over there."

We were talking about a move of ninety yards to the next skyscraper over, but to me I was relocating to Calcutta. "I'll just be so far from everyone I work with—I don't have many projects with those guys." I thought of Sandy, my "next door neighbor" and unofficial surrogate mother in business operations; Gretchen, the head of network administration who went with me for coffee most mornings; and Emily, who'd taken over as head of publications after I'd left the position.

"Oh, it'll be fine, and then I don't have to come over here to see you," she said, her smile now gone. We had worked on the same team for five years. Her kids came by often and loved my office because I had the bowling set, a wind-up toy, a foreign coin collection, and other things that were far more amusing than their mother's stapler and adding machine.

I put everything in a metal cart and walked with Denise over to the new wing.

"So, how's Susanne?" Denise asked me.

"She's great," I said, trying to keep the boxes on the cart as it rattled down the hall. "She invited me to some dinner party she does every year with a friend."

"Wow, how do I get invited? If only I could get Ed to host a dinner party."

I smiled, thinking that women, on average, probably didn't pick their men based on dinner hosting or baking capacity. Unfortunate, that.

* * *

I'd performed an impressive trick in that my coworkers still all thought I was female. I was tempted to drop bigger and bigger hints and then, at the moment that someone finally asked me if I was transitioning, I'd have a chorus line of gay bears, dressed in pink tutus, come bounding into the room, kicking their hairy legs out and presenting my insightful colleague with a check for sixty-nine dollars. It was too hard to line up the dancing bears, however, so I gave up on that plan.

My coworker Emily walked into my office and sat in a chair next to my desk. "You look all nice today. What's the occasion?"

"That commission meeting is tonight. The one where we try to get a vote on the new regs." I'd told my coworkers about the activist group I was in; they just presumed I attended as an ally. Emily knew we were trying to get anti-discrimination regulations on the books on behalf of trans people. These regs would give the expanded Human Rights Law some enforcement teeth.

"Oh, right. That's so cool. I hope you guys win." Emily was a Yale graduate who'd found a job here straight out of school. Putting together technical reports on science indicators for the National Science Foundation probably wasn't what the former history major had had in mind for her career, but the congeniality of the place grew on everyone after a while. I'd thought, as the person who hired her, that she'd quickly tire of the company, but six years later, she was still here. She still looked every bit the twenty-two-year-old greenhorn, so it was nice to know that not everyone felt stressed to work here.

"The commission's been in favor of changing the regulations for a while, so we're all pretty confident they'll go through," I said, sounding more sure of myself than I felt inside. The butterflies were starting to collect for their regular conference in my stomach. "There's this board member of another organization who got his hands on the draft regulations the day before yesterday and is now throwing a fit about them."

"Oh, man, that sucks." She frowned at the thought.

"I mean, everyone sees through him, but I worry anyway."

"Well, good. I mean, DC's such a liberal town."

I nodded.

We talked and complained about work for a while. I knew her really well. I felt badly that I hadn't told her about the trans thing going on with me and promised myself for the seventy-fourth time that I would tell her soon. I had a long list of people on my guilty conscience list.

Finally the end of the day rolled around. The metro train I boarded zipped through the tunnel, and I watched the people in my car. The majority of them didn't give me a second look. I'd had enough run-ins by that point to know it was the ones who continued to stare at me that should raise my red flags.

I rode the escalator up to the administration building and waved at another coalition member, dressed all in black, a male-to-female transsexual. I wondered if strangers could figure out, looking at the two of us, which of us was the FTM and who the MTF. Good thing I had a reputation for giggling, because she didn't ask me what I was thinking about.

More people trickled in to the space at the top of the escalator, all supporters of our cause. I started to sense the strength of our group. *Why don't I feel this tough by myself?*

Susanne walked by, studying the piece of paper with my apparently poorly written directions. I ran over to her to stop her before she wound up twenty blocks away.

"Hi, baby," she said in a slight singsong. I kissed her cheek.

"We're over here," I said, pointing to the group. She held up the address I'd given her and grinned.

"Yes, well, we're over here," I said, looking sheepish. I was learning, however, that she never scolded, much less yelled.

Somewhere between climbing in the elevator and stepping into the conference room, the sky suddenly darkened. We were on the eleventh floor and could see the layout of the city, the Capitol building giving us a sense of perspective as a background element among the cityscape. It was the kind of distance that could at once make a lawmaker feel immensely important but not attached to any of the actual lives she would affect with her power. Fortunately, we had brought our actual lives into the building.

"Why are we waiting?" someone asked me, over my shoulder.

"The commission doesn't have quorum yet," I answered.

The questioner, a young trans woman who'd told us downstairs that she'd just started hormones the day before, looked nervous.

"It's early still," I said. "They know they have a big vote tonight—they'll show up."

We sat around the table and waited for them to do all of their other business first. Finally two more commissioners arrived, making quorum. Nearly ninety minutes after we sat down, the chair of the commission finally got to their rulemaking and our regulations draft. She clearly was in support of our cause, and I breathed a sigh of relief. I had known this already but had fretted anyway.

The man who opposed the regulations spoke as the first public witness, and I marveled at his thinly veiled transphobia. He spoke, and thunder clapped outside; hard rain pelted against the windows. His three minutes of allotted time ticked by as I gripped my hands tightly under the table. Next a supporter of our cause spoke, and I relaxed because I didn't have to listen to someone who hated us and our cause.

"Next is Everett Maroon," read the chair from our signup sheet. I raised my hand, and people passed a microphone down to me.

"I am Everett Maroon," I began, trying to remember to breathe. "I am transsexual. I am gender variant. I have a good sense of humor. The lack of these regulations is an oppression in and of itself," I said. There was something else I wanted to add in my last thirty-two seconds, but it escaped me, so I handed the microphone back to the woman handling the transcription. I sat back in my chair.

I felt a warm hand on my leg and turned to see Susanne smiling at me. She blinked slowly. "I'm proud of you," she whispered. I gave her a grin.

We listened to the stories of others—people not allowed to use either segregated restroom at work, teenage trans women who were bullied out of school and who had little to no prospects for a decent job. A friend of the naysayer got his three minutes and made more doomsday predictions of bathroom assaults if people were allowed to use the restroom that concurred with their gender identity or expression. My head started to throb with the preposterous concept of roaming bands of male sexual predators wearing floral print dresses to fool law enforcement.

After three hours Susanne and I headed outside into the rain, which was lightening up.

"You did well," she said to me, squeezing my hand as we walked through the city. The smell of wet asphalt permeated.

Perhaps the coalition could win this battle.

*　*　*

"I started writing a letter to my family," I said to Robyn. My mom, my sister Kathy, and my brother David each had a big personality and a boatload of opinions.

"Oh?"

"Yeah. I don't know, maybe it's too much, but it's helping me clear my thoughts."

"Is it a letter to send or just a letter to organize your ideas and help you talk to them?"

Good question.

"I haven't decided yet on that. I think I'll send it to them. It's more practical."

"How so?"

"Because if I call one of the three of them, that person will call one of the others as soon as I hang up the phone, and I won't get to be the one to tell each of them. This way everyone will have the same information from the same source." I sounded so rational. It was like one of those children's puzzles—cross the river with a fox, a bird, and a cat, but only take one at a time, and don't leave two animals on the other side who might eat each other. I wasn't sure which animal I was in this scenario. Probably the canary.

"Well, that makes sense," she said. "Let me know if you want me to look at it. If you don't, that's fine too. I'm just here if you need me."

"You really have been," I said, wishing I'd brought a soda with me because hers looked particularly refreshing. "Thank you for everything."

"Well, it's my job," she said, smiling. I could tell she liked being appreciated, which made her a pretty normal person.

* * *

I walked around my apartment, making sure everything was ready for my sister, her kids, and her boyfriend. She referred to him as Maybe The One, so I wanted to greet him with open arms, though I would check out how he was around the girls. Callie, the older daughter, just hitting adolescence, was a bit of a bookworm and had a dry sense of humor that she revealed only sparsely; Jess, the younger sister by sixteen months, was primed to be the most hell-raising stuntwoman in Hollywood someday. Despite their personality differences, they looked like carbon copies of each other, with gazelle-long limbs, carelessly perfect blond hair, and an affinity for tiny clothing. Though they bickered like an old married couple, they looked out for one another.

Susanne and I walked up to the corner in Bethesda not far from where I'd been spit on months earlier, waiting to meet up with my sister and her entourage. They'd agreed to have breakfast with us at a little pancake diner, a hard to find place that got busy after nine o'clock in the morning. Susanne, ever the night owl, had slept most of the car ride over and was still rubbing the sand out of her eyes.

"Is that them?" she asked, focusing on several people who were still a couple of blocks north of us. A couple holding hands and two tall blonde girls on some kind of rollerblade-sneaker combination were out in front, looping around in a vague attempt to move forward. The smaller girl waved at me.

"Yup, that would be them," I said, smiling.

Jess rolled up to me. "Hello, hello, hello, hello," she sang.

"Well, hello, silly goose," I said. "What are these things you're wearing on your feet?"

"They're Heelies, duh," she replied. She moved her long hair away from her face and sized up Susanne.

Introductions and hugs went all around, and we walked—save the girls, who "heelied"—to the diner. It was like a little bit of suburbia in the urban landscape of almost DC.

We sat down at the table, holding enormous menus with thirty-nine kinds of pancakes, and Jess kept staring at me.

"What's up?" I asked.

"I'm gonna call you Bob," she announced.

I worried I'd break out into a nervous sweat any second. "Oh, you are, are you?"

"Bob is fine," said Susanne, patting me on my shoulder.

"Bob, what are you having?" inquired Jess, now smiling all the way across her mischievous face.

"The apple pancake," I answered, smiling behind my menu.

"Bob is having the apple pancake," Callie echoed.

"Oh, there's an apple pancake," said my sister. "Bob would know what's good here."

"I might have to go with Bob on this one," said Ross, the boyfriend.

Susanne held my hand under the table and squeezed.

We ran the children ragged all over DC. We went paddling on the Tidal Basin in plastic boats that had taken on whatever smells the swamp water had to offer. The girls insisted they would paddle productively and, for the most part, they kept their promise. Afterward, we wandered among the cherry blossoms and onto the Mall, which was not the kind of mall the girls had assumed it would be. They loved the subway, with its repetitive announcements and shiny vinyl seats, and they were fascinated by the statue in Lincoln Park. Finally we made it back to my apartment, rough cobblestones somewhat incompatible with Heelies. Susanne headed back to hers on her own, a few blocks away. "You go have fun now," she said, kissing me quickly on my cheek.

When the girls collapsed on the couch, the cats scrambled away, taking refuge under my bed in the next room, should beanpole-like humans start trying to braid their hair or dress them in ribbons.

I brought beers out for Kathy, Ross, and myself.

"So, that Susanne is awesome," she said.

"Isn't she?" I agreed, taking a long sip from my bottle.

"Whatever happened to Patricia?"

"Oh, you know, it just got nasty. And now Patricia is Pat." After I said it I wondered why I thought that would be helpful information to give her.

"Oh," she said, looking confused. "Is she a he now?"

"Yes," I said, doing my stare-in-the-bottle routine. As a strategy it never failed to fail me.

"Oh Jenny, please don't become a man and grow a penis."

"Uh, okay," I said. Another nail in the coffin of my life. I knew, once more, that this whole sex change thing was just impossible.

* * *

Lori had joined me for a drink at the swanky gay bar; Jeffrey was to join us when he could get off work in his downtown office.

It was spring, on the cusp of shorts-wearing weather, when the seating would start its cacophony of farting noises again, but we were both in pants, so we had a quiet spot on the foam-filled bench.

"I have to tell you something," I said, bracing myself.

"Okay. What is it?" Lori asked.

"I'm transitioning," I said, knowing she knew the meaning of the shorthand.

"Oh. You are?" She took a sip of her drink, not betraying her thoughts to me.

"Yes. I've been thinking about it for a while."

"How long?"

"Years, I guess." I wanted to drink faster but resisted the urge.

"Since we were together?" *Ah, the important question,* I figured.

"No. Some time after." She nodded in understanding.

"Why are you only telling me now?"

I thought for a second. "Well, I didn't want to start telling people until I was really sure. It's not that I didn't trust you."

"Okay," she said, looking into her martini glass. "What's your name now?"

"Everett."

"Everett?" she asked, saying it slowly and turning it over.

"Yes. Everett Daniel."

"Everett Daniel. Isn't Daniel the name your parents were going to name you?"

"Yup."

"Hmm. I like it." She flashed me a grin and patted my knee reassuringly. "Who knows so far?"

"Um, Susanne knows. Niles and Syd. My therapist, of course. Some people online."

"Not Jeffrey?" Lori's eyes opened wide, in something approaching shock.

"Not Jeffrey. I'll tell him soon."

"Not anyone at work?" She was seeing whom she could talk to about it and whom she couldn't, I gathered.

"Nobody at work, not my mom or brother or sister. Not any of my bowling mates." I listed other people we both knew. "It's a short list of people I've told." This seemed to make her happier, somehow.

"When are you going to start hormones?"

"Well, I was on T for about eight months last year, and then I stopped."

"Really?" Now I felt like I was in trouble. This was harder than I'd imagined, and yet I felt some sense of relief.

"Why did you stop?" she asked, sensing my fear.

"I wanted to see if it was working for me, and then after a time, I didn't want to do it in the closet anymore. I want to do it with my friends and family knowing."

"I wish you'd told me earlier, but I'll try to get over it," Lori said, then asked if she could tell Barbara. I told her that was okay.

Jeffrey walked up to us. "Jesus, you two look like Debbie Downer and Debbie's sister Denise. Get another drink!"

I smiled and shuffled to the bar to do as he said, trying not to think about how many more conversations like I this I was going to have.

Chapter 18

Nervous, I re-read the letter to my family three, four, five times, changing little words here and there that didn't affect the meaning at all. I pressed Send. And then I tried to find the number for Hotmail technical support so I could get the email back.

Susanne knew I wanted to tell everyone about my transition before my birthday in June. After years of getting proposals, reports, and web systems out the door at work on someone else's timetable, I needed a deadline to get through this. She was careful not to ask how it was going but listened when I told her about a person I'd disclosed to. I continued to be happily surprised by her support, which I didn't take for granted.

I hadn't figured out who to tell first at work but decided to start with my HR representative, Wendy, since she was pretty cool in her own right and way more intelligent, in my estimation, than the actual head of HR, the "sexual expression" lady as I called her to my friends. I also had a short list of coworkers I was closer to, so I'd need to tell them before any announcement went out.

Most on my mind, however, was my family. I'd emailed them late at night, giving myself a little reprieve before they opened their email. But I figured I'd hear from them soon enough. Maybe I could live in denial about telling them in the meantime.

Meantime, however, passed very quickly.

* * *

I heard the phone ring and saw on the caller ID that it was my mother.

"Hi, honey," she said, avoiding my name.

"Hi, Mom!" I exclaimed as if I'd just been released from the last day of kindergarten. The orange tabby opened up one eye as if to chide me for waking him.

"How are you?" she asked.

How did she think I was?

"I'm fine," I said, waiting for the crying I'd expected. "How are you?" *Just how long are we going to have this insipid conversation?*

"I'm okay. A little surprised. Both Kathy and David called me this morning. They said they love you, but they just need to process this news. I mean, we all love you, honey, and we're just sad that you've been sad all these years." That touched me.

"Oh. Oh. Well, that's okay, I mean, not that I've been sad, it's never okay for people to be sad, you know, like that unhappy bloop character on that antidepressant commercial, but just that, you know, we all have stuff, right?" *Stop talking!*

"What?" she asked, confused.

"Nothing. It's nice to hear they love me."

"I just am going to have a hard time calling you Everett."

My heart sank. "Oh. Well, you can give it some time. It's okay."

"Why Everett?"

"Why the name?"

"Yes." She waited for me.

I told her my pat answer about syllable counts, unusual names after carrying a name as common as Jenifer, the whole story. She seemed not to believe me, like I'd picked it in order to win a million dollars from some crazy organization out to get everyone in the world to have some odd name so they could rescue the planet from aliens. I figured it might be a while before they would use my chosen name.

"So, how does Susanne feel about this? Are you two going to break up?"

Now I was genuinely surprised.

"What? No, Ma, she—she's known all along."

"Oh. Good, then. So she's okay with you becoming a man?"

"Uh, yes. Actually, she kind of sees me as one already."

"Oh."

The increasing absurdity of the discussion was starting to get to me.

"Well, good," she said again, talking mostly to herself, "because you don't need that kind of loss right now, and Kathy really likes her. Be good to her and try to keep her around."

"Yes, mother."

"Okay, kid, I need to go now. I'm hosting a Bible study tonight."

Bible study?

"Sure, Ma, I'll talk to you later. I love you."

"I love you too, honey."

I hung up. I felt better and somehow worse.

My brother called me next. He said he'd always love me but I'd never be a real man, so I shouldn't go through with this. I held my tongue and didn't respond, other than to say, well, I have to go through with this. This was the brother, after all, who would hold my head under water in the neighborhood pool until I couldn't hold my breath anymore, and then he'd shove me under again as soon as I'd gotten a bit of air into my mouth. I told him he should take some time and thanks for calling. I hoped he'd come around at some point.

My sister was mostly sad that she was losing her sister; she'd loved having a little sister all these years. I felt her sadness. I tried to explain that I was the same person inside—which I'd said in the letter but which was probably not apparent to her, because the phrase "sex change" was kind of an upstaging hog on screen. Hard for anything like "I love you all" to seep through that. But she too told me she loved me and was honest about needing some time to think it through.

I hung up the phone for the last time that night and thought that as initial reactions, it had gone pretty well. Nobody was mad at me. There'd been some dismissiveness, but heck, I'd said the same thing to myself, hadn't I?

Perhaps they had to transition, too. And I was twenty steps ahead, so I should give them time.

*   *   *

I finished my bite of avocado burger, washing it down with a sip of stout beer, and told Jeffrey I was transitioning.

"Huh," he said, "I didn't see that line of conversation coming."

I laughed, trying to cover what was now a constant sense of unease.

"I mean, you're just so masculine already," he said, his mouth trying to determine if it should frown to show his skepticism or smile to cover it up. "What do you get by transitioning?"

I wasn't ready for that question. "Well, I don't think, even as a masculine woman, that I'm happy. I see myself as a man."

"I see." He paused. "Who else have you told?"

Why was everyone so concerned with who knew? Were they going to have a conference on my gender identity, or were they jockeying to host the celebration party?

"Uh, Lori knows as of last month. I just told my mom and siblings."

"What does Susanne make of all this?"

Really? Again?

"She's known from the beginning."

"Oh. That's some time."

"Well, it seemed good to tell her at the outset."

"Why haven't you told me before now?"

I got the distinct impression I was being interrogated, and he was looking for me to slip up in my story. *No, it's not that I'm trans, it's that I'm a serial killer looking to thwart Interpol. Don't mind me.*

"Look," I said to him, trying to express the degree to which this was important to me, "I told people online first because they didn't mean anything to me. I had to explore with people who didn't know me any other way. Someone like you, you're an anchor in my life. I needed to hold on to Jenifer while I figured out if I could let her go."

And also, you haven't been so great about the trans thing with other friends. But what I'd said was true, if not complete.

"I just thought I knew you better than this," he said, and we ate in silence for a long time after that. He wasn't reassured.

*   *   *

The Contessa, Michael, was more understanding.

"Wow," he said, "I've always seen you as such a strong woman. But good for you."

"Thanks," I said. "It hasn't been easy. But butch only was taking me so far."

"You know, I've never really thought of you as a butch."

"Uh, really?" Just when I thought I could predict the arc of these conversations, people threw curveballs at me and beaned me in the head. "Were you blinded by my love of lipstick and Aqua Net?"

"Oh, I don't know," Michael said, looking up as he answered. "I guess I think of butches as tough, leather dykes, you know."

"Ah. I'm more of a flabby intellectual," I said.

"Exactly! Which I guess you could do in either gender."

"Indeed," I sighed.

"Okay, it may take me a while to get the pronouns right," he warned me. I thought of that person in Brooklyn a couple of years earlier who'd chastised me for presuming which pronouns I should use. I resolved not to be hardheaded about it.

"That's okay. I need some help with them sometimes, too," I said.

*　*　*

I opened up my email inbox and saw that the new organizers of the DC Dyke March—Pat was no longer in charge of it—wanted to know if I'd handle my annual training of the fire-eaters. I said sure, but they'd need to supply the white gas fuel. I'd bring the coat hangers and the cotton string for the torches. We set a date a few days later, since the June march was around the corner, and I drove to the address in the Petworth section of DC, near Howard University.

They lived group house style in a crumbling building. Dirt and weeds pretended to serve as the front lawn, bad cover for the used condom wrappers and dusty malt liquor bottles. Half of a fence stood proudly next to the sidewalk, the other half carried away some time ago.

"Thanks for coming," said the organizer, meeting me at the front door. She knew me from the last two marches. She had a funny smile on her face that bothered me, though I didn't have a reason why.

"Sure," I said, pulling out my equipment. "You have the gas?"

"No, we forgot to get it," she said, and someone giggled.

"Okay." I was curious about what was so funny. "I have some extra from last year."

We made torches, and I showed them the prep and safety considerations. Nobody introduced me to the people I didn't know, even though I told the organizers in my email response that I was going by Everett now. So I guessed I'd just be some nameless stranger who showed up and cajoled them into putting fire in their mouths. That sounded safe.

About an hour later, I watched as everyone had memorized the standard Lesbian Avengers fire-eating chant, and they swallowed the torches successfully, looking astonished and happy with themselves.

"Really, the aftertaste from the white gas is the worst part," I told them.

"Thanks," said the organizer, shaking my hand.

"Sure, Sara, no problem," I said.

"Pat told me before I emailed you that you were transitioning," she said, looking guilty.

"Ah. Did he?"

"Yeah. He said you were changing your name to Bennifer."

"Seriously?"

"Yeah, I figured he didn't mean it."

"Well, that's pretty offensive, actually."

"Yeah, I feel bad for laughing."

"It's okay," I said, and I put my hand on her shoulder. I couldn't be mad at an eighteen-year-old kid. It was Pat who should have known better. "Anyway, now you all are ready for the march. Remember, don't do it if it's too windy. Please."

She gave me a hug. "Thanks for helping us out, Ev."

I waved goodbye and walked back to my car. *Bennifer, please.*

* * *

My thirty-sixth birthday came and Susanne made me a rich chocolate cake with chocolate butter cream frosting that somehow held up against the early summer heat. Everyone I knew was at the party, and all of them were using or trying to use my name Everett. I was grateful for them; after years of struggling with this, maybe everything would be all right.

There were still some cousins and other relatives I hadn't told, and all of my coworkers, but the list of who didn't know was now shorter than those in the know. I knew from announcing I was gay a decade earlier that the coming out process never really ended, though on the transgender front it was a little different. Some people transitioned and then never told anyone, or told only their partner and then nobody else. It was called being "stealth." I wasn't sure where I stood on it, other than not to presume I knew anybody else's business nor what went into their decision making about such a personal choice. But online, battles in the community raged. As they always would, I guessed.

Michael and Jeffrey clung to each other a little, not mingling much with Susanne's friends, or Lori and Barbara, who they'd known for some time. I told myself not to worry about the interpersonal dynamics and just enjoy myself. I still experienced the pull of Jenifer and Everett in different directions. I'd drawn and quartered myself.

As had happened in my twenties, a cramp snuck up on me, and I realized I needed to go to the bathroom. *Are you kidding me?* my brain asked itself. *A period? Really?*

"Really," I said to the mirror above the sink. I dug and dug in the cabinet, looking for tampons, not remembering when the last time was that I'd needed any.

What kind of man has a period? You're such a charlatan!

I detested my bathroom. I considered burning some sage in it, to purify it of whatever evil had moved in when I'd gotten depressed. Except I hated the smell of burned sage.

Finally, I found an ancient feminine hygiene product. It was in a crumpled wrapper. Maybe it was worth money as the first known tampon in earth's history; only carbon dating it would tell. I washed my hands, splashed some cold water on my face, and headed back out to the party.

Chapter 19

"I want to go back on T," I said, expecting a raised eyebrow from Robyn. It was I, after all, who'd decided to stop the T. Wasn't I just fickle, and didn't that mean that I had some other illness, some not-trans, not-gender dysphoric problem? Maybe I was a closet borderline personality, like Kathy Bates in *Misery*, and I'd fooled everyone. And now that I'd clued in to myself, I'd have to kill anyone I suspected knew the truth about me, or at least dismember them at the ankles.

But the eyebrows on her face stayed put. "Okay," she said. "It shouldn't be a problem at this point."

She meant that because I was an adult and had already been on T, doctors wouldn't have a problem prescribing it for me. But perhaps she didn't realize that I was just as unconfident as any eighteen-year-old trying to get birth control in their doctor's office with their unsuspecting mother in the waiting room. Even less confident than some of them, I thought.

"Well okay then," I said, overcompensating for my nerves. "I'm sure there won't be any issues, then."

I was wrong. One call to Dr. Travers's office, and the receptionist refused to put me on his schedule.

"I can't put you in," she said tersely.

"What's the issue?" I asked.

"You have a balance due of forty-five dollars."

"Uh, okay," I began, clearly confused. "So here's my credit card number."

"It's been an outstanding balance for more than ninety days."

"Well I haven't been in his office in months. I'm sorry. I didn't know I owed you anything. Let's just pay the balance now."

She took my credit card number and processed the payment, then resumed her icy demeanor. What is she looking for? *Transsexual blood? My first born?*

"So, when can I see the doctor?"

"I can't make an appointment with you," she said.

"But why not?" Now I was annoyed.

"Because you had an outstanding balance for more than ninety days," she said like the recording I began to presume she was. She had skipped into past tense now, having just processed my balance. "I have to contact the doctor and see if he's still willing to see you."

"Willing to see me? All this over forty-five dollars?"

"That's our policy."

"Well, will you ask him for me?" He'd been so nice in person; I couldn't imagine he would say anything other than yes.

"I'll see when I can talk to him. I'll call you tomorrow." The phone clicked off. She'd actually hung up on me.

She never called me back. At this rate of disappearing doctors, all of the country's physicians would be gone before the last American glacier was due to melt into nothingness in 2020.

*　*　*

I'd asked to get funding from work to take a week-long class at the University of Michigan in Ann Arbor. To my happiness, Mary approved it, so I told Susanne that I'd be spending a week in July in her home state.

"Hmm. Maybe you could meet my family," she suggested casually one evening.

"Oh, they're close to Ann Arbor?"

"Not really, but close enough." A few weeks earlier, she had told her family she was dating someone, and she had explained to her two brothers that I was transgender. One of them apparently had searched online for the term, not knowing what it meant, which meant that I had to try it out myself to see what kinds of web pages popped up. *The Rocky Horror Picture Show* was near the top, as were some Christian sites on how to "fix" transsexuals, and a few sites on how to dress like the other gender. For all her older brother knew, he'd be meeting an immoral, Goth, recently ex-lesbian with a penchant for black leather corsets and a shaky singing voice. *Perfect.*

"Well, it would be nice to meet them." I thought back to the days when I was with Pat, and he'd remarked that it was good I'd never meet his family because they'd just think I was too fat. *Perhaps I should work out before I head up there,* I thought now. Maybe I could drop forty pounds in two months. Maybe flying pigs would perform painless liposuction on me while I was sleeping.

* * *

Online, I'd found the name for another doctor, this one an endocrinologist, not an obstetrician with a concentration in endocrinology. The only difference this made for my life was that I wouldn't look out of place in the waiting room. But once again I was dealing with a receptionist gatekeeper for the practice.

"How can I help you?" she asked. *So far, so good.*

"I need testosterone therapy." That seemed clear and straightforward.

"Are your levels low?"

"Desperately!"

"Oh ... okay." I had lost her in the morass that was my sense of humor.

"Actually, I'm transgender."

"Oh, okay," she laughed. "Do you have a letter from a therapist?"

"I'll have one with me." This was my way of saying, "no, but let's make the appointment anyway." If I'd wanted to give myself E-cup breasts I'd have needed no letter from anyone.

Two weeks later I hopped off the Metro in downtown DC, hearing superhero music in my ears. *Dum da da dum! Here comes SuperT! Amazing muscles from nowhere! A voice like a baritone! Rippling lines of—*was I walking in the right direction? *Oh, dear.* Now I was two blocks farther away. I turned around and walked right by where I'd just been. *Dum da da dum dum! Here comes SuperT!*

Ace was a strange first name for a doctor, I thought, much less a person. It smacked of 1950s-era comic book villains, the kind of acne-riddled, angry teenagers who drove around in a black Caddy and terrorized the wimps and geeks of the high school. But this Ace was nothing like my imaginings. Older, with a carefully shaved beard and a New York City accent, his office was covered in awards, much like the last doctor's office had been. I started to suspect that there was a catalogue out there, and doctors everywhere selected awards for their offices like they ordered desk blotters. Endocrine awards, however, were not nearly as interesting as the OB/GYN awards had been, probably because nothing is as outstanding as a crystalline uterus and fallopian tubes. Endocrines, on average, just didn't have that kind of appeal.

"So you have been on T already," he asked me in the form of a sentence while looking through the forms I'd filled out.

"Yes." I figured shorter answers were better, as if I were in court, on trial.

"Well, you look like a man to me. What else are you trying to achieve?" His point-blank stare was a little intimidating, but I sensed that he didn't intend to come across that way.

"Well, I've had some changes, yes, but I'd like to continue."

"You want beard growth," he said, assuming the rest of my sentence. He unconsciously touched his own beard, in a way that I could have interpreted as mocking if I'd been in a worse mood. It dawned on me that he had absolutely no sense of humor. Maybe this arrangement wasn't going to work.

"Yes, I'd like that," I admitted. "My face is still very smooth except for a bit under my chin and some passable sideburns." I smiled to show him that I was actually dealing with my hairless cheeks fairly well, but my comment went unnoticed.

"How's your penis size?" he asked, now reading from my folder again. That he called genitals a penis meant he had some cultural competency, but as I'd never had a conversation with another human being about this exact topic, I was unprepared to respond.

"Uh, is any man happy with his endowment?" I asked, hoping to avoid the issue.

"Well, I think I can help you with that," he said.

I almost asked if he had a special penis-growing pill in his desk but bit my lip.

"I spoke with Dr. Zeiger before your appointment today," he announced. I was glad he'd spoken with Robyn but was a little confused as to why she hadn't mentioned the conversation to me. "She spoke very highly of you."

"Well, of course she did!"

He stared at me.

"I mean, that's nice."

"You're a funny guy, huh?" he asked, standing up. He motioned for me to follow him.

"I try," I said, and we went into the exam room.

"Let's just do a little blood work, and if it comes back okay I'll call in a prescription for you, all right?" He wanted me on a gel version of testosterone, so I could get an even, daily dose of T as I had before. And then I'd be back on track. I nodded, not really caring what the method was. I just wanted it back in my veins.

*   *   *

Chocolate, apparently, was the way to Susanne's mother's heart, so I stopped at the Krön Chocolatiers in Georgetown for the best truffles available in the city. I thought about the quarter-pound package and then asked for the half-pounder. I didn't want Susanne's mom thinking her new boyfriend was a cheapskate.

On the flight to Detroit, I held Susanne's hand most of the way, admiring her sweetness, and I got a little mad at myself for continuing not to expect it. I supposed it was better than taking her for granted six months into dating.

I took a deep breath as we pulled into the driveway, a winding monster that Susanne told me ate cars in the winter with the snowfall and again in the spring with its mudflows, as if it insisted on a perennial two-course meal of vehicles. This was why Susanne didn't mind the crazy driving patterns of DC—she'd learned to drive via navigating around the steady stream of potholes in her home county.

"Ready?" She took my hand and squeezed it.

"Sure, I'll just head to Ann Arbor, and you let me know when you want me to pick you up."

"Come on," she said, laughing. "We'll get our bags in a minute."

We walked around to the back door—with fields on two sides, and an apple orchard on another, the back door was the one used more often. Her family heard us pull in, since there was no other ambient noise to drown out even a sedan engine. As we crossed the threshold, we were greeted with a receiving line of Susanne's immediate family. I walked through, shaking all the hands like a politician at a pick-up campaign event. In the space of five seconds, I met her mother, stepfather, two brothers, one sister-in-law, two nephews, and a niece.

And then there we were, standing in the kitchen, talking about the flight and ride in, as people do when they don't know what else to say. I looked around the house, which was laid out in an open manner. A staircase heading down to the finished basement was the only thing that interrupted the living room, kitchen, and eating area. A deck looked out on the aging orchard that Susanne had told me still bore a little fruit each year. All of the walls were varnished wood, the kind of knothole-stubbled boards that could teach counting to small children. Her family seemed as down to earth as the home. Inside of five minutes, though, Susanne's mother said she needed to get a few things from the grocery store, and she left us to chop up some radishes in the potato salad she'd been preparing. I'd never heard of radishes in potato salad, so I had no idea how to cut them.

I leaned into Susanne's ear and whispered, "How should I chop these?"

She shrugged. "Little cubes?"

I made tiny cubes. They looked weird and unappetizing.

"Mrs. Hughes," I asked as she headed out of the kitchen, "how do you want these cut?"

She looked at the pile of radish cubes on the cutting board. "Well, that's ... fine."

"Well, now, they're not fine. That's okay. Just tell me how you'd like them cut, and I'll do that."

She looked astonished for a split second, and I worried that I'd blown the whole trip with three sentences. And then she smiled.

"I'd like them sliced thinly," she said, holding up her finger and thumb millimeters from each other.

"Sliced, can do," I chirped, and I started slicing them to show her how excited I was to cut tiny radishes. *Such a sycophant.*

Susanne waited for her mother to leave and then turned to me. "That may be the most direct communication she's ever had in this kitchen," she said, smiling at me and patting me on the shoulder. Bullet dodged.

Chapter 20

Starting to use men's rooms gave me a whole new perspective on being male in America.

First of all, they were disgusting in every way imaginable. In women's restrooms, there was the occasional "hoverer," the woman who didn't trust sitting on the toilet seat, lest it was dirty in an invisible, germ-infested way, and thus would squat over it and spatter her urine on it, ironically—and for the rest of us, frustratingly—making it much dirtier than when she'd found it. And hoverers never dried up the seat after doing their business, because this would break their cardinal rule not to touch the toilet.

But the gross habits of hoverers aside, women had nothing on men's public facilities. The urinals, I was surprised to find, were not the dirtiest parts of the space. The first stall was. I wondered if there was an underground community that intentionally destroyed the stalls closest to the door and then posted pictures on the web.

I had a problem using any restroom facility, actually. Women chased me out of women's rooms, men glowered at me for looking too effeminate or female. I tried to gauge how I was being perceived at any given moment so I could identify which room I should use, but my days were now filled with a nearly even mix of ma'am and sir, so I wound up avoiding them altogether.

"That's not healthy," Lori told me over lunch one day. "You can get a UTI that way."

"I know, but I don't have another choice right now."

"That sucks," she said, mulling her experience in restrooms as she slowly chewed a chicken salad sub. We were back at the Korean-run deli near her work. "I got yelled at by an old lady last week. I threatened to show her my tits, and she shut up."

"How clever of you," I said, laughing.

"Well, I thought so," she said, smiling as she ate.

* * *

The week in Michigan gave me a reality check about DC, what I was achieving in the city, and what I wanted out of my life then and in the immediate future. DC was a fairly high-stress, high-energy place that, instead of being a bastion of activism, was more about back-door, small-town politics and rampant materialism. Thinking about the topics of conversation I'd had at parties—with queer and straight people, filled with nonprofit staff, lobbyists, lawyers, academics, IT professionals, and data cruncher types—it broke out something like:

- The House I Bought
- The House I'm Remodeling
- The Vacation I Just Took/Am About to Take
- The "Insert Luxury Item Here" I Bought
- The Promotion I Just Got
- The "Insert Random Legislator's Name Here" I Talked to Today
- Random Political Issue
- The Weather in DC and How It Sucks the Big One

Traveling to another city was, at the very least, a break from that.

Whether people saw me as male or female varied the whole time I was away, but I supposed it did at home, too. I'd figured out that it was less about what I was doing, wearing, or saying than about the reference point of the person perceiving me, but it was a little taxing to be ma'amed on one street and get the man nod on the next. I reminded myself that none of us have any control, really, over how others read us. I made my attempt at unscientific data gathering. But in this transition so far I'd met a variety of people and their responses.

I figured DC was a better place than many to transition, in that it had doctors who knew what transsexual meant, as well as other resources, but it still felt like a small town sometimes. It was never more provincial than when I heard from acquaintances that Pat had told them I'd forced him to be trans because I'd wanted to do it myself all along.

I got hot under the collar whenever that got back to me, but I tried not to respond to something so ludicrous, which would only give it merit. On one sunny evening, I was having a beer and hamburger at a tavern in Eastern Market, near where I lived. I looked up as someone called my name—Everett. It was a woman I'd met through Pat, now several years ago.

"Hi, Tammy," I said, trying not to be unmannerly with food in my mouth.

"Wow, it's been a long time! You look great!"

"Thanks," I said, half-excited to see her and half-worried that whatever I said would get back to Pat.

"Mind if I sit down with you a minute?" *The joys of sidewalk eating.*

"No problem. Catch me up on stuff."

"Well, I've got a new girlfriend and we moved in together a while ago. She has a child and a dog, so it was like instant family."

"Wow," I said. *Everyone has their shifts, I suppose.*

"I'm sorry I haven't seen you. You know," she said, lowering her eyes and voice, "Pat went around to all his friends when you guys broke up and said, 'You can either be my friend or his friend, so you have to choose.'"

"Really? That sucks."

"Yeah. And so I picked Pat, but that was stupid."

"Well, you knew Pat first," I said, trying to let her off the hook.

"Well, just so you know, his life has fallen apart since you were together."

"I wouldn't wish that on him." *Okay, maybe a little. Be honest.*

"Anyway, I'm sorry I did that," Tammy said.

"You had to do what you had to do. It's okay. I've moved on." This was true, wasn't it? I felt a little lighter, letting go of some of my anger at him.

"It would be great to hang out with you soon," she said shyly. I gave her my new number and waved goodbye as she walked back to the corner and across the street.

★   ★   ★

I had a new prescription for T and a brand new box of Testim testosterone gel. I drove home quickly from work, where I'd again had it delivered, as excitedly as I had that first day with the T cream. Opening up the box in my bedroom, I saw that it was filled with lots of little tubes that looked like oil paints instead of man gel. I punctured one and squirted it onto my stomach, trying to turn my nose as far away from the awful alcohol smell as possible but knowing that I couldn't get far without cutting off my own head. Which of course would defeat the purpose of putting the gel on in the first place. Making matters worse, some of the gel spurted out at an unpredictable angle, so I had to scrape it off my right biceps and wipe it on my belly. The cats grimaced at the stench and ran out of the room, cowering across the apartment by the front door.

"Sorry, guys," I said to them. I had to do this every day?

Within a few minutes the alcohol had evaporated and the intensity of the smell dwindled. I itched where I'd rubbed it in, but I dismissed this and got up to wash my hands in the sink. Susanne and I had dinner plans at one of her favorite restaurants, a Pakistani place on Pennsylvania Avenue in Eastern Market. I had grown to enjoy walking around my neighborhood. DC felt like less of a too-cool gay scene and let more of its farming town roots show through in this part of the city. I called Susanne to say I was leaving to come see her.

We met up where our paths to the restaurant converged and then walked over together. I loved it when she took my hand and swished her thumb in my palm.

*   *   *

I took a breath and walked into the office of the HR representative, Wendy.

"Hi, Jenifer," she said, and the name sounded fake to my ears. "What's up?"

"Well, I wanted to let you know as my HR rep that I'm transitioning and will be going by the name Everett." I knew she'd understand this terminology because Aidan had gone through a sex change here years ago. Wendy had handled his paperwork.

Wendy and I had attended many a happy hour work event. She was kind enough to laugh at my jokes and knew how to drink most of our coworkers under the table. In years past, we'd talked about wanting to have babies. She didn't miss a beat as I ended my sentence. She smiled.

"What can we do for you?"

Cool! Maybe this will go better than I'd thought it would.

Chapter 21

I hummed with energy and scoured the apartment, then made a batch of chocolate chip cookies. It could have been summer or maybe the smelly T I was taking, but I felt young and strangely virile, if that was the right sentiment. It was hard to name something I'd never experienced before. I told Robyn about my newfound motivation and drive, in part to share, but in part to make her aware of it in case my mania wasn't healthy.

She changed the subject.

"How did you like this doctor?" she asked. I knew she wasn't happy about how I'd been treated by Dr. Travers's receptionist.

"Other than being too serious, he's fine," I replied. "I follow up with him next month to make sure my levels are okay."

"How was he toward you?" she asked, another question I hadn't expected. She was fishing for something.

I wasn't sure what she wanted to hear. "They were all very respectful and called me Everett the whole time. And the lady that stuck me for my blood was very good."

"Good, then. It's just that you've had your share of crap with medical providers, so I wanted to make sure this was going well."

"Yeah, so far so good. The stuff I'm using stinks to high heaven."

"Ah, the price you pay," she said, laughing.

I told her I'd talked to HR, and next I was going to tell Chris, my VP, and Mary.

"That's wonderful. Oh, this has been such a long time coming, Ev."

"I hadn't thought about that. I guess it has."

She looked surprised. "Oh, sure, it's been two years since you've been seeing me, give or take. You've worked really hard to get to this point."

I wanted to bask in my own glory for a minute, but since I didn't know what that point was, I didn't know how to appreciate it, or even if I should.

* * *

I had presumed that smearing an alcohol-based gel on my stomach was an endeavor that created itchiness. After all, wet stuff evaporating off of a large area of skin wasn't a trivial process. But my need to scratch myself silly was, after only three months of using the gel, increasing daily. I couldn't dig under my shirts to relieve myself in the middle of the workday or commute home.

Undressing after work one day, I saw that the itchiness had evolved into an actual rash. This was no simple shingles rash. This was a side-to-side eruption of fine red dots all over my stomach.

I had polka dots.

I called the doctor's office, and a couple of hours later, he called me back.

"Yeah, that sometimes happens with Testim. You're allergic to it."

"Oh. What do I do now?"

"I'll just switch you over to the other brand. You may have to argue with your insurance company for a little while, but we'll put a note in the system to help you out."

The system? I said okay, and he told me not to take any more of the Testim.

I was allergic to transition. I figured it wasn't worth wondering what my rash meant metaphorically.

* * *

I had decided to tell some of my closer colleagues about my news—even if it was old news to me—before my boss Chris sent out an email about me, lest they think I'd snubbed them or left them in the dark. I wasn't prepared for the variety of responses I received.

Gail, a VP and one of the company lesbians, looked at me. "Thank God we were never lovers, because I would miss your body parts." It was only after I looked at her, dumbfounded, that she asked, "That was inappropriate, wasn't it?"

"Well, yeah, kind of," I said, "even though I generally appreciate honesty."

"Sorry," she said, looking at her hands.

"No worries," I said, smiling too big for what I'd intended and walking away. Exactly which body parts was she talking about, anyway?

Gretchen, the head of network services and a tomboy, nearly shouted. She pushed her glasses up her nose and grinned.

"Wow, that's so cool! Wow, that's so cool! You're so cool! What are you gonna do first?"

The head of the testing group, a real femme fatale and a woman of color who never held anything back, asked me, "Oh my god, Jenifer, are you gonna put one on?"

I laughed, not comprehending what she meant and hoping it had nothing to do with genitalia.

A gay executive I'd gone out with on occasion told me, "Boy, you weren't kidding about being in the Gay Mafia, were you?"

Denise, who was on the same team with me said, "Okay. Okay. Okay. I'm a little freaked out. But it's good. Okay. Weren't you going to have a baby?"

"Yes," I answered, giving the rest of my answer slowly, "but I just couldn't wait any longer. I'll have to have kids another way."

A colleague who ran the fantasy football league every year and used to coach our softball team was delighted.

"Oh, that is so cool! You'll be the best man around here, you know." I thanked him for his kindness.

One of the technical directors who lived half a block from me was excited and then nervous.

"Wow! But hormones are dangerous! And oh no! Susanne! Is Susanne going to leave you now? Isn't she a lesbian?"

"It's okay, Lea," I told her, "Susanne's known all along. She's okay with it."

"Oh, okay, then. Oh, good. Because she's really nice and you need to keep her around."

"I totally agree," I said, patting her on the forearm.

Emily, the head of publications, had her usual feline air of detachment.

"You know, that's great. It's not like it's a big difference, anyway. In fact, why didn't I ever notice before now?"

Fatima, the front desk receptionist, though, was the one who took me aback.

"Come on, Jenifer, let's run to the ladies room so you can show me your dinkie!"

"Fatima! Absolutely not!" I saw that she was holding my arm, as if prepared to drag me off to the restroom with her. She could sooner have towed a semi up Capitol Hill.

I suppose it could be worse, I thought, driving home. Nobody yelled at me or told me I was fired. People seemed genuinely happy for me, even if they were a little over the line with some of their comments. But everyone had been honest and forthright, and I knew where I stood.

Why didn't I do this earlier?

*   *   *

The second time on T, I noticed changes again, most notably a loss of hair on my head. The new gel evicted hair from my head and forced it into a life of regret over on my shoulders and upper arms. More interesting, and far less upsetting, was the realization that I felt different about using T. I felt celebratory this time. I couldn't find any guilt to speak of, and I certainly wasn't worried that I was stepping on Susanne's toes, since she couldn't have given a fig if I were on T or not. She would love me no matter which path I decided to take.

Free from my own anxiety, I enjoyed the body changes much more than I had the previous year. Okay, I didn't like the ballooning stomach from my fat redistribution. My facial and body hair seemed to be growing more on one side of me than the other, and I tried to remember what puberty had been like when I was a teenager, but I couldn't recall if my development had been symmetrical or not. No matter. *It's not like hair growing on my right side means I have to join the Republican Party, right?*

Something new was on the horizon, though, something I needed to plan for, that seemed bigger than anything I'd done to this point. I needed to go under the knife for chest surgery at some point. I had put off thinking about it seriously, knowing it would cost several thousand dollars and require at least a couple of weeks of recovery. Vacation time I had. A spare eight grand in U.S. currency I did not.

Sitting on Susanne's building's deck, I broached the subject.

"I think I should get top surgery," I said, mesmerized by the sunset behind the Capitol. Congress was still in session, we could tell, because the light at the top of the dome was lit.

"Okay," she said. "Were you thinking of a specific time frame?"

"Not yet, no. Next year, I guess. I need enough time to pay for it."

"Do you know who you'll see for it?"

"I think I'll schedule a consult with Dr. Fairchild, who's near Baltimore."

"Well, good, honey," she said, and she leaned in so her head was on my shoulder. "I'm proud of you. If you want me to come with you to the appointment, let me know."

"Thanks, sweetheart." She did not allow any nicknames, so it was either honey, sweetheart, or her name.

Having broken the news to my family that I was Everett, I'd thought my stress level would decrease and life would feel easier. But I hadn't gained much confidence in talking to them. Getting a chest reconstruction was definitely going to be a difficult conversation. I thanked my stars for Susanne's support.

*　*　*

After talking to HR and my boss, Chris, who was nonchalant about my transition news, we decided that I would write up the announcement and he would email the staff. I pondered what I'd written. I stopped by Chris's office, around the corner from mine.

"It's in your inbox," I said, wanting to run away, squealing like a stuck pig. I stood tall instead, projecting confidence.

"Okay, I'll copy it and send it out," he said in his usual *laissez faire* fashion, as if he were emailing a client about a statistical report we'd just finished.

I walked back to my office and waited. And waited. I refreshed my inbox nineteen times in four minutes, knowing that Gretchen would see my insanity on her mail server log and shake her head at me.

Finally, it went out on broadcast. Why hadn't I just left the building to get a coffee so I didn't have to be around for this? What a dumb ass.

Denise poked her head in first.

"I see the email went out," she said, and she grinned at me as if we shared a secret. Some secret. More than 1,000 people now knew there was a transsexual in their midst.

"I told Noah and Cassie about your transition last night," she said, referring to her two children who knew me.

"You did? What did you say?" Curiosity bit me.

"I said, 'You know Mommy's friend, Jenifer?' And they nodded. So I said, 'Well, she's changing her name. Now she's going to go by Everett.' And I waited to see how they took this in."

"Yeah, that makes sense. So what then?" She continued to smile.

"Noah said, 'Well, okay.' And I said you were also changing so that you're going to be a man now and not a woman anymore. And Noah asked, 'Oh. How's she going to do that? I didn't know you could do that.' So I said, 'Well, I think she has to see the doctor about that.'

"Then I asked if they had any questions. And Cassie said, 'No, but it must have been a difficult decision for him.'"

"Wow," I said, "aren't kids cool?"

"Kids are totally cool," she said. "Anyway, congratulations again."

I thanked her and looked back at my monitor. I had eight emails from coworkers who said they were excited for me. *Adults have their moments, too.*

I left for lunch and walked back to my office barely twenty minutes later. Fatima had changed the name plate outside my door to read Everett Maroon. Touched by the thought, I also liked how it looked and put my hand on the sign as if Fatima would sense me thanking her from the other building.

It was really happening. I really wasn't Jenifer anymore. I felt a pang of sadness that I presumed was the sensation of letting go. And immediately after, I laughed.

*　　*　　*

Having come out to my friends and family and exploding the closet door at work, I had some momentum, telling anyone I ran into—like the cashier at the lunch counter or the owner of the convenience store in the lobby. Overall, most people seemed really happy for me. Very few were skeptical or negative. I had managed not to run into Arnold at work, who had limited time in our hallowed halls since announcing a semi-retirement, but I guessed that he would have had one of the more memorable comments about all of this.

Behind my desk, I started packing to go home; it was intimidating to think that there were four more days of work in the week. As I started thinking about my evening, one of the senior project managers stuck his head in my office.

"So, Ev," he began, shutting the door behind him, "when, uh, when new guys start over in this wing, they get a little, uh, talk." He fidgeted with whatever was in his pockets.

"Oh?"

"Yeah. When you use the men's room—"

Oh, here it comes. We don't want you to look at us in the urinals, we want you to announce you're coming in, what is it?

"—make sure you don't go after two in the afternoon."

I blinked a few times, as if that would help me hear better. "I'm sorry, what?"

"I mean, Kendrick goes in there every day at two. You don't want to be in there afterwards."

"Really?" I couldn't believe this. "It's uh, it's that bad?"

"It's that bad," he said slowly, giving each word emphasis.

"Okay, Dave, thanks for telling me."

"Oh sure," he said, visibly relieved our conversation was ending. "So aren't you dating someone?"

"Yup. A lovely graduate student."

"Well, good on you. She's cool with this?"

"She's cool, yes."

"That's great. Congratulations." He waved and was gone.

I wasn't sure if I'd been congratulated for transitioning or having a girlfriend or having a girlfriend who didn't mind I was transitioning, but it didn't matter. Now my question was when would my curiosity get the better of me, forcing me to check out the restroom in the afternoon?

I drove home thinking that men's style of communication was actually a little crazy. Maybe it was just the men I'd met. I was used to speaking my mind because feminists told me I should. How did I need to shift? If I wanted to stay true to my bleeding heart principles, now I needed to give women space to talk in meetings and talk less myself. That seemed like a fair challenge for an extrovert like me.

I pulled up outside Susanne's building, a small bundle of flowers in hand. I walked in the lobby door and pressed the code on the buzzer machine.

"Hi, honey," I said to the metal box.

"Hi, Ev," she said. "Come on up." The door latch hummed, and I walked to her elevator. At least she was smart enough to live somewhere that had a modicum of accessibility.

In the hall I saw a mother and young boy coming out of the laundry room. I held the elevator door for them, thinking that the kid was a bit of a handful.

"See," she said to him, motioning with the basket at me because she didn't have a free finger to point, "that's what men do for ladies—they hold doors."

Well thank God someone told me what men do before I got too far down this road. I gave her a small smile, knowing I was confirming her nineteenth century version of chivalry. Now was not the time to explain that a crazy trans man was modeling manners for her child, I presumed.

Susanne let me in her apartment and kissed me, squeaking a little at the bouquet.

"So how did it go today?" she asked.

I plopped down on her futon. "I'm glad it's gone so well at work, but I would really, really like it if I could have five minutes where I don't have to talk about my gender."

"Oh, yeah, that must be exhausting." She poured water in her tea kettle. Susanne drank many glasses of tea a day, something that must have been passed down to her by her mother, who had many a teapot and kettle in her house. "That will go away, I'm sure."

"I'm just wiped out mentally. And I've been working to midnight and getting into the office a little early, then working for nine or ten hours, and stressing about my finances, and worrying that I need a new timing belt."

She walked over to me and sat down. "Honey, just breathe."

I did as she said. I didn't tell her I was worried about getting depressed again, but the thought was nagging me. And here I was, making positive moves in my personal life, doing well in the company, so why now?

I smiled and kissed her just below her ear.

Chapter 22

Work continued to be a changed place, as if I could feel that all of the atoms around me had been reassembled in a different order. It was strange to think I'd hidden this big thing about myself, and now I wasn't pretending anymore.

My hair continued to fall out, and I made a mental note to ask Ace for a prescription to stop hair loss. If I'd been a non-trans guy, I'd probably have been bald by twenty-five. Perhaps it was a lesson in moving past my vanity.

With all the shifts going on, I looked forward to the second week of bowling in the new season. Routines were good. I needed something stable, other than the terrible traffic to battle to and from work. Bad traffic did not count as stabilizing.

Later that week, I emailed all of my government clients, sending almost the same email as had gone out to the staff. Five minutes later, two had replied to me saying that they really liked my work and didn't really care what name I was using. By the end of the day, I'd heard back from most of my clients, all of whom were at least moderately supportive. *Check that box,* I thought.

The 24/7 coming out fiesta continued. Maybe when it was all over I'd turn to Susanne or Jeffrey and say, "I wish someone would congratulate me again," but I suspected that day would never come.

I looked at my watch and saw it was 6:45, well past the time when I would have normally left to go home to my corner of the city. I got up, grabbing my keys so I could use the restroom, but remembered my coworker's warning. Surely it couldn't be that bad. My bladder sounded an alarm. I spent three-tenths of a second pondering snagging the women's room key from the communal kitchen, but I chastised myself. I'm doing this a hundred percent, damn it.

Nobody had ever walked to the men's room with such an air of determination, I was sure. I marched up to the door, unlocked it, and voila.

I realized my miscalculation right away, and as a bonus, finally understood the reason for the overpowering orange rind cleaner in use in this office tower, on this floor.

Clearly, Kendrick needed a funnel, or a vacuum, or some kind of waste disposing technology not yet otherwise invented. I backed slowly away from the stall, covering my mouth and trying not to inhale the stench, which was difficult given that my shock made my brain tell my lungs to gasp for air.

Air was not to be found here.

I took the elevator down to the lobby, walked over to the other tower, and took that elevator to my old floor, where I'd worked before the bosses had moved me. Two other men from my new tower were in the men's room. We nodded silently at each other, the grim understanding of our situation between us. This was a sick hazing ritual men had for themselves.

* * *

I was starting to adjust to my colleagues calling me Everett.

Before I could lose myself in my inner monologue, up popped an email in my inbox from an old colleague, Gus, who'd taken a Federal job a few years earlier.

—How's it going, Jenifer? What's new?

Hoo boy. I replied:

—Going well! I guess my news is that I'm having a sex change and am now going by Everett.

I filled him in on the work scene, seeing as he knew these people, and told him about one new challenging project I was working on. A few moments later, he sent another email.

—Congratulations! That's great, Ev. So I was wondering if you were interested in joining us here at the agency. Would you like to send me your CV so I can pass it on to the guy who's doing the hire? We need to get someone in here before the new fiscal year on October 1. I think you'd be perfect for it.

Hire? Leave the company? The company I just came out to? With the supportive colleagues yet not a great salary?

I emailed him my resumé, figuring I should see what the offer might be.

I thought they'd look at my background, I'd get back to my tasks at work, and that would be that. Not more than an hour later, however, my old pal called me to say they loved my resumé and I'd be getting a call. The next day I talked to the hiring manager, Darrell, on the phone for a bit more than an hour, comparing our approaches to work, sharing some office war stories, and talking about my experience supervising staff. He and I talked salary, and in this collapsed, tight time frame for making a decision I didn't have the chance to over think anything. He asked what salary I wanted.

I was shocked, realizing that one month into my transition at work, more than fifteen years into my career, someone was asking me this question for the first time. *This sexism crap is real,* I thought. *Like really super-real real.*

I named a number I thought was somewhat absurd and was grateful the phone didn't communicate how far my jaw dropped when he agreed. He asked when I could start, and we agreed on that, too.

"So I just need your Social Security number and pay stub," Darrell said, and my heart sank. *Here's where he backs out.*

"Just so you know, my legal name isn't yet Everett, even though I've started the paperwork on that." My mind flashed to my foyer table—somewhere buried in the pile of bills, junk mail, old birthday cards, unsent letter to Pat, and free Pride condoms was the application for the name change, filled out halfway.

"Legally, my name is Jenifer, but I don't go by that anymore." *There you go, just put it out there like this happens every day. I don't care what his response is.*

"Okay," he said casually, "we'll only use the old name on your paperwork until we don't have to, but everything else will be Everett."
Don't drop the phone.

"Can you get me a couple of references?" Darrell asked.

"Oh, sure." I figured quickly that I could count on Denise, Sandy, and my colleague Lea, who also was a life coach and knew me pretty well.

"Okay, great. Let's see, it's the end of Thursday," he said, and I heard him flipping through paper, probably a calendar. "You should hear from the recruiter on Monday, I think. We have to move quickly because it's end of year." The Feds operated on an October to September budget schedule.

"No problem," I said, giving him my cell phone number. Part of me didn't really expect a phone call from them. More probably I'd get a Dear John letter saying that, hey, it didn't work out after all, have a nice life but I'm taking the goldfish and the DeLonghi coffee maker.

Was I ready to say goodbye to people I'd known for nearly seven years and throw myself into an entirely different organization and new set of people? Would I even have that choice to make?

It hit me then that this year had seen a lot of changes. I had wanted to completely refurbish my life. Well, I was looking at some mighty fine new draperies, wasn't I?

* * *

Driving home, I wasn't sure what to think. Was I rattling a hornet's nest? How could one group of people know me as female and another group not know I'd ever been a woman? That was impossible. I would walk into work on my first day, and people would see right through me, but telling them I was transgender also seemed problematic; it was none of their business, and it was too awkward to bring up.

"Hello, I'm Everett. I was Jenifer a couple of years ago, but, you know, that got old." *Not good.*

"Hello, I'm Everett, the new transsexual in the office! Nice to meet you." *Way too geeky and creepy. Greepy.*

"Hello, I'm Everett. Gosh, I can't wait until I cut these darn breasts of mine off!" *Total overshare! Do not point out the breasts to people!*

Yeah, I wasn't seeing a way to tell them. Wouldn't they just know?

Susanne, Lori, and Barbara thought otherwise. We'd met up for dinner at a pizza joint in the city.

"Ev," Susanne said, lowering her head and sizing me up, "do you think you look female?"

"Well, sure," I said.

They giggled.

"You don't look female anymore," said Barbara. "I really don't think they'd know."

"You have to bind everyday if you work there," Lori pointed out.

I nodded. "I have to do that now, anyway."

Barbara, the lawyer, considered her thoughts for a moment. "You know, if I were you, I'd see if you can get a counter offer, if the government really comes back with a definitive offer for you. So you could stay under better terms. Or, you could just start somewhere fresh."

Somewhere fresh. That sounded like it had possibilities.

*　*　*

I sipped from my mug and looked around the new coffee house in the heart of Eastern Market. Susanne and I were starting to talk about moving in together, which gave me goose bumps every time the subject came up. My cell phone buzzed in my pocket, and I excused myself to Susanne and went outside to talk.

"May I speak with Everett Maroon, please?" asked an unfamiliar voice. I glanced at the caller ID. It read "Federal Government." *I wonder if they know how foreboding that looks.*

"Well, this is Everett."

"Everett Maroon?" she asked. *Because there's a whole house of Everetts answering this phone? I'm not one of George Foreman's four sons named George.* I figured she needed my whole name.

"Yes, this is Everett Maroon."

She was the recruiter, calling to offer me the job. The entire process had taken from Thursday afternoon to the following Monday evening, just like Darrell had predicted. Who knew the government could work this fast?

I'd been interested in a government job for years, hearing stories that people came to work in their pajamas, that they didn't have to work the sixty-hour weeks of contractors, that they called the shots and had the most secure jobs in the country. I didn't want to say goodbye to my colleagues, many of whom I'd gotten close to over the years, especially after they were so supportive of me. But thinking about how many of them had left for other opportunities, I thought it was fair to take this chance.

The recruiter offered me a start date a full month later, in part to give me time to get my name changed legally and in part to get me in with the rest of the newest agency staff, so we would all have the same orientation days.

"Okay," I said, thrilled that she was so flexible. "Let me find out from the court when I can declare my name, and I'll get back to you."

I walked back into the coffee shop and sat down at the table with Susanne. I told her they were giving me the salary I'd asked for, plus a little bit of a signing bonus. She screeched her happiness. And then I told her that they were giving me time to get the name change processed.

"Oh, wow, they're savvy, too?" she asked, clearly impressed.

"Apparently," I said.

"So you said yes?"

"I said I needed to sleep on it," I said, remembering that my parents had told me never to take a job the same day it was offered. But I had no reason for delaying a response, now that I thought about it for three seconds.

"Wow," Susanne said, reaching across the table and taking my hands in hers, "I am so happy for you! You deserve this."

I smiled. I told myself that I had to be willing to accept all the good things in my life and not apply my usual hand-wringing anxiety to them. My very next thought was, *Oh my God, I just got hired for a job I can't do. I wonder when they'll see through my facade?*

Some habits died hard.

* * *

The next day at work, I walked into my boss Chris's office and sat down. He was reading a report and, though he acknowledged me by waving me in, he wasn't ready to start talking yet. Finally, he finished his paragraph and asked me how I was.

"I'm fine," I said. "I got a job offer to work at the Social Security Administration. I wasn't out there looking, really."

"Oh, damn. Well, good for you. Are you going to take it?"

"I think so, yes." I immediately felt guilty and miserable.

"Well, that's exciting news for you. You know we don't make counter offers here. We can't set a precedent."

"I didn't know that, since I've never said I'm leaving before," I said.

"Do you have a last day yet?" he asked. He twiddled a DC Capitals embossed pen in his fingers.

"No, not yet, I'll give more than two weeks, though."

"Oh, okay. Well, let me give Mary a call." He reached for the phone. We were done.

Crap, I thought, *Mary*. I should have told her myself.

"I just, you know I've loved working here. It's nothing personal."

He stopped dialing and flashed me a quick grin. "I know, mate. People need to move on sometimes. You're critical around here, but it's good for you and it'll help other people move up."

I wondered if I would ever have that kind of dismissive detachment that other men had. I doubted my ability to do the new job. Maybe my boss had been waiting for me to leave because I now made him uncomfortable. I walked back to my office, shut the door, and realized that I hadn't cried in a really long time. It would be a nice release, but it just wasn't happening. I wondered abjectly if I should blame testosterone.

*   *   *

Jeffrey and I were late to bowling. By the time we got to the alley, there were only five minutes of practice left. This was additionally annoying because in each of the previous weeks in this new league we'd joined, they had run behind schedule on the practice and start of play. Not so this week. No sooner had I sat down to put on my shoes than the president of the league was sitting next to me. Buddy was a round, older, very smiley man who was every bit as laid back as the last president of the other league was over-engaged. I liked Buddy.

Buddy looked serious. "Everett, can I talk to you about something?"

I looked at him with a jaundiced eye because his tone was so off. I focused on tying my shoelaces. From the corner of my eye I could see that Jeffrey was listening in. He was on the lookout for me.

"What's up? I asked.

"Well, someone saw you in the men's restroom last week and came to me with a complaint."

At this point I flashed back to last week. I washed my hands in the men's room at the end of the evening to get the lane grease off of me. I also went into a stall once and adjusted my binder, which presumably nobody could see. I didn't do anything objectionable like killing a kitten, I was pretty sure.

"He said he was uncomfortable with you in there."

"He what?" I wasn't ready for this. I was somebody's problem?

"So the officers and I got together."

Got together?

I wondered if they were going to ask me to use the women's room.

"We decided that you should use the restroom that's off of the meeting room. It's got a single stall in there. If you were later in your transition, it probably wouldn't be a big deal, but for now, let's handle it this way. Okay?"

"Are you serious?" I had a million questions, but that was the first one. I saw that Jeffrey had come over and put his hand on my shoulder.

"What about me made him uncomfortable, anyway?"

"I don't know," said Buddy, looking around the room instead of at me. I figured he knew this wasn't acceptable to me. It must have sucked to be league president.

"You didn't even ask him? And you made this decision based on that?" In fact, he hadn't talked to me, either, before deciding where I could wash my hands.

"Look, I'm not happy about it. I didn't really know enough about transgenderism to know what to say to him."

"Transgenderism? Look," I said, trying not to shout, "this is a cowardly decision, Buddy. And very disrespectful toward me. I haven't disrespected anyone here. Shit, I'm not comfortable using ANY public restroom, but you don't see me complaining."

"Look, I'm trying to make everyone happy here," he began.

"I'm not happy," I said.

"If you were just further along."

"And then what happens? Everyone starts pretending I have a penis?"

"I'm just trying to work this out." He looked like a cornered rat on a sinking ship.

"Well, you failed. I'm gonna get a practice shot in now if I'm still allowed to play."

I stood up and walked away, picking up my bowling ball from the ball return. Before I turned to face the lane, I looked at my fellow players, searching their faces. How many of them had been included in this conversation about what to do with me? Who had been the complainer? I threw a practice ball down the lane too hard, half-wanting it to hit someone.

I saw Jeffrey getting ready for a practice throw, his usual cool demeanor turned down low enough to cause frost to settle on the ball. Whatever banter we usually had as a team was absent. My chest had tightened into a constrictor knot and refused to budge.

We bowled out the evening, figuring the team we were playing deserved to get to play and not go home early with three forfeits. Being pissed off worked well for our game, and we bowled well above our averages, taking all three games for the week.

I packed everything up, and Buddy motioned for me to come over to him. I presumed he wanted to make himself feel better about the whole situation. I ignored him and walked out of the bowling alley, never to return.

Getting in the car, I ranted.

"I am so sick of privileged people who use whatever oppression badge they have to be bastards to other people, I may seriously knock the next asshole in the head. And how much more work do I actually have to do on myself because other people suck?" Tingling in my fingers told me I should loosen my grip on the steering wheel.

"I just can't fucking believe it," Jeffrey said. "Stupid white men. I want my money back."

I got home that night, grateful for the affection of my cats, and called Susanne.

"You are fucking kidding me," she said. "Someone's not comfortable because you're washing your hands, and you have to use a special restroom? Virginia sucks." Most of the DC-area gay bowling leagues were there, as were the ones we'd been bowling in. She told me to come over.

Sitting on her futon, otherwise known as the couch of graduate students, I wrote a letter to the officers who oversaw all of the gay leagues. I caught my anger and played reasonable, saying people should be entitled to use the bathrooms that agree with their gender identity, that bowling members who are ignorant about transgender issues don't have a justification for their intolerance, and that as gay people, we should be wary of people who proclaim us not man or woman enough.

* * *

Work the next day was a welcome relief. I was in my office when Chris came in and sat on the end of my wrap-around desk. Goofy newfangled office furniture. Maybe I wanted a little bit of wall without a counter against it so I could put a chair or filing cabinet there. Instead, executives were forced to sit on my work space.

"So, I spoke with Mary," he began, and I suddenly felt sad again.

"Yeah?"

"She wants to make a counter offer to you."

"Wow, really? I thought you didn't do that here." *Shut up, Maroon*, the more intelligent portion of my brain said to the dumber part.

"Well, she wants to make the offer. We'll pay you what they offered."

"That's great," I said, and still, I felt like a traitor. "Can I sleep on it?"

"Yes, of course," he said, turning to leave. "Mary said you were really special."

"That's kind of her," I said, thinking that he was trying to convince himself of her sentiment. I wasn't sure why he would do that.

I was grateful I had an appointment that evening with Robyn. I had a lot of news to relay to her.

She was livid about the bowling league.

"No offense," she said, red at her collar clawing up her neck, "but men are so weird about their penises."

I laughed. "No kidding. I think the only people with actual penis envy are men. Is that what this is really about?"

"I think so," she said. "He wants only men born men in his space." She shrugged.

About work, there wasn't such a clear-cut response in the room from either of us. I told her I was weighing my options.

"I just had my performance review last month, and apparently money was tight," I said, thinking back. "So maybe this month everything is different."

"You get what you ask for," said Robyn, and I realized I'd just jumped over the wage gap, again, and this time with the company that knew me.

"I don't know, maybe I'm ready for a change," I said. "I think I'm ready not to be in the beginning of transition anymore. I feel like I've been beginning for forever."

"Well, you've been coming here for more than two years, Everett. I'd say you're not beginning transition anymore."

*   *   *

Everyone had an opinion about whether I should stay at my current company or join the government, and it was beyond difficult to make a decision. I had gone back to Chris and Mary and told them somberly that I would be leaving in mid-October. It was too good an opportunity, and it would let me do some new things. They congratulated me and wished me well. I walked back to my office, sat down, and wondered if I would ever feel at home again. I'd known these people and these halls for nearly seven years.

So much was changing—my body, my home, my work. I would have been hard-pressed to find something that remained stable at that point. I tried to remember to breathe. I had wanted things to open up for me, and they had. I just had to deal with what that meant in my day-to-day life.

Chapter 23

I stood in line to submit my civil paperwork with about a dozen other people holding various papers and wads of cash. I kept the paper turned in on itself so nobody would see my old name or that I was a chubby transsexual. Not that anyone was trying to peer at me. It looked a little like the papers teachers would pass back to me in grade school.

Finally, I made my way up to the window, and I passed the paper and money to the cashier. She looked it over. She was a youngish African-American woman with carefully coiffed hair and an electric blue, bedazzled shirt. She had a different understanding of "business casual" than I'd ever considered for myself, but she seemed to know her job well, and she didn't have disdain for this long and probably ungrateful line of citizens.

"Oh, good on you," she said, looking at my sheet. She leaned close to the glass. "You look great." I had a flash image of me behind a peeping tom glass, being asked to dance all sexy like. There was a reason that nobody had actually ever asked me to do that.

"Why thanks, I showered this morning," I said, only then realizing what she meant.

She laughed. "This one has a sense of humor," she said to her colleagues, who only responded with a jaded "huh" in her general direction.

"Okay," she said, getting serious, "you need to run a weekly ad in a newspaper here in DC in the legal notices section of the classifieds. Do that for three weeks. Bring in a copy of the notices on the date you're scheduled to come back in, and your name change will be final."

"I don't have to use the *Washington Post*?" I thought about how expensive it probably was.

"No, you don't have to use the *Washington Post*," she said, and she handed me a new piece of paper with my notice of publication on it and the date I should return to the court.

I thanked her and walked out, wondering what part of this whole transition process happened in one step. Nothing, apparently. But I would come back on October 30 and get confirmation that I was now Everett Daniel.

* * *

The president and treasurer of the bowling league, apparently, were sad to see me and Jeffrey go. In their joint email they made clear that it wasn't another member of the league who'd had a problem with me using the men's room; it was the alley management. Since this bowling alley was in Virginia, there were no legal protections for sexual orientation, gender identity, or gender expression. The whole experience made me think I should have a small part in the next documentary on transgender people and public facilities. I wanted my four-second sound bite: "I stopped bowling in a gay league because they wouldn't let me pee or wash my hands!"

I appreciated that Buddy had come to my defense, but he'd negotiated without me and didn't seem to have the best grasp of how to advocate for me. Lesson learned, and, like he'd said to me that previous week, when I passed as a man all the time, who would notice or care?

Sure, I thought, reading the end of the email, *that's true. But what about all the people who don't look like the gender they say they are?*

* * *

Susanne had never in her life visited New England. This seemed a travesty to me, so we headed to Connecticut for the weekend, to go to my sister Kathy's house and take in the scenic vista that is the western part of the state. They'd had a wet summer that year, so the colors of the trees were beyond vibrant, which was nice. And we kept the "nature" to a minimum, although somehow in mid-October I managed to freeze my ass off at the man-made lake near Kathy's house.

It was my first time seeing my sister since I sent her and my brother and Mom an email about my transition. Kathy's original response to me on the phone, the day after my email, was that she'd rather talk to me in person than via email to discuss something so life-changing and intimate. It took me a few months to have the wherewithal to go there and have the conversation.

Susanne did her best to be a great role model, and while I felt somewhat guilty, like she had to carry the weight of representing People Who Are Cool with the Trans, she said it wasn't any burden. This only made her more appealing. Kathy did look at me when Susanne left the room at one point and leaned in, saying, "She's a keeper."

"I know, she's great, isn't she?" I kept looking in the spot where I'd last seen her, as if the air might still contain some remnant of her.

"And she's okay with this whole transition thing?" Kathy asked, clipping off the ends of green beans over her sink. People who knew us commented that we didn't look much alike, but it was our different coloring that threw them off. She with her Polish father had blue eyes and ashy brown hair, but we sported the same chin, mouth, eyebrows, and cheekbones.

"She is indeed. We're moving in together next month, in fact."

"You know, you've always been guyish."

"Yeah, I know."

"I knew you were gay before you did," she added.

"I remember. You bitch," I said, and we laughed.

"I just want you to be happy."

"I know, Kathy. I want you to be happy, too."

"I just don't know if I can call you Ev and he. It's really hard." Her eyes welled up with tears.

"Well, just give it time," I said. *I had a hard time getting there too, Sis, but you'll come around.*

"Are you going to have some kind of surgery?" she asked, looking at my face. Was she seeing the five-year-old me? Or someone she had to get to know all over again?

"Yes, I'll have a chest reconstruction at some point. I don't know about anything else. I mean, I may need to have a hysterectomy at some point."

"This isn't a phase," she said to her hands.

"This isn't a phase," I said, and I hugged her.

Somewhere in the time since my niece Jess had decreed I would heretofore be called "Bob," the girls and my sister had reached a new

name for me: "Ancle Evy." It was a step closer and a symptom of
wanting not to change at the same time. I smiled to hear it, though,
because it was an acknowledgment of sorts, and I knew that they
were trying to make their mother and me comfortable in the use of it.
It didn't seem like a name that would make much sense in public,
but I would burn that bridge when I got to it.

The girls turned in for the night, and I threw another two logs on
the fire in the living room. Susanne and I dunked ourselves in the
hot tub outside and talked about the quaintness that was New
England.

"It's kind of like I imagined," Susanne said, trying to spot some
star formations in the hazy night sky.

"The big dog, the kids growing up, the energy of a one-parent
household?"

"Connecticut," Susanne answered.

"Oh. I knew that."

"Yes, dear," she said, indicating she knew I was full of shit.

We moved quickly from the wet heat of the whirlpool to the dry
heat of the fireplace, faking out the goose bumps that formed during
the twenty-five-second interval of deep and abiding cold. We talked
about packing and moving, and our excitement, and my terrible
misery at having to find new homes for my cats because Susanne was
too allergic to live with them. I knew from the outset of our cohabiting
conversations that I'd have to give my babies away, which would be
incredibly, heart-renderingly painful. I'd told her I could only do such
a thing if this relationship was the real deal. And she'd nodded her
head, saying she would never ask for such a thing from me if she had
anything less than complete commitment to us and where we were
journeying as a couple. Even so, I'd started the mental countdown of
my days and nights left with my boys. I made too many countdowns,
but I couldn't help myself.

* * *

I thought she was nervous, and Lori thought I was nervous.
Probably we both had some nerves, because this was her wedding
day. She didn't want anything to go wrong. I focused on not
dropping the rings when the rabbi asked for them.

We changed into our tuxes in a back office at the vineyard, which she and Barbara had picked for the big day.

"How are you feeling?" I asked Lori, who was struggling with her cuff links. Silently I took them from her and clipped them to her sleeves.

"I'm fine," she said. "I want it to start already."

"I'm really happy for you, Lori."

"Thanks."

"Where are the rings?"

"In my backpack." She pointed, her hand shaking a little.

I fumbled around and found the box with the rings. Inside the black velvet box, they were like twin stars shining in the night sky.

"Okay, whose is whose?" I asked.

"The top one is Barbara's and the bottom one is mine," she said, pulling out two yarmulkes for us to wear. I stooped over so she could clip mine on my head.

"Ha, you look Jewish now," she giggled.

"*Oy gevalt,*" I said, winking.

We walked into the bright light, soaking up the sun in our tuxes. I looked out at the vineyard from our vantage point at the top of the hill. Off in the distance I could see a range of trees, the October sun just starting to encourage them to show some color. Just before the rows of vines stood the outside altar where we would hold the *chupah.* I felt a tap on my shoulder. It was the rabbi.

"You're the best man?"

"Yes, ma'am." *Yes ma'am? Who are you, the butler?*

"You used to be a woman." She said it as a statement, not a question.

"Um, yes."

She looked at me and squeezed my hand. "God loves you. He has given you a difficult but rewarding journey."

"Thank you." She sensed my nervousness and kindly changed the subject. We talked about a lot of things, none of which stayed in my head. I appreciated her dedication to her brand of Jewish feminism and her extremely colorful religious dress. It hurt my eyes a little, but it took risks. I had to give her credit.

* * *

The drive to Social Security wasn't too bad, though I reminded myself that I wasn't driving in at rush hour. I followed the directions the cheery recruiter had given me and turned into a massive parking lot of what looked like 15,000 cars. The Federal Government was no joke.

Trying to make sure I wasn't about to get lost on a twenty-building campus, I asked where the Annex Building was, and someone pointed it out for me.

I'd spent fifteen minutes at home making sure my binder wouldn't blow at any moment, lest Becky and Bertha decided to meet The Fingerprint Man, as he was known. I was not about to press them into an ink-soaked sponge.

My recruiter met me after security called for her, and she greeted me standing just on the other side of the metal detector.

"Welcome to SSA, Everett," she said, smiling and shaking my hand.

"Thanks."

She walked me back to a room where other new recruits sat filling out their background check applications.

"List all known aliases and any former legal names," instructed the form. It was one requirement out of many, including attestations that I not had taken illegal drugs in the last ten years and that I not be a risk to the security of the nation. *How nice of them to check before they hire us.*

But crap. I should have expected this name stuff, I thought sullenly. I wrote in both names, the one I could start using next week, and the name I'd had with me my whole life.

My recruiter had handed me off to The Fingerprint Man and another HR representative, a squinty-eyed, shorter man in a neatly pressed but cheap suit. He looked over my application, stopping at the section on names and aliases.

"Your legal name is Jenifer?" he asked, his finger pressed on the page.

"Yes, but please call me Everett."

"I see," he said, seeing more, perhaps, than I'd have liked him to.

He led me back to the fingerprinting room, where a machine the size of my car determined that I did not have a criminal record.

"So," Weasel Eyes asked me, "what, uh, grade are you?"

"GS-12," I said, not sure why he was asking.

"Huh."

"What?" Did I have an aptitude test to take or something?

"Nothing," he sighed, clearly annoyed with me. "I'm only an eight, and you're a twelve?"

"I guess so," I said, smiling, hoping he'd take the hint to back off. *Yes, my sex changing ass will be paid more than your non-trans ass. Deal with it on your own time.*

* * *

I sat in the Clerk of the Court's office, having already given them Form 893A, affidavits from everyone I had met in the last seven years, and a pint and a half of my blood, high sodium level and all. In walked a small man, and my first impulse was to presume he was transgender. To be more specific, he emitted a pulsating sound and light show all around him that everyone else in the room was oblivious to and which I later suspected was the cause of a six-hour splitting headache. Perhaps the Bush Administration was trying to stifle the queer and trans movements by surreptitiously implanting these devices in our necks so we couldn't hang out with anyone else in the LGBT community, but I didn't have real evidence for this.

He found a chair and snuck glances at me, not flirtatiously, but in the hmm-he-could-be-trans way, and I was grateful that I hadn't shaved in four days and so had a ridiculous-looking beardette to help clue him in.

The overworked woman behind the counter called out, "Maroon," because she either didn't know what title to affix to my name, or because we were all just surnames to her. I was just happy she didn't pronounce me Moron in front of the assembled crowd. After I'd been in this room a few times, I began to realize there was always an assembled crowd at room 4220 of the Superior Court Building. It was two doors down from the room where lawyers who have passed the DC bar get sworn in, and that room was always empty every time I was in the building.

I stood up, and at the same time they called up Mr. Maybe Also Trans, and I saw he had requested a name change as well. The Ben Sherman shoes and bright green Tommy sweater with complementary pink Oxford shirt were one thing, but the mini-beard put the probability over the top. I saw I had a duty to perform. I would not be swayed by things like personal space and polite silences.

"Psst," I whispered to him in a stage-like fashion, "Are you transgender?"

He looked at me, seemingly taking in the word. T-R-A-N-S-G-E-N-D-E-R. I immediately flashed to a memory of the Electric Company and how helpful it would have been to show each syllable of the word floating over my head in seventies, orange, sans-serif font.

He nodded. "Yes, I am." *A man of many words.*

"Well, then do you know that gender identity or expression is now covered as part of DC's Human Rights Act? You're protected in employment, school, and housing." I had broken out the PSA language.

"Oh. That's good. Thank you for the information."

Well, okay, great, he was glad I told him, but there was more to say. Now my choice was to nod like a bobble head idiot and get back to collecting my court order—which was exciting, honestly—or go on and tell him about the regulations now in effect. I couldn't help myself. We'd worked so hard on putting these in place, how could I not tout their existence a little?

"Well, and in addition to the law," I continued to whisper, "there are now regulations on the books so that you can use the men's restroom in any commercial or municipal establishment in DC, not be harassed at work by people who intentionally use the wrong name or pronouns, and you can use the men's locker room at the gym." Because clearly this scrawny guy was a closet gym rat.

"Great. Thanks for the information." *A real Cyrano de Bergerac, this guy.*

"Sure. Anytime." Anytime, Everett? *Don't mind me, I'll just stand on the corner and be accessible to anyone with questions about the regulations.* I could have slapped my forehead. I in fact did not slap my forehead. I waved goodbye to him, and he seemed torn between genuine gratitude for hearing about his rights and a strong need to get away from the large trans guy with teenagery facial scruff.

I tuned him out and stood in the Clerk of the Court's office, holding my name change order from the judge. In typical impoverished DC fashion, it was on regular paper stock, with a pressure seal in the corner and a stamp from the clerk to prove I had the real deal and not a photocopy. If I'd known, I would have brought in linen resumé paper for their weary office.

It had been a simple process, if I didn't think about the sixty dollar processing fee, seventy-five dollars worth of ads in the Moonie-owned *Washington Times*, and twenty dollars in postal fees to let the people I owe money to know that I'd be an Everett now. Then there were the 34,179 responses to people's questions about why on earth I'd want to rid myself of a perfectly good name.

I nodded to the clerk, done at last, and slinked off with my new official name.

Bye bye, Jenifer Leigh. Long live Everett Daniel.

Chapter 24

Niles had just moved back to Brooklyn after living in DC for a couple of years. He emailed me to say he could adopt the little gray cat but probably not the big orange one. I'd had a friend of Samantha's come by to meet my furry friends, but she wound up declining, saying she had a lot going on right now. *Tell me about it.*

I picked up the phone and called a local rescue club president. I gave her my story but was unprepared for her response.

"You people," she hollered at me, "you think living beings are just disposable!"

"Uh, no, I don't—"

She cut me off. "You can't just throw away a cat!" My heart suddenly was racing.

"I'm trying to find a home—"

"Having pets is a commitment," she went on, shouting, like I'd called Dial-A-Rant. Meanwhile, my cats sat on my lap contentedly, unaware of my upcoming betrayal.

"I don't think you understand," I tried to say.

"Oh, I understand," she said, "it's people like you who ruin the world!"

I hung up on her, not feeling the least bit guiltier for it. I petted Sebastian and Ulysses for a long while. Why did everything good have to come with such hardship?

After a couple of hours, I calmed down. The cats looked over-caressed, now full of static and mashed fur. I called Susanne to see what she was planning for supper. It seemed easier to go to her place than stay at my own.

"That's terrible. Nobody should scream at a stranger like that," she said, holding my hands.

Bumbling into Body Hair 205

"Well, I wouldn't think so," I said. "I think she's probably seen a lot of out and out abandoned cats. Even Samantha said I wasn't making this a high enough priority."

"Oh, honey. You're doing the right thing and trying to find homes for them, and you have spent a lot of time on this."

I looked at the lovely dinner on her kitchen table, not wanting to eat any of it.

"I know. I love them so much."

"I know you do, honey," she said, petting me like I touched my cats, "and I'm so sorry I'm asking you to do this."

"I know. I wouldn't do it for just anyone," I said, thinking briefly of Pat. "This better be the real deal," I told her.

"Oh, honey," she reassured me, "yes, you're the real deal."

* * *

I was a rat in a maze when it came to walking around the cube farms of the Social Security Administration on the west side of Baltimore. Disorientation was the order of the day. The building for us techie geeks had been architected by someone who'd created a lot of malls, and it showed in the glass atriums, open winding staircases, and Plexiglas banisters that kept pedestrians from falling three stories to the bottom floor. I wanted to put up a sign that read "Cinnabon," because no mall is complete without one, but I found no support for this idea among my new colleagues.

They didn't know me, but because I was now only inches and pinkish-plastic cube walls from five other staffers, I could hear them talking to each other. One single, younger employee was having a birthday, and his friends had chartered a bus so that they could ride from pub to pub, drinking but not driving. How thoughtful yet tacky of them. One middle-aged man, in heart-breaking fashion, was doing his best to communicate with his senile parent about why she had to take her pills. A young mother attempted to set up day care with a private provider until a space opened up in the center here at work.

I heard all of their stories, but they weren't *told* to me. I wondered how long it would be before people would start opening up to me, and I asked myself if I was putting out some kind of vibe to keep potential new acquaintances at bay.

As had been the custom at my old job, sign-up sheets went up around the campus for people to bring in holiday cookies. I put my name on a sheet, not thinking twice about it, because at my last job nearly everyone signed up, and we all gained a few pounds from all the confections streaming into the office.

Looking at the list a few days later, I saw I was the only man on the list. I thought about the handful of conversations I'd had so far with my male colleagues: football, cars they wanted to buy, baseball playoffs, basketball pre-season, which work project sucked the most. These were certainly not bakers. Was I going to be boxed in? Would they think that instead of wolves, I'd been raised by tree sprites?

No, I decided. I'd brought in cookies for years at my old company, I was going to contribute cookies here, and they were going to enjoy them. I wasn't going to spend every minute sweating over blowing my cover, as if I were there to inspect their gender roles.

I brought in perfectly round, delicious, lemon and ginger cookies, taken from the annual Christmas Cookie magazine from *Good Housekeeping*, which I bought every year. If asked I would say I read it for the articles.

Our team had a couple of tables for things like cookies, potluck dishes, and fundraising event notices a few feet away from my cube. I'd been working there for six weeks, but very few people knew who I was or where I sat "on the floor." So I wasn't surprised to overhear a conversation about me.

Two women taking a break had come to sample some of the cookies on the table.

"Ooh, this one is great," she said, the cookie obviously still in her mouth from the sound of her enunciation. "Who made this?"

"Mmm, it is good," came an answer. "Everett made them, I think."

"Who's Everett?" the first cookie eater asked.

"He's the new guy in usability," said the second. I smiled at my desk.

"Is he gay?" asked Cookie Eater Number One. To this I raised an eyebrow.

"No, I think he has a girlfriend," said Number Two, and I finally recognized her voice. We'd been in a few meetings together.

"Hmm," said the first one, still munching, "well, either she made these, or she is in for a big surprise."

They didn't see me nearly choke on my soda.

*   *   *

I didn't have the heart to put the cats in the crate again, certainly not for a five-hour drive to New York City, so I brought them to the car one by one, panting as I went up and down the three flights a few times, getting everything I needed for the trip. On a Saturday morning, I put a little litter box, fresh water, and food in my car and spread clothes across the back seat so the boys could sit on something that smelled like me. True to form, they wandered all over the interior except there, presumably not enjoying the smell of their Judas. I pretended we were going on a vacation together. The cats just sat there stewing about seeing the vet again, but once we were on the highway, they settled down and curled up together on the passenger seat and napped.

The plan was to take Ulysses to Niles's apartment in Brooklyn and Sebastian to my sister's house in Connecticut. That plan disintegrated somewhere around exit 7A on the Jersey Turnpike, when Kathy called to say she couldn't take Sebastian; she just had too many animals. I raced to think of other places to take him and settled on begging Niles, outside his apartment, to take him in for a little while until I could find the tabby a permanent home. That it was cold and raining when I pulled up only added to how desperate I looked. He said okay. I had successfully punted.

I'd gotten an email the day before, a nasty letter from a friend of Marcus and Samantha's, who'd seen one of my many postings about the cats. He said I was the most irresponsible person ever and that he hoped I'd never have a pet again. Couldn't Susanne just take a fucking pill, he'd asked. Susanne, reading this over my shoulder, became livid. I wrote back to him.

—You have no idea what you're talking about, asshole. These aren't mild allergies. If you don't have anything constructive to say, fuck off.

I was no longer going to tolerate being taken to task over giving away my cats. Was it too much to ask that we could move in together after ten months? The agony I'd gone through over my babies, without anyone being judgmental on top of it, had been terrible. I wanted them in new homes, happy to start the next chapter in their lives, and I hoped I'd have that, too.

*   *   *

I had a very large check to deposit into my account, so I walked across the street on my lunch break and made my transaction at the ATM. A couple of days later, I got the check back in the mailbox. "Name discrepancy." I sighed. I hadn't updated the name on my account, and the check had been made out to Everett, on the promise from the teller that it would be okay. I stuck the check in my wallet and reminded myself to go to the bank again with it.

The next day, I waited patiently for a bank official to see me.

"Hi there, how can I help you, sir?" he said.

"Well, I have this check to deposit."

"Okay, we can help you with that." He took a look at the check, and I waited for the shoe to drop. "What's your account number?"

I fished my bank card out of my wallet and watched his face scrunch up in a classic show of confusion.

"Okay, so you're ..."

"I'm Everett."

"But this account is for Jenifer."

"I was Jenifer, and now I'm Everett," I said. I stifled the urge to say, "Ta da!" I unfolded my name change order from the court in DC and handed it to him. "I legally changed my name."

"You're, uh, you're Jenifer?" I guess I didn't look like a Jenifer.

"Yes."

"Well, this check is for Everett."

"Yes, that's me, too."

"I can't deposit someone else's money in here."

"Right. But you can deposit my money into my account, I'm sure."

He flashed some relief. "Well, yes, I can do that. So you're ..."

"I'm Everett. I used to be Jenifer," I said again. "I changed my name."

"I need both Jenifer and Everett here to authorize this."

"They're me!"

"What does it say on your driver's license?" he asked me.

I showed him my license, which still bore my old name. I also had my laminated Federal badge with my new name and smiling face, but he wouldn't accept it.

"I can't change the name on the account until you have an ID, other than that one, that says Everett."

I had to leave without depositing my check. Because god forbid I steal my own money from myself.

* * *

I had not yet accrued leave time at my new job so had to spend a Saturday at the Division of Motor Vehicles. I knew better than to provoke the intake staff at the DMV, lest they purposefully give me an incorrect form so I'd have to keep starting the process all over again.

Two hours and forty minutes after arriving, I was at the window with my name change order, which was getting a bit battered at this point. I presumed the vast majority of people doing this were recently married women who were changing their last names. The bank official had even told me that if all I'd wanted to change was my surname, that would have been much easier. *So nice to know.*

The DMV clerk typed my life story into his computer.

"Mmm," he said. He typed a little more. "Ah." Ten more pecks at the keys. "Okaaaaaaay."

"What are, uh, what are you seeing there?" I hoped I wasn't about to be mistaken for someone on the FBI's Ten Most Wanted list.

"Well, I can't change your name," he said, sighing.

"What's the problem?" I tried to read his screen, but I needed the neck of a spotted owl to see anything.

"You have an outstanding ticket with Virginia." He looked at me for my response. I wasn't sure if he expected I would slap my head and shout "D'oh!" or deny the charge, or melt into a puddle of DMV failure.

"Oh," I said, trying to recall getting a ticket in Virginia. It was entirely possible. "Where do I need to go to resolve this?"

I shot way up in his assessment because I didn't yell at him and asked for further instructions. I was a civil servant, too, and I'd already been through basic training in navigating thick layers of bureaucracy.

"You need to go to the Arlington court house," he said. "Bye, man," he said as I waved goodbye.

I left for the next stop on my identification change journey.

Chapter 25

Robyn asked me how I was, the typical question to start all manner of conversations.

"Sometimes I find it hard to be an extrovert."

"Oh?" she asked, not missing a beat. "Why is that?"

"I think to quieter people we can be annoying. We step all over them, we talk too loudly, we seem unapproachable and over-enthusiastic. I think some introverts think that we don't have time for them or that we'll just assume they're snobs. So they don't bother to talk to us."

"Are you feeling isolated?" Robyn asked, leaning in and frowning. She was trying to figure out where I was coming from. Unfortunately, so was I.

"See, I think I recharge my battery through interacting with other people. And it's been hard to talk to anyone at this new job. It's like by the end of the day, I'm dying to talk with just about anyone."

"Okay, that sounds frustrating."

"I guess it is. It's weird, it's like I feel … repressed. But now I'm a white man. I have all the benefits the world can throw at me. At least until people figure out my history."

"Repressed?" She was going to make me talk through every inch of this.

"I just don't see a lot of room to talk about my feelings." After bottling up my words all day, now I struggled even when I could speak.

"Why do you need to talk about your feelings at work, Ev?"

"You know, like if something is frustrating, or I'm excited about a new project. I have emotions. But no men at this job ever bring them up. It's like the Village of Stepford over there. I'm trying not to compare them to my old coworkers, because I'm not the me from my old job, either."

"Tell me about how your new coworkers interact with you," she said, and I felt myself calming down a little. I was invested in making this new situation work, but I that worried I'd made a big mistake leaving my job for this one two months ago. I didn't even have my cats to greet and pet anymore.

"People only talk about work with me. At my last job, I knew all the names of my colleague's partners and children, which towns they lived in, what their hobbies were. I could ask Kevin about his golf game or Sandy when her first grandchild was due. I only know that my new boss loves Jesus because she wears it on her scarf."

"Her scarf?"

"Yes, she has a scarf that says 'I love Jesus' all over it in Arial Black font."

"You know the font on her scarf?"

I shrugged. I was losing my train of thought.

"Nobody comes by to chat. Nobody asks how I am. Nobody tells me about their kids. I think folks felt fine chatting with me at my last job because I was a woman. In this new job, people don't 'chat' with men. They just work with them. And I can see why."

"What do you mean?"

"A lot of the men there are sexist. And they don't even see it. They just, they just put men first. I think I'm different than them—not that I'm better—but I see things they don't see."

"Well, then you let that make you a better man, Ev."

I would think about that idea for a long time.

* * *

My plight at work fell on deaf ears when I tried to discuss it with Jeffrey.

"You're just now realizing this?" he asked me, sipping his gin something-or-other. He looked at the glass. "This isn't Bombay Sapphire." The waiter noticed the Diva's discontent and came over, taking the drink back to the bar and scolding the bartender. We'd gone out to a gaucho-style steakhouse and were having a few drinks before Michael and another friend came to join us.

"Well," I said, "perhaps I am. I knew things would be different as a man, but I didn't anticipate this." I wasn't sure why I felt on the defensive, but I did.

"You think men have it easy? You may have gotten more than you bargained for."

"I wasn't trying to get an upgrade on my gender, Jeffrey. I'm fine with there being consequences to having a sex change. I just didn't see this one coming. I'm trying to adjust."

He relaxed in his seat and was happy to take the next crystal glass from the waitstaff. "Ah, now this smells correct." He paused. "Look, I'm just saying, yes, women get to talk and express their emotions, and men don't. So being a gay man in the good old U. S. of A. is tough. We're caught in the same set of expectations. But you're not really gay, anymore, anyway." He took a long sip.

"I am really gay, Jeffrey. I don't think being with Susanne changes that."

"What do you think people see when you walk down the street? A gay boy and his hag? They see a straight couple."

"But that doesn't make me straight, any more than it would make you straight if they didn't realize you were gay." He seemed so angry and tired.

"Let's drop the subject," I said. I didn't know what else to say. Our friendship was unraveling, and I didn't know how to catch the thread. I hoped the Contessa and company would show up soon.

*　*　*

It took a long time to get to Social Security headquarters even with the benefit of a reverse commute. I passed the time in the morning listening to NPR, but in the evenings, I felt rough around the edges.

The question Jeffrey had asked me had been stuck in my head since our night out a couple of weeks earlier. I hadn't seen him since, though not for my lack of trying. He was too busy, or I'd asked him at "the last minute," or he couldn't tell me what his plans were so far in advance. There was no way to get a yes out of him. The buddy I'd holed up with at the beach two summers ago was gone. I repeated the question to Susanne, asking, "Do you think we're straight?"

She looked at me, guessing why I was asking and cueing up a response for me, and asked simply, "Please. Have you seen our sex?"

Why yes I had. I hugged her.

"I just feel like I'm lying at work. Like I could be discovered at any moment."

She looked at me.

"I'm not planning on dropping my pants in the office or anything."

"Good idea, honey."

"I just hate changing up the pronouns if I tell an old story from before I transitioned. Stuff like that."

"Honey, you're still adjusting. And you'd be adjusting anyway, even if you didn't have the trans stuff to go with it. You're not lying, you're doing what you need to do to move forward."

I thanked her. She made sense. Why didn't I think of these things on my own?

* * *

We drove up to the northwestern outskirts of Baltimore to see a surgeon who was one of a scant dozen or so in the country to perform chest reconstructions on female-to-male transsexuals. I wanted to know what my options were for surgery and to figure out the exact cost. I'd heard a lot about Dr. Beverly Fairchild. Now I would see her in person. I tried to play cool, but I could feel my nervousness and excitement eking through my skin.

I wasn't ready for this surgery to happen in the very near future, but I did want to hear her thoughts on how she'd do it and what she wanted me to do in the meantime. Wearing a binder ten hours a day for the last six months (and before that, binding for a two-year period) was taking a toll on me. My breathing was compromised for hours at a time, I had to replace the twenty dollar neoprene binders every other month, and I was always ready to overheat. Being big and red in the face must have made people worry I was going to have a heart attack.

We pulled into the medical building, which in actuality was a suburban strip mall. Snuggled in between a dentist's office and a weight loss center, its placement/location suggested a strange prioritization of body modification. Through the windows from outside the office looked a bit like a pricey beauty parlor. It had a sparkling row of what looked like high-end salon chairs. I supposed

the Botoxing bonanza went on at her practice. We made our way to
the receptionist's desk, noticing a lot of breast art on the walls—
delicately curved plaster bosoms, painted in womanly pastel tones.
Any one of these heavy art fixtures would have won in a cage fight
with Dr. Travers's ovarian crystal awards. Clearly her main dollars
came from boosting breasts to a bigger size, not lopping them off.
Having researched her background, I knew her training was
impressive. She was a past chief resident at Johns Hopkins, with all
the board certifications one would want a plastic surgeon to have.

A woman stood in line ahead of us, having a conversation with
the receptionist or intake nurse that would have been more
appropriate behind closed doors. I did not need to hear about this
woman's areola size, nor in what compass direction she wanted
them to point. I sat down next to Susanne.

We met the doctor after I filled out the requisite seventy-four
forms. She and her head nurse, Nurse Barbara, were very nice.
Barbara checked me over first.

"How long have you lived as a man?" she asked me, up close to
me as she gauged my blood pressure.

I had to calculate, and figured it had been about two and a half
years since I first started disclosing to people online. *Wow, has it
really been that long?*

"Well, you look like a guy to me," she pronounced. I didn't
know what to make of that, so I took it as a compliment, which was
probably how she intended it. Who else walked in here asking to
have a guillotine chop off their Beckies and Berthas?

The doc came in, greeting us. She was tall, with red and blonde
hair, teased up so she resembled a lioness. I wanted to know if she
was a Leo. We introduced ourselves and she measured me with a
breast surgeon's version of a protractor. *If fifth grade straight boys
knew about this device they might be more motivated in math class.*

Surgery was less about having a specific aesthetic or looking
great on the beach and more about not wanting the back pain that
binding was giving me, worrying about what I was doing to my
body by compressing my breast tissue, and worrying about my
binder breaking when it would be inconvenient, like at work.
Binding wasn't a long-term or sustainable solution. She said that in

the thirteen years she'd been doing this surgery, only one person's nipple didn't survive the procedure and make it to the newly constructed male pec. Poor unlucky nipple.

"When do you think you'd like to do this?" the good doctor asked me.

"I'm thinking about late October/early November."

"Whatever you like," she said. "I'm sure I'm available then."

We walked back out to the lobby and I paid a $1,000 deposit, picking Halloween, about nine months away, for the big event. Becky and Bertha would be no more. I waited for my receipt, taking in the curtain valences and the faux Louis XIV furniture. Just because she had an interior decorating aesthetic that I didn't share didn't mean I'd walk out of the operating room looking like the Sun King.

Susanne had her notes in her hands, and I saw she had another pamphlet with her. I looked at it as we got back in the car.

"Luscious Lips, honey?" I raised an eyebrow in her general direction.

"Honey, have the sexy lips that every woman wants!"

"How many times did you read that pamphlet while we were waiting to be seen?"

"I lost track after three."

I laughed, and we made the two-hour trek home.

*   *   *

I called the Contessa as I walked to the very large parking lot at work.

"Michael," I said, "it occurs to me that I drive by your town every day on my way to and from work."

"Yes, you do, Everett," he said in his careful lisp. "Why do you bring this up?" I thought I could hear him smiling.

"I bring this up—thank you for asking—because I think that we should share dinner sometime. Why don't we do that?"

"I think that's a lovely idea," he said. We made plans for the following week. It would be good to see him. I valued the people I knew from before my transition in a new way, because they knew all of me and I'd gotten to see the best of them.

I drove home and plopped down on the coach. Opening my

email, I saw I had an email from the Syracuse University Alumni Association about updating their database. Boy, did I have stuff to update. I called the number in the email. And then I proceeded to have what was possibly the most unusual conversation the Alumni Data Entry Person probably had that day.

Unsuspecting Alumni Data Entry Person: Okay, Miss Maroon, did your last name change?

I heard the clickety clacking of keys in the background.

Me: Oh, no. That's the same.

UADEP: Okay, Miss Maroon, so what would you like to update? *Click click clack click.*

Me: Uh, the first and middle names.

UADEP: Oh, okay. And your first name? *Click click clacking click.*

Me: E-V-E-R-E-T-T. Everett.

UADEP: Okay … E-V-E-R-E-T-T. That's interesting. Middle name?

Me: D-A-N-I-E-L.

UADEP: Oh. *Click cla—* You have a lot to update! (She giggled.)

Me: Yes, I suppose I do.

UADEP: So, uh, um, uh, um, uh. Should we change the "Miss?"

Me: That seems appropriate.

UADEP: (Giggling) Okay, great. What would you like?

Me: Can I get "His Highness?"

UADEP: Um, have you been bestowed with that title?

Me: (Wondering about what it would take to get such a bestowment) Well, no, only among some friends and a bartender in the city. But I don't suppose he counts. How about Mister?

UADEP: (Sounding exhausted all of a sudden) Mister it is. Now then, have you been doing anything since graduation that I should mention in here?

Me: Have you not been a part of this conversation? (Shared laughter)

Chapter 26

When I learned that my mother needed a knee replacement, I called her to tell her I could visit afterward to help take care of her. After some prodding, she agreed, one of the stipulations being that I bring my lovely girlfriend about which she'd heard so many good things. Kathy must have gone on about Susanne after meeting her twice. So I'd made the arrangements, booked the tickets, gotten the time off of work, and packed my bag.

Talking to my mom the night before we left for her house in Arkansas, she said she was excited to see me and meet Susanne. Something was off in her tone. I asked her what was wrong.

"I just don't know what to do about neighbors who come over to visit. I've never told them about a second son."

"I see." I had to mull this one over. Something told me suggesting I'd been a secret teenage birth wouldn't go over well.

"I mean, I can't introduce you with your old name." I was glad she'd caught on to that. "So I suppose I'll tell them you're my friend."

I nearly dropped the phone. *Her friend?* Her friend, whom she's never mentioned before, thirty years younger, bearing a striking resemblance to her, is dropping in on a town so small and isolated it had no four-way intersections, to take care of her after she acquires a titanium knee joint?

I guessed it was better than being introduced as her daughter.

* * *

Mom's incision and stapling were done well, but she contracted a severe and dangerous staph infection. By the time we got to her house, thin red streaks trailed out from her staples like skeletal fingers taking hold of her leg. Her doctor gave her a prescription for a strong antibiotic and by Sunday it had cleared up considerably. She was emotionally tired and a bit zonked from painkillers, but she was happy to see us.

"She's just precious," Mom said about Susanne. I agreed, although I wondered if there wasn't a blurry boundary between opinion and opium right at that point.

Her fear about explaining me was well founded, because she knew a lot of people from her church, and they had made it a point to bring by meals for her. While their intentions were good, some of the entrees looked less than edible. One dish consisted of boiled chicken breasts atop a glimmering field of Minute Rice with canned peas and sliced jalapeño peppers stirred in. I recombined ingredients from the craziest offerings so that they more closely resembled food that the four of us could eat.

At one point Susanne and I were playing cards at the dining table, in clear sight of the front door, when a church friend stopped by to drop off bread, bread pudding, and amaretto cream, and neither my stepfather nor Mom introduced us. So we were just random strangers playing cards in her house, or perhaps figments of this man's imagination, since neither of my parents acknowledged we were even in the room.

Afterward they both looked like guilty children.

"I like the name Danny," my stepdad Gary said, shuffling the card deck.

"I've always liked that name," agreed my mother, who wrote down my name as "Ev" on the points list for our card game. She called me *he* once or twice that evening. She also cried later, saying, "I just can't call you Everett." I understood that she was conflicted, even ten months after I sent her my letter. She fretted that she'd "made" me wrong. I told her I was happy and hoped that she would find comfort in that.

"That Susanne is pretty great, though," she said the next day as I changed her dressing.

"Yeah, isn't she?" I said.

"I mean, not a lot of people could deal with, you know," she said, trailing off.

"You know, Mom, I told her about me on our first date. I'm glad she's okay with who I am, but she's not a superhero or anything. She's great and I love her. We try to keep everything in perspective."

"Perspective is good," Mom said, nodding off.

We cooked up a storm for her—making my favorite Italian rice balls, squash mac and cheese, a pot roast, and some chocolate chip cookies. After the first couple of dinners, Gary remarked that they wanted us to move in for a while so we could just cook for them.

"As long as we call it Susanne and Ev's B&B, fine," I said, smiling. He clapped me on the back and laughed.

* * *

I gave Jeffrey another call to see if I could cajole him into spending an evening with me, but he seemed disinterested, and, unfortunately, I was getting used to it.

"Well, so what's going on for you these days?" I tried to ask casually.

"You know, the same." He was waiting for me to come up with another sentence or to hang up. It seemed like a control thing. *Why are you so hostile?* I wondered.

"Well, I'm still adjusting over at SSA," I said, forgetting how it had bothered him the last time I'd brought it up. And then I recalled his reaction and wished I could take the words back.

"You know, maybe you'll never really understand being a man. It's not like you're a real man, after all. You'll never have a penis, and you'll never really know what it's like with your little lesbian girlfriend to be a man in this country. So just stop."

I looked at the phone. I heard dead air again on the line. I collected myself.

"Jeffrey, that was really over the line." My hands shook.

"I'm sorry," he said slowly.

"Look, I'll just, uh, I'll talk to you later. Have a good night." I waited to hear him say goodbye and I hung up. *Who is he? Is he right?*

* * *

I left the office in Baltimore early to see Dr. Ace and get my quarterly blood level check, decked out in a pinstripe suit and tie and holding my black briefcase. I had inadvertently transitioned into a DC lobbyist. I spotted a tiny, older lady of color trying vainly to hail a cab. One by one they passed her as I walked toward her on the sidewalk. At least three of them had no passengers.

I stepped to the curb and put up one arm, and two cabs pulled over within seconds. *Gotta love M Street and 19ᵗʰ,* I thought. I opened the door. I motioned for the woman to get inside.

"Oh, thank you," she said excitedly.

The cab driver started to protest.

"She's my mother," I shouted at him, and watched as he pulled away.

I had a superpower.

* * *

I'd looked at many, many websites on diamond rings, and I finally settled on a fair trade, sustainably mined, non-conflict, Canadian diamond, via a gay jeweler in San Francisco. That ought to be politically correct enough for Susanne. I made the purchase and set the delivery for a friend's house in Virginia, since on any given day, Susanne might be at home to receive packages. I grinned as I made the purchase.

"Whatcha doing?" my next-cube neighbor asked me.

"Buying a ring to propose to my girlfriend," I replied.

"Oooh," he said, leaning in to look at the specs. The rumor that I might be gay kept crawling around the office. It was one way for them to explain why I seemed different from most of the men who worked there. He seemed relieved but also genuinely happy for me.

"When are you going to ask her?"

I had a plan. "We have a beach vacation coming up," I said. "I think I'll ask her while we're walking on the sand at night."

"You're a romantic! That's so sweet." He put one hand on my shoulder. "Whatever you do, Ev, do not drop it in the surf."

I had not considered that as a possibility. It sounded horrifying in its great plausibility. Perhaps I should come up with another way of giving her the ring. A small, white room, equipped with a metal detector, ought to suffice.

Meanwhile, other coworkers heard the news, since we were all piled on top of each other's desks. Soon I had six people in my four-by-three-foot cubicle, all congratulating me and smiling. I told them not to put the cart before the horse, and they told me I was full of nonsense. They had opinions of me that I didn't know existed. How had they seen me these past six months?

I hoped I would someday have a clearer understanding of myself and who I had become.

* * *

Michael and I were having dinner at a British pub, one of many different restaurants we'd tried since I started working in Baltimore. Once a demanding customer who had no problem sending back dishes if they weren't what he had "expected," the Contessa had mellowed and become more forgiving, even if he was still a picky eater.

"So I bought a ring," I told him.

He gasped, holding three fingers to his mouth. "Really? What did you get?"

I told him about the carat, the cut, the gay jeweler, and he smiled at me. "Did you give it to her yet?" He held his head to the side and made an inquisitive expression, because apparently lightening his voice at the end of the sentence might not have been enough of an indicator that he was posing a question.

"Well, I'd intended to give it to her next week when we go to the beach, but, uh, that plan was foiled."

"She found the ring?" His eyes were as big as moons.

"No, actually," I said, "she found the ring cleaner, which was wrapped with a bow, and then wanted to know if it was a present for her."

"Well," he said, "what did you do?"

"What could I do? I said it was for later."

"And?"

"And she said, 'Oh, laaaaater. A present for me for laaaaater.'"

He sighed, knowing I'd told her. "So pray tell, what did Ms. Beechey say to the ring?"

"She said yes."

"Congratulations!" The Contessa then proceeded to tell the other patrons and waitstaff near us that I was now engaged. They applauded, almost as if on cue.

"Michael," I said, lowering my voice, "would you be my best man?"

He thought about something and then said, "You know, I guess I thought you would have asked Jeffrey. But you two aren't that close anymore."

I was sad. "Well, I'm not asking you as second fiddle. I'd honestly love to have you be my best man."

"Do you mind if I ask why?" Of course he wanted to know. Classic Contessa.

I fiddled with my drink glass, enjoying briefly the way it moved against the white linen tablecloth underneath. "I think that what I'll need on my wedding day is a calming, loving influence, and I don't see anyone being that more than you. Plus I have to see you in a tux."

"I can get into that," he said, taking another bite of his well done steak. "I think it's disappointing, though, that you and Jeffrey aren't really friends these days. He just can't get over how long it took you to tell him. He said he realized he never really knew you if you knew this for years and didn't tell him."

"Really? Is that his problem?"

"He hasn't told you that?" Michael seemed surprised.

"He's never told me there's any issue at all. I mean he went off on me on the phone a while back, but I thought he was having a really bad day. He just won't accept any of my invitations to do things, and I'm getting tired of initiating."

"He told me you don't even ask him to hang out anymore."

"That's just plain not true." We sat in silence for a minute. "I think I can't fix whatever his deal is."

"I think you've struggled with it enough," said Michael, chewing. "Some people are friends for a lifetime, and some for a season. Maybe this was just your season."

I nodded and finished my steak. Moving on was hard, but I could do it. I had other exciting things to look forward to, and I wanted to share them with people who were happy for me.

*   *   *

Susanne and I checked out a possible site for the wedding and reception. We didn't have a date yet, but we thought something like a year away would work for us, after she'd defended her dissertation. One place we looked at came with a vivacious party manager, who said repeatedly that we were the "cutest couple." *Ever?* I was taken aback by the thick air of heterosexuality, and refused to be the stoic, uninvolved groom to be. Figuring I could just channel a little bit of the Contessa, I asked questions about which of the furnishings could be whisked out of the room so that it wouldn't interfere with our color scheme.

"Oh, what colors have you picked?" asked the venue manager, genuinely interested in such minutiae.

"Light blue and chocolate brown," I said.

Susanne interjected, "Well, I'm not sure if those will be the colors, yet."

"Well, those are very hip this year," the manager said, and I liked her immediately. "What a man you have here, Susanne."

I beamed in Susanne's direction, and she rolled her eyes at me.

* * *

I was back up in Connecticut visiting my sister and embarrassing my nieces by talking like a pirate all day. I knew Callie, the older niece, secretly liked it. I found her on my sister's porch.

"What kind of pizza do pirates like?" I asked. "GARRRRlic pizza!"

"Oh my God, stop," she protested.

"Where do pirates like to go on vacation?"

"No, not another," pleaded Callie.

"ARRRRRuba!"

"I so don't know you," she said, walking away from me.

Later we held hands in the ShopRite. In the produce section, we tried bagging apples with our free hands, which was strangely cooperative and fun.

My sister made no attempt to use Everett or male pronouns for me. She looked at me dumbfounded when I referred to myself in stories as male. I wasn't sure how to broach the subject with her, because I knew she'd been trying to switch over months earlier.

Later in the evening, Kathy walked into the living room and asked, "Is Aunt Jenny going to start dinner soon?"

I snapped at her. "Not until you stop calling me 'Aunt Jenny.'"

She walked out of the house to her front lawn, upset. As was our family style, the leaving was brief, for she came back into the kitchen and started yelling.

"Not everything is about you," she said. I frowned.

"No, not everything. But my life is about me!"

"I changed your diaper," she said, crying, and I could only imagine what that memory held for her. Nothing like trying to stick up for yourself when someone is recalling wiping your ass.

"This is so hard. I don't think I can ever call you my brother. I've loved you as a sister and I've always loved having a sister."

I hated to see her cry. My frustration with her crumbled. I walked up to her and hugged her.

"I'm still me. I'm still here. I wouldn't have done this if I didn't really, really have to. I wished it didn't have to be this way, but it does. And I'll never not love you, even if I become a turtle next year."

That made her laugh a little, and she held onto me a little longer before leaning back and standing on her own.

"I love you," she said.

"I love you, too, and if you wanted to change your name tomorrow, that's okay with me."

"Good to know," she said. She ruffled my short hair and we got to the business of preparing supper. I was tired.

It was going to be a great engagement party with my family in attendance.

Chapter 27

It was time for my annual physical; it had been well over a year since my last exam. Dr. Min was away on vacation, so I got another doctor in the practice that I'd seen before when Dr. Min wasn't around. Since I'd told her about starting T two years earlier, she'd read up on gender identity disorder and hormone management. Dr. Min had indeed come a long way, and it made me feel good to know that there were conscientious practitioners like her.

I pushed through heavy traffic and passed two accidents, arriving ten minutes late for my appointment. Apparently the office staff was thirty-two times burned, sixty-four times shy about late arrivals, so they were at DEFCON 3 when I walked in.

"Well, can you make an appointment for another day?" the receptionist asked.

"What? I'm only a few minutes late."

"I'm not sure he'll be able to squeeze you in now."

"I can't believe this. We're talking ten minutes here."

"He's in with another patient and he's booked all morning. You're welcome to wait to see if he can see you."

"You know, I have been a patient here for years. I've always waited in this lobby past the start time of my appointments. I'm late once by a little bit and you think you can treat me like this?"

"You're welcome to wait or reschedule," she told me.

I sat down, figuring I'd give them their own ten minutes, and then I would find another doctor. Lo and behold ten minutes later, I was at intake.

The nurse told me to get naked down to my waist and to take off my trousers. It appeared men didn't get the crunchy paper gown to wear. Once I was alone I searched the cabinets for disposable gowns, but there were none, so I kept on my undershirt and removed my binder.

Not Dr. Min came in and sat down. He looked a little younger than me, with perfect, chiseled features and a careful hairstyle, as if he'd placed every hair exactly where he wanted it on his head.

"I only have a few minutes because you're late for your appointment," he announced in a stern voice.

"Excuse me," I said, "are you lecturing me?"

"Well, now, being on time is important."

I growled at him. "I just told them outside, I've been a patient here for seven years. I was stuck behind multiple accidents on the way here"

He continued to argue with me. I interrupted him.

"If you're so freaking busy, then let's not spend your limited time arguing about your late arrival policy." That seemed to surprise him. So he checked my blood pressure and temperature, which were fine. He listened to my heart and lungs through the undershirt. He told me to lose weight. Then he asked me if I'd "had the sex-reassignment surgery" yet.

"Which one is that?" I asked. "It doesn't work that way for female to male transgender folks."

And hello, can you not see the two breasts in the room? They nearly launched themselves off my chest like dumbass-seeking missiles.

Apparently what he meant by this question was whether I'd had a hysterectomy yet, or would I need a pelvic exam and Pap smear today. I heard, "hell no, we won't go" in my head.

"Oh, I'll just make another appointment with Dr. Min for that," I said.

"Oh, okay," he said, visibly relieved.

I told him I'd be getting chest reconstruction at the end of October and he nodded, seemingly newly aware that I hadn't had it yet.

Susanne suggested, when I relayed the story to her later, that he could perhaps read up on cultural competencies for medical practitioners sometime, you know, when he was waiting for late patients.

* * *

My surgery was now less than a month away. I wasn't panicked about it. I also hadn't yet mentioned it to my mother. I had a lot of work to finish before I took leave from my job for two weeks.

While I was looking forward to the results of the surgery, I'd been under general anesthesia enough times to know I would wake up really sick. And even though I always told the doctors this and insisted they just put a little something in my line when I'd be in recovery, they never listened until I started hacking like a cat with a hairball. I also had a resistance to feeling intoxicated, and painkillers made me loopy. I wasn't looking forward to the loopy. But there were things I thought about fondly, besides the chest itself. I wouldn't have to bind anymore, no more daily sweater vests to create a smooth chest line—I'd be more comfortable and less overheated without them, much as I liked them. I also looked forward to being able to tie my shoes without popping my binder or feeling like I was going to pass out from the lung restriction. What would it feel like to have a flat chest? I could only imagine.

I had to call Mom.

*　*　*

The house was immaculate for our engagement party—I had spent the last four days scrubbing everything inside the walls, for not only was my soon to be mother-in-law about to visit, but my own mother was coming. Susanne and I were happy that they would meet; better now than nine months from now at the wedding.

"Okay, I think we're ready," I said, looking around the living room. I'd even made sure the throw blankets looked inviting and fresh.

"Honey, I think we can relax now. Everything looks great."

Relaxing was not in the cards. No sooner had we finished the prep than we headed off to the airport to collect our various parental units.

One lovely evening of expensive fondue dinner later, a clear pattern emerged between our parents: my mother would call me "she," and Susanne's mom would find a reason to use male pronouns or "Everett," as in:

Michael: Everett, these ribs taste fantastic!

Mom: Isn't she a great cook?

Susanne's Mom: Everett cooked for us when he visited last year, and he made a really lovely supper.

I could see that Mom was trying. She wanted to be in touch with my life, and she could see that I had caring friends. She, Kathy, and Susanne's mother helped us set up for the party, putting out appetizers and mixing up drinks. Our friends started arriving, some bringing presents, everyone hugging and introducing themselves. *Happy people make a lot of noise,* I thought, enjoying the mood of the house.

Mom wound up quizzing my closest comrades.

"Michael, those are adorable pants," she said, patting him on the back. "Are those whales?"

"Yes, Margie, they are," he answered. Michael was always happy to show off his Brooks Brothers whale pants. How could whale pants not be a crowd pleaser?

She lowered her voice and leaned in to him. "Michael, did you know Everett when she was Jenifer?"

"Yes, I've known Ev for years now."

"Hasn't it been hard not to call her Jenifer?"

He looked at her kindly. "You know, it was a little at first, but it got easier." He watched her take this in. "I know he really appreciates your support."

"Oh, does he think I'm supportive?" she asked, obviously pleased. She smiled, tears forming in her eyes.

I was laughing with someone when she sneaked up behind me and hugged me.

"Hi, Mom," I said.

"Honey, I love you," she told me.

"I love you, too," I said, wondering what brought this on.

"I'm just really proud of you."

We'd come a long way since she'd called me, crying.

* * *

The parties kept coming. We'd decided to hold a low-key "surgery party" for me on the last Saturday in the lives of Becky and Bertha, and it was heartwarming to enjoy my friends and have their support. I had a moment of disappointment that Jeffrey wasn't there, but I was okay with it.

A breast theme permeated everything, from the shape and color of Susanne's famous sugar cookies, to the cards people gave me, to the conversation. It was like my breasts would be going on a trip around the world, sending back postcards from all the places they visited. *Becky and Bertha See the Taj Mahal.* I wondered whether I would have been more fond of them if they'd received such fanfare upon their arrival into the world, but I knew the answer to that.

One friend brought over every episode of *Buffy the Vampire Slayer*, *Xena: Warrior Princess*, and *Firefly*. "Excellent television," she proclaimed.

"Thanks, Jody," I said, looking over all of it and wondering if I really had enough hours to see all of this. Maybe if I didn't spend any time doing anything else, like pouring a glass of water or going to the bathroom.

Someone else brought a fun pack of the kind of stuff I used to get when I was a kid in the hospital, so I was eager to tear into the Laddergrams. As one person put it, "Who doesn't love Laddergrams?"

Ethan, Niles's friend, came up to me and put a hand on my shoulder, which was a little bit of a stretch for him since he was a good seven inches shorter than me. He leaned in and said, "You'll wake up afterward and think, 'This is the best decision I ever made.'"

"Really?" I asked him.

"Really," he said. I hugged him.

I sure hope so.

* * *

We were in the "early banter phase" that happens before the start of a meeting. I was in the room with several folks from my team, a few programmers, and their managers. One of the managers said suddenly, "Oh, Everett, I heard you're having surgery next week. I didn't know! I thought you were going on vacation! Is everything okay?"

This comment could have meant a few different things. She could have been saying something like, "Egads, surgery!" She could have really wanted to know what kind of surgery I was having. She could have been concerned for my general health. But because twenty-three other coworkers had asked me in the weeks leading up to my surgery date, "What surgery are you getting?" I no longer much cared. I'd told them things like, "I'm having some extra tissue removed," or "I'm just dealing with a problem I've had for a while." Yeah, like two puberties in one lifetime.

So without batting an eye, I looked at her and spoke, knowing everyone in the room was listening.

"Really, Ashley, I'm just a big transsexual, and I'm going to get a nice, new man chest." I patted my binder for extra effect.

She laughed in my face, soon followed by the rest of the staff. One staffer held his sides, he was laughing so hard.

"You are such a jokester! Oh my God! Fine, fine, Everett, don't tell us what you're having! Sheesh!"

Later that night, when I relayed the story to Susanne, she choked on her tea, looked at me, and said, "Well, they can never say you didn't tell them."

* * *

A new guy on our work team, relocated from upstate New York, spoke tersely but directly and had a very dry sense of humor. He hovered at my cube entrance, talking about work and his cat, and then abruptly asked when I would be going out for surgery. He tugged at his goatee as he waited for me to respond.

"Next Wednesday," I said. "Halloween."

"So what surgery are you having?" *Couldn't people just confer on my answers? Should I write an email to everyone?*

I looked at him and said in a serious tone, "I'm having some extra tissue removed."

"Oh, like an unformed twin inside you?"

"Okay, you need to stop watching so much *Medical Incredible*."

Susanne thought there must be a pool at work on what my surgery was.

Chapter 28

Painkillers were strange beasts. The effect of Vicodin wasn't like drinking. It was more like having someone hit me on the head with a frying pan, repeatedly, only without the actual skull-crushing part. If asked, I would have said yes, there are little blue birds flying in circles around my head.

I watched the ceiling move past me as they wheeled me into the operating theater, and gasped when I saw, among the surgeon's tools, a very large stainless steel hammer. What the hell was the hammer for? The anesthesiologist giggled at my shock, and then I was out, the frying pan beginning its chemical assault on my skull.

The next thing I knew, a woman in pink and green scrubs was calling my name, trying to get me to put on a shirt. *Hey, those are the original Syracuse University colors,* I thought. *How about that?*

Her mouth was moving. "Everett, come on, you can do it," she urged me.

Susanne somehow got me to the car. I struggled out of the wheelchair and flopped, yelping, into the passenger seat. I clutched the surgeon's letter that would allow me to change all of my identification to "male." Then we were in a nearby hotel, where I would recover for the first day or two before heading back home. Susanne must have taken us there. *Sweet, lovely Susanne. I love her,* I thought.

Walking down the hallway to our hotel room, I suddenly needed to make acquaintance with the toilet bowl. *Oh, toilet bowl. Be my friend. I love you, toilet bowl.*

The pain either wasn't as bad as I thought it would be, or pain medication worked far better than I thought it would. As sternly instructed, I hadn't taken off the surgical vest to see what was underneath. I didn't even want to touch the thing, which would have required moving my upper arms away from my body, and I wasn't prepared to do that at T-plus four hours.

In one of my more lucid moments, I saw Susanne sitting on the couch while I opened up my laptop to send a note to my people. I had an email from my sister Kathy.

—**Hey Ev, I'm thinking of you and I love you.**

I love you too, Kathy. I fell back asleep.

*   *   *

A few days later I was still in bed, but by this point we'd come back home and I was grateful for that. We had yet to open up the dressing, since that wouldn't be allowed for another couple of days. The drains were hard to navigate—they hung down from next to my armpits, and they required regular emptying into the toilet when I didn't feel much like getting up. Certainly not an aid to my still-nauseated stomach was the concept of pouring out significant quantities of body fluids.

In this haze, the phone rang. It was my mother.

"So honey, is there anything new in your life?" Her voice was high-pitched, as if she was forcing innocence.

"Well, Susanne got a job interview. I guess that's new." Fortunately for me, Mom had asked a question I could answer honestly, if not completely. Incomplete truth-telling was now my reluctant modus operandi.

"Oh, great. Is she there now?"

"No," I said, trying to focus. Vicodin made that difficult. "She goes out there in a couple of days."

"Out where?"

Crap, where was she going again? "California," I answered. *Success!*

"Well, that's nice," she said, suddenly sounding disinterested. "I've got to run. I've got my volunteer time at the hospital now." *Ugh, hospitals.* I wondered why I should mind them; after all, I hadn't been to a hospital for this. I'd been to a strip mall.

"Okay, Ma, thanks for calling."

"I love you, Jen— kid. I love you, kid."

"I love you too, Ma." The phone conversation was too much for me, and I passed out again, about to be a repeat victim of my own drool.

The next day, strangely enough, she called again. While I did talk to her frequently—anywhere from once every couple of weeks to a couple of times a week—I didn't typically hear from her two days in a row.

"So, honey," she asked in that same overly sweet tone, "what's new?"

What was going on with her?

"Well, Susanne has a job interview later this week." *Plausible.*

Her lilt disappeared. "Yeah, you told me that yesterday when I asked."

"Oh." Damn those Vicodin, I had no memory.

"So is there anything else going on right now?" she continued. "You know, new in your life or new to you? Like, something that's changed? Something you have that you didn't have before, or something you no longer have?"

Holy cannoli, she knew. I mean I knew she knew, but she really *knew.*

"Mom, what are you asking?" My filter for subtlety was offline.

"I just mean, if there was something big going on for you, I would want to know about it. I would want to be there for you if you were going through anything that, you know, you'd want a mother for."

"Ah. I see."

"I mean, you could tell me whatever you wanted and I would be happy to hear it."

"Really? That's great, Mom."

"Really."

Okay, one doesn't get an opening this big without it being a calamity like oh, the Black Hole of Calcutta, very often, so I took it.

"Well, I had surgery a few days ago." *Cue sound of bomb dropping.*

"Oh. What kind of surgery?" she asked, practically cooing. She asked her question with the same inflection one would use with, "Oh, what color?" to the declaration that one had just bought a luxurious cashmere sweater.

"Well, I had a double mastectomy with a chest reconstruction, and it went very well."

"I'm so glad it went well!" I heard a pause, not common in conversations with my relatives. "Honey, are you happy?"

"I'm really happy, Ma. I'm actually surprised at how happy I am." I didn't add that perhaps the pain pills were inducing euphoria, but I knew I was actually happy nonetheless.

"Well, that's great, dear. I really just want you to be happy and healthy. You know, I realize that I haven't been there for you, and I'm sorry. I'm not going to give you a hard time about this anymore. I think you're a great person and I'm thrilled to be your mother. Honey, are you crying?"

"Just allergies," I stammered.

*   *   *

A little more than a week since Becky and Bertha went on their once-in-a-lifetime trip to the great pathology lab in the sky, I was climbing the walls. My drains were my new constant companions. I was supposed to monitor how much was coming out every day, and when I was under a certain amount, report to the surgeon's office to have them pulled.

I was way over that threshold and still oozing out more than I should have been at that point. What was the point of getting off the couch if I was still a fluid making machine? I called the doctor's office and told them how much I was still draining on my right side.

"Stop being so active," said the nurse who answered the phone. Well, I'd try this weekend, I told myself. I was supposed to go back to work the next Thursday, after all. Actually, going to work sounded like the best concept in the world.

With nine days' worth of hindsight, I could see that I was glad for having the surgery. I was really happy with how it looked—of the three square inches I could see. Loopy after surgery, I'd apparently told Susanne in the recovery room that "this was a good decision." It would simplify my life considerably if I could just have faith in my decisions before I made them. Hey, I would take my insights as I got them.

Maybe my drains would come out soon.

*   *   *

Lying in bed or on the couch, around the clock, time stopped having meaning. I went off the Gregorian calendar and started one of my own. On Day Twelve of the Drains from Breasts of Yore, they started accumulating a cloudy brown fluid. However one defined "good," this wasn't it. I called the doctor's office twice in two days, but both times they said to be patient, slow down, stop being so active, wait until they're putting out less fluid. Two nights later I checked the right drain. I had obviously transitioned to Kermit the Frog, looking at the green fluid in the floppy drain cup. After thinking about how few things in the human body made it to that part of the color spectrum, I called the doctor's answering service. Nobody called me back.

When I'd called on Friday, otherwise known as the Day Before My Bodily Fluid Celebrated St. Patty's Day, I told them that my partner was heading out of town this weekend and if I'd need a person with me to get the drains out, could we please do it now? She said not until the drains were producing less on both sides.

"Now, you're in Philadelphia, right?"

"No, I'm in DC," I corrected.

"Well, still, they need to be making less fluid."

The following Monday, now called the Day of the New Week of Oblivion, Nurse Barbara called me to say, "Your drains have been in a long time. Come in today so we can take them out." I asked, gently, again, if I needed someone to come with me. "That would be advisable, yes."

I hoped I'd be much happier once the drains were out, if only because cleaning myself wouldn't continue to consist of a series of soapy and wet washcloths while standing over a sink.

* * *

The fluid saga had not ended. I was getting dressed for my first day back to work, which, three weeks post-op, included stuffing my surgical vest with maxi pads to increase the compression on my hurt chest and help speed healing. Maxi pads, to their credit, have a nebulous outer layer kind of like a black hole that sucks in material at terminal velocity, crushing it into an infinitely small, infinitely dense piece of matter. When connected to wormholes, by the way, they deposit all of this material into a new location. Thus it was possible, I theorized, that our universe had been formed by the big bang of millions of crushed maxi pad deposits.

Getting dressed, I snagged a suture on the maxi pad. It hurt beyond description, which I articulated by screaming. I couldn't get the suture out of the maxi pad, so I tiptoed to the bathroom, holding up the vest/maxi pad combo, because I'd stuck the pad's adhesive to the vest. I tried not to jiggle the suture; fortunately, brand new man boobs weren't prone to actual jiggling. I cut the suture, still feeling pain, covered the cut end with some paper tape, and finished getting dressed. I got in my car, oddly thrilled to be commuting again.

Four hours into my workday, I felt a searing, stabbing pain that prevented me from thinking about anything else. It felt like I'd pulled a muscle or cracked my sternum. I muddled through the rest of my day—my supervisor had kept my workload light—and left a little early. The second I got home I ripped off my shirts in a "get the leeches off of me" way, not an exotic dancer way. Nothing looked wrong. The tape was still there. The incisions were clearly healing. But it felt like something was pulling the sutures out. It was a little like when I'd had shingles. I took a few ibuprofen, but the pain got worse. I called the surgeon, who said that pulling a suture may have damaged some of the scar tissue, and that it was a painful thing to have happen but should be better in one to two days. She thought ibuprofen was a good idea, since it's also an anti-inflammatory. I didn't sleep well, but I made it to 5:30 a.m.

I awoke with a new friend: the return of Bertha, my old right breast! It was the morning of Breast Resurrection Day.

Bertha appeared to be irate at my choice to excoriate her. She was red, hot to the touch, and something like a B-cup. As the day went on, Bertha installed an addition under my right armpit. I called the surgeon's office again, and one of the nurses said, "Oh, you can't have an infection this late. Just rest up and don't be so active." Always with the "not so active." What were they, paid by the junk food lobby? And what was that about a two-week recovery period again?

In two more days, otherwise known as the Day of the Breastal Revolt, Bertha had turned hard to the touch. She felt like the pectoral muscle of the statue of David. Only this was not what I'd had in mind for rock-hard musculature. I called the doctor's office again. I got the nurse to agree to call in another antibiotic prescription for me, and she sighed while I said I had to look up the number of the pharmacy near me. She reminded me that it's "very, very rare to have an infection this far out." More likely it was an allergic reaction to the sutures. But who could know without looking at me?

Susanne flew back in Friday from her interview in California after getting bumped off of her original, earlier flight. I felt like death in a frying pan. That night I woke up several times with the chills. I sat around all weekend, sick of something being wrong. I renewed my full work schedule. Monday and Tuesday I'd been signed up at work to go to an annual recap of the literature in my field, so I figured if I could sit at home, I could do it in an office building, too. I went home early the first day and kept cursing myself for not feeling well. I couldn't make it past six hours of sitting. *Why am I such a baby?*

Wednesday morning I had my quarterly visit with my endocrinologist, who was also an internist. Susanne and I were happy that a medical professional was going to actually see my face. Ace looked at me with my shirt off.

"Holy shit, Everett!" This, the man with no sense of humor or intense expression. He ordered me to call the surgeon, and I told him I couldn't seem to get past the nursing staff. I'd only managed to get to the doctor once on the phone.

"Look, she took you to the dance, she can take you home. No other doctor is going to go near this."

"Hey, you watch how you talk about Bertha there."

He grinned. "Just go up there and insist that she see you."

Oh my God. It must really be bad.

I left his office and called the surgeon's office once more, getting one of the nursing staff.

"I've got a 100-degree fever now," I said.

"Well, a 100-degree fever isn't that high a fever," she replied.

What, I was going to need to cough up a kidney before they said yes to me? Was there a magic word I was missing here? *Open sesame!*

"My internist told me I had to come see you."

She suddenly got interested. "Oh, is that an option? Where do you live? Are you local?" Had I not told them I lived in DC in each and every conversation?

Of course, I thought, *people fly in for this from everywhere. They probably don't do a lot of follow-up on FTMs.*

She told me to come in the next two hours. She didn't realize I was still in my car, illegally on my cell phone. I saw that snow was starting to fall. I had to get out of the city, fast, before people started walking around with A-frame boards pronouncing that the end of days were nigh. The first winter snow in DC always brought out the hysterics.

I spent the next ninety minutes driving in the left lane behind nervous drivers going thirty miles an hour. My chest throbbed, and my pulse, which was already too high, was pounding. I still felt terrible, and I walked into the surgeon's office. They took me to an exam room, and I undressed and showed the nurse my chest.

"Those are stretch marks," she said, looking at the red lines streaming across my torso from the incision line.

"I don't have stretch marks," I muttered. *Wow, I feel like crap.*

"Sure, you have lots of stretch marks," she argued.

"I don't have stretch marks in the middle of my chest!"

Yelling did the trick, and Nurse Barbara left the room, dismissing me with her departure. Another more daring nurse came in and saw me.

"You have cellulitis."

"Itis," I knew, was a suffix that means, to us laypeople, infection. Cellulitis is an infection under the innermost layer of skin, and it is bad news, because it quickly becomes septic, meaning that it can travel to one's bloodstream, and then one is in for a bad ride. The surgeon came in, scrubs on from just finishing up someone else's top surgery. Her smile disappeared as she took one look at me, and she immediately started ordering all kinds of supplies to the room, things with names I didn't understand. They took off my opened-up shirts, and the doctor gave me a local and then opened up a few of my stitches. This is when I peed out of my rib cage—at least it felt like peeing, as I felt a sense of relief and of warm liquid streaming over my skin. As I was being aspirated, I felt a big dose of happy as the disgusting ooze left my body. It was a strange experience to watch my chest deflate. I could almost hear Bertha screaming like the Wicked Witch of the West, "Nooooooo, water, nooooooo, I'm mellllllllllllllting!"

The surgeon looked at me kindly as I side-urinated. She put her hand on my shoulder. "I'm sorry, Ev, you're the one percent outcome."

"I'll go buy a lottery ticket," I said.

They gave me an IV bag to re-hydrate me—all my liquids had been going to Bertha the Undead—and a strong antibiotic. They put in a new drain on that side, a floppy plastic tube with no collection cup. I lay in the dark room for a couple of hours, drifting in and out of sleep until the IV bag was empty. I returned two days later to get my side rechecked. It looked much better, even though I had some more recovery to do now. I saw the surgeon again a few days later, now that I was clearly on her radar screen. She'd even given me her home number so I could call her directly. And I had finally earned my VIP pass with the nurses.

* * *

There was nothing quite like taking off one's pants to do one's business in the men's room, only to see one has dropped a nipple on the floor. Okay, not a nipple. A nipple scab. I picked it back up, not really knowing why, but feeling badly for the little guy, who'd been protecting one or the other for seven weeks. Since I had no physical sensation on my chest, I looked inside my shirt and saw that it had come from my left, non-infected side. Normally I would never reach down and pick anything up off a men's room floor, but for some reason I just couldn't leave it there. I looked it over, while still sitting on the john. It was kind of cute, circular, like a little dried blood UFO.

Maybe the drugs weren't yet out of my system.

Two days later at work, I was washing my hands at the sink, when I felt the other scab fall all the way through my shirt, into and down my trousers, landing three inches from my foot. *What should I do? I wasn't alone in my stall this time. What if I bent over to retrieve it and someone came in? Geez, how bad would that look? How would I explain it? Oh, I'm just going through my biannual nipple molt, don't mind me.*

* * *

My reissued birth certificate arrived in the mail, with my new legal name, a gold seal, and a male sex marker on it. There was no baby footprint, but I still had the one from my birth year. It didn't say amended anywhere, it just presented itself as a birth certificate, like a replacement for one I'd lost in a fire. *Go New Jersey.* Not a bad state in which to have been born, if I did think so myself.

I laughed as I read the name of the county of my birth, and I showed Susanne.

"Of course," she said, smiling as she read the form. "Middlesex."

Now I could go and get everything changed to say male. I wasn't just Everett now, I was legally male. Or actually, I was as legal as any clerk of the court would support me in being legally male.

Chapter 29

On primary election day I went to my polling place shortly after the polls opened in DC. I felt good about fulfilling my civic responsibilities, when I remembered that I'd changed my name and address since the last time I voted. *Oops.*

Not really sure which name they'd have me filed under, I searched through my wallet for my voter registration card. I knew I had to tell them which party I was voting for, this being a primary and all. I wasn't sure if they'd want proof, even though I knew they weren't supposed to.

I made out my old legal name in half-faded and blurred crappy dot-matrix ink. Now I was faced with a choice: which name to give the election official. I had a vague memory of filling out the registration after my name change—DC, in fact, had sent the registration to me, acting like an actual government or something crazy like that—but I had no memory of mailing it back to them.

So I simply said, "Maroon." I mean, it wasn't a common name. There are only 50,000 Maroons in the whole country. I was betting I had the only one in this voting district. My aunt and cousins lived way across town.

Unlike the election officials for the A–G line and the O–Z line, this guy held up the top of the book so I couldn't see the names on the list. *Darn H–N guy!* I stood a little to the right and looked at it from the side.

He was looking through the Marshalls and going in the wrong direction. Not sure of the requirements for election officials and now suspecting that being able to alphabetize wasn't one of them, I waited patiently. His line was the longest. There was nobody in the A–G line and I furtively wondered if I shouldn't take Susanne's surname when we got married so I would never have to stand in this line again, but logic took over to remind me that while there are a lot of H–N people out there, I wouldn't, in fact, ever stand in this line, right here, again. So I chilled out.

He'd found it, he thought.

In unison, we each said a version of my name.

He looked at me, confused. He reached up and plucked my voter registration card out of my hand.

Studying it, he said, "Ma'am, I don't understand."

Crap, he was talking to me. I said, kind of quietly, "Oh, Everett is right."

"It's right?" Another furrowed brow from him as he stared at the list.

"Yes, that's the name."

"But this card says Jenifer Leigh, not Everett Daniel."

"I—" I stammered a little because I wasn't sure if I should let the giggle happen or just whisper to him. I didn't want everyone in on my business, but by this point, every person in a twenty-foot radius knew what was going on. Damn me for not cleaning out my wallet. "I changed my name," I said, simply.

"You CHANGED YOUR NAME FROM Jenifer Leigh TO EVERETT DANIEL? I DON'T UNDERSTAND."

The last threads of discretion were vaporized like a delicate flower in a vast, all-encompassing, radioactive mushroom cloud.

"Yes, I did."

And then I noticed, since he was no longer physically protecting the voter roll, that although DC had updated the name, they hadn't updated the address. My guess was that I indeed never sent in the registration update, and they had just entered the new name because their superior court regulations ordered it, or something, along with the legal name change. Clearly DMV changes—my new address was on my license—did not work the same way.

"Okay … but where do you live?" he asked, reading my mind. *Darn, I wasn't supposed to think about my new address! He knows I have a new address! He knows I'm an election spoiler from Alpha Centauri!*

"I just moved around the block."

"You CHANGED YOUR NAME and MOVED?"

He said "and moved" like Bill Cosby imitating his wife having a conniption.

"Yes. But I'm in the same voting district. It's just—"

"You MOVED."

"—around the corner."

We looked at each other. The rest of the H–Ns were getting restless. I refused to explain why I'd changed my name, even though that little tidbit of information would surely help him put it together. Wasn't it self evident?

"Please, here's my ID." I knew I didn't have to show this to him. "I just want to vote. I live here. I'm registered right there."

"Okay, okay ma'am," he said to me, though I wore a pinstriped navy blue suit and light blue tie. He kept staring at the names, floating in front of him like they were born of a painful acid trip. "I am really confused."

He handed me my card, and I voted.

*   *   *

My sister and I had started a game years back in which we would take the first syllable of someone's name and call them by another word that also started with that syllable or sound. So for Kathy I would call her "catheter," and for me it was often "genuine." When it started being "genitalia," I put a stop to the tradition. But it was standard practice for us to pick up the phone and say "catatonia!" to say hello.

I called her one night and said, "Catheter!" And without even thinking she said, "Eveready!"

I smiled. Things had mellowed out for the both of us.

*   *   *

I called my sister Jayne to tell her about my upcoming nuptials. I didn't speak to her as often as Kathy; she lived in California and was a lot older than me, so we hadn't spent a lot of my childhood together. Despite our lack of proximity, we were a lot alike and had the same booming, bring down the walls laugh.

I couldn't send out a wedding invitation to anyone who didn't know about my transition, what with the huge "Everett Daniel Maroon" on the top of it. So I told her, "I had a sex change."

"Really?" she asked. "Why?" That was the first time anyone had asked me that, in all this time. I had to think of a reasonable, short answer.

"Because I wasn't happy. Now I'm happy."

"Oh, good. Okay." A brief pause. "Hey, you know I was just talking about this the other day. Do you watch Oprah?" The "pregnant man" was all over the media on a book tour.

Holy God in heaven, really? Can I get five minutes without hearing about Thomas Beattie? It was like when people would come up to me and say, "Hey, you hear about that guy Jared who lost 200 pounds? Maybe you should try Subway."

The conversation shifted to family news.

We had a nice, if not poignant moment when she mentioned how she missed Dad. "I can't believe it's been so long," she said, referring to his death in 1995. I agreed. She said she had to run to go take care of her grandkids, and we gave verbal hugs, then hung up.

*   *   *

On a Friday I took time off of work to go to the clinic the DC Government said was a good place to get the premarital blood test for syphilis. Susanne and I pulled up across the street, checking the address many times, initially not believing our eyes.

The place we went to could only be described, in technical terms, as a shit hole. There were tears in the rippled carpet, unexplained stains on the ceiling, faded, crooked pictures on the walls, and a myriad of services advertised in faded, handwritten signage next to an open doorway in one corner of the room, exclaiming "Passport $5," "TB Tests, $15," "Marriage blood tests," "Form line here." It was so bad Susanne said it wasn't a lab, it was a place of bloodletting. And really, it looked like a crack-house-turned-vampire-hostel from *Buffy the Vampire Slayer*.

Meanwhile, DC had at the time the worst HIV infection rate by far in the U.S., with one in twenty residents HIV-positive. That they tested for syphilis was ludicrous; also, did they think the "premarital" couples weren't already sleeping together?

We decided that if the room where they drew our blood looked clean and orderly, and if we liked the nurse, we would stay and get it done. If it continued on like Pig Pen's Needle Sticks, Inc., or I saw a den of succubae, we were out of there. But the nurse had on fresh scrubs and a proper phlebotomy set-up, as it appeared to us laypeople. We did note, however, that nobody, at any point in the process, checked our ID.

We each received a piece of paper for our trouble, declaring that we were incapable of communicating syphilis to another person "at this time." As if we would rather have such a capability? Strange sentence construction, the form had. Further down was another curious sentence:

> NOTE: The sentence above does not mean you have syphilis. It is required by law. If you had syphilis you would not have been given this form to take to the Marriage License office.

We told ourselves we were reassured.

We showed up at the court after battling with 273 insane or out-of-town drivers, which is the same difference for whomever is stuck driving behind them—in this case, me. An hour later we showed up at the courthouse, having had to go around a large area that was suffering through a power outage. Why were we trying to do this on Friday the thirteenth, exactly?

We walked in and saw a couple we'd seen earlier at We Bleed You Cheap, LLC, and they joked that we should have driven over to the marriage office together. Some other random woman was demanding a name change because she'd put the wrong name on the license application, and she became a bright light of customer service, drawing in more and more civil servants like moths. So we waited. And waited. We were sitting in different gently stained chairs, this time within three feet of a trellis filled with silk roses and plastic ivy, which was apparently the entrance to the den of civil marriage services. My first thought was wow, see, governments need gay marriage, if only to get rid of the awful decorations the heterosexuals have put up in courthouses across the country.

The couple we'd been tailing got into a discussion with yet another woman about whether the Bible said women could be preachers or not. The other woman was waiting to get a copy of her parents' wedding certificate. As we watched the debate take shape, a man from another couple joined in, more intimidating and angry about it. There was a flurry of Bibles out of people's pocketbooks like righteous light sabers, and I realized that now would not be the time to chime in about whether God thought the transsexuals should marry, and wasn't same-sex marriage a blessing on all of us? I could see Susanne ready to slap a hand over my mouth, or kick me in the shin, but I knew better than to mix it up while sitting in the marriage license office. I studied the back of the chair in front of me, pretending interest in the artificially designed grain pattern.

I heard the car meter expiring three blocks away, and Susanne left to feed it. Finally they called our names to come up to the counter. I signed the application and made a civil ceremony date. Once again nobody asked for ID. Heck, they didn't even need Susanne there. I could be Jack the Ripper, for all they knew, and Susanne my slave bride. *Holy crap,* I thought, *gay people have no idea how lax these straightniks are! Institution of marriage my ass.*

But I was so excited to see what the inside of the ceremony room looked like, wondering what could possibly be behind the rose wrapping papered door. Maybe Monty Hall.

*   *   *

I'd babysat Lori and Barbara's baby, who was cute as a button, and was driving back home. As I accelerated onto a major highway, the Check Engine light glowed on the dash. Worse than the notification was the cause for it: the transmission suddenly popped out of gear and into neutral. Trying to get the clutch to engage, I struggled for many seconds and realized I was losing speed and needed to pull over. I looked for the safest place to ditch it, right at the end of the merge. I crossed my fingers that nobody would plow into me. I dialed AAA, and a tow truck pulled up forty minutes later, which was arguably record time for getting a tow in my long experience of broken down cars. The driver jumped out of his truck and took a quick look at my car, then maneuvered his tow and had the car on the bed inside of five minutes.

"You need a ride, I guess?" he asked me.

"Yup," I said, feeling much, much less masculine than him with his bulging biceps and dirty, crumpled ball cap. To add to my emasculation, he began telling me absolutely disgusting stories about his sexual escapades when picking up distressed cars and, apparently, the women who drove them. Slowly he started weaving in some information that he had moderately bad erectile dysfunction. *What the hell am I supposed to say about this? Is this the "man conversation" I always knew I'd have to participate in someday? Was this what Jeffrey had warned me about?*

Worse, in the back of my mind was a nagging question. *There's no way he's going to discover I don't have a penis, right?* This was quickly followed by: *Aren't transmissions expensive to replace?*

Chapter 30

I was in the run-down grocery on O and 7th Street Northwest on my wedding day, because we needed soda pop for the reception that afternoon. I didn't have cold feet so much as I was nervous that everything wouldn't go off without a hitch. I was making myself a little crazy thinking about the day ahead and what could go wrong. I admonished myself in the checkout lane, saying, *just take it all in, enjoy this day. Just smile.* But the people in line didn't seem to care a fig about me, somehow not understanding that I was pulsing out copious quantities of getting married aura.

I put the bags in the car and drove to the Quaker Meeting House where we'd be getting married. We'd gone through the checklist earlier when we'd woken up. Programs, tux and dress, dress shoes, water bottles, overnight bags, all of it packed in the new car.

I met Michael, Susanne, and the soon-to-be in-laws for lunch, forgetting in the midst of the chaos to eat anything. It was nice to have time to visit, and the Contessa was quite the calming influence I'd hoped he'd be.

"Are you ready for your big day?" he asked me, wiping his brow and taking a sip of iced green tea. In the last hour the weather had turned stifling.

"Yes, indeed I am. In fact, I'm ready for the ceremony already. But I also don't want to rush it."

"Are you sad Jeffrey isn't coming today?" I'd gotten the regrets from him only a few days earlier, as expected.

I thought about Michael's question for a moment. "I'm disappointed we're not friends anymore, but I'm thrilled that everyone who's coming is really excited to be there." I hugged him one-armed, leaning over from my chair.

Just then Susanne came over and kissed me on the cheek. Her hair was set in pin curls, and she had the look of a 1940s actress. It looked a bit out of place, since she was still wearing her street clothes. "I'm so happy to be marrying you today, Everett."

If there'd been a mall bench nearby, I would have walked into it.

"Oh, honey," I whispered, "I'm hysterically happy. We're going to have a great day."

We finished lunch and then split up into our respective parties to get dressed in our formalwear. Michael and I met up with Lori and walked to the changing room in the church. We compared our tuxes and told ourselves we looked very dashing, even though none of us wore whale pants. I tried keeping the heat at bay by sticking my face directly in front of the wall AC unit. Later, my mom, sister, and brother showed up, all in the wedding color scheme, which made me a bit teary.

The musicians started playing, and as I looked out at the slate-lined patio, Susanne and her entourage walked up and greeted me. I caught my breath at the sight of her. She had, with the wardrobe change into her dress, transformed from starlet to Greek goddess.

"Are you ready?" I asked.

"Totally," she said, kissing me.

"Hey, that's for later," I said. She responded that I was a silly monkey. In my tux, that wasn't far from the truth.

We stood behind the large white doors that separated us from the congregation on the other side. I took stock of the people who were about to walk down the aisle with us—my mom, Susanne's parents and brother Kurt, several nieces and nephews, Susanne's college friend Jessica, Lori, and Susanne's best friend Jesse. Everyone looked excited and prepared to walk without tripping. I gave Susanne a last pre-marital kiss, since apparently that was okay, karma-wise, and we lined up. With the doors open, we could see everyone, the bright sunlight intensifying all of the colors in the room. Mom held onto my arm as we walked in, and I seated her near where Susanne and I would be standing.

I watched Susanne walk in, her parents on either arm. The ceremony was lovely, a blur that I tried to absorb carefully, like trying to pick out flowers in a field from the vantage of a speeding train. I looked at everyone—our friends and relatives—and thought, *this is our family, all of these people.* I smiled at Susanne, who beamed through the whole event and then grabbed me around the neck and pulled me down for our kiss. I turned to her father, who was performing our ceremony and was speaking about us to everyone gathered in the room.

"And now," he said, "I'd like to introduce my new son and my favorite daughter."

The congregation laughed, as most of them knew that Susanne was his only daughter. Then they clapped, and we walked past them holding hands and grinning.

*   *   *

It was a day of moments: looking at all of the guests in the Quaker church and realizing they were there for us, watching Susanne say her vows to me, walking in to the cocktail reception room (complete with piano player), cutting the cake, taking the first dance.

I talked to one of my best friends from grade school, a smattering of cousins, Susanne's aunts and uncles, my siblings, and so many good friends. Everything went the way I'd hoped it would—I mean, there were a few things here and there, but it was mostly as planned. And then.

I was dancing, and I needed a drink, but I kept getting pulled back to the dance floor. Trying to be Mr. Fun, I went past my limit and felt a snap-pop in my left knee. My leg caved under me like a broken doll's and wouldn't take any of my weight. To everyone on the dance floor, it looked like I was doing a fake move to my knee. In actuality I was trying to stabilize it. Then everyone realized I was really hurt, and the room died.

I motioned to everyone to keep dancing. To make sure they understood this directive, I employed the rather effective phrase, "Keep dancing!" To my relief, they complied. Susanne's Canadian wrestling cousins pulled a chair over for me, and I sat down. Watching everyone have fun, it was nice to have some time to appreciate the party.

Ninety minutes later, I hobbled to the elevator on a pair of crutches a friend had dashed out to buy. I got out to the street, where one of Susanne's friends was waiting with her car. The friend and Susanne's Canadian wrestling cousins came with us to George Washington Hospital, ten blocks away. I must have looked a sight, rolling in wearing a tux and announcing that I'd gotten married that day. The triage nursed looked at me.

"Did you do a split?" Triage nurses must have great senses of humor, I thought.

"I didn't mean to," I answered.

I rolled to the intake cubicle, noting that it was larger than mine at Social Security. It also had cooler toys. The nurse put a cuff on my arm and a pulse monitor on my finger. I looked at the screen and gasped.

"Why does it say 190 over 140?" I asked, clearly afraid.

"That's from the last person," she said, unruffled, "it'll change as soon as I push this button."

"Were they like, having a heart attack?"

"I think so, yes."

Okay, so some things are worse.

Susanne continued to look stunning in her wedding dress and perfect hair. They must have had space in the ER, for they sent us to a private room to await the radiology orderly who would whisk me to the X-ray room. We all sat in the room, talked about how we were doing, blown knee aside, and ate some leftovers from the reception.

"Wow, the lamb kebobs are really good," I said. I hadn't eaten anything all day, I realized. We passed them over to Susanne's Canadian wrestling cousins who had come to the ER with us. They laughed that they finally had a chance to catch up.

After an X-ray, the doctor proclaimed it a dislocation that had relocated itself, but a month later it was properly diagnosed as a torn ACL.

We got dropped off at our fancy hotel, and I crutched to the elevator. The lovely staff had set up a bottle of champagne for us. This I drank with careless abandon, while Susanne enjoyed the in-room hot tub. I couldn't even think about getting inside it, much less subjecting my swollen knee to its heat, so we took up residence, one of us in the tub, and the other on the luxurious bed with seventeen plush pillows.

"Honey," I called out to her, "I love you."

"I love you too," Susanne said, the sound of bubbles roiling around her.

"Thanks for marrying me," I said.

"Thanks for marrying me," she said.

"Sorry I blew out my knee," I said.

"Sorry you blew out your knee," she said, "although I honestly can't say I'm surprised.

More Great Reads from Booktrope Editions

Sweet Song, by Terry Persun (Historical Fiction) This tale of a mixed race man passing as white in post-Civil War America speaks from the heart about where we've come from and who we are.

Don Juan in Hankey, PA by Gale Martin (Contemporary Comic Fantasy) A fabulous mix of seduction, ghosts, humor, music and madness, as a rust-belt opera company stages Mozart's masterpiece. You needn't be an opera lover to enjoy this insightful and hilarious book.

Memoirs Aren't Fairytales by Marni Mann (Contemporary Fiction) a young woman's heartbreaking descent into drug addiction.

Billy Purgatory: I Am the Devil Bird by Jesse James Freeman (Young Adult Fantasy) A sweet talkin', bad ass skateboarder battles devil birds, time zombies and vampires while pursuing Anastasia, the girl of his dreams (and they aren't *all* nightmares). Funny and compelling.

Throwaway by Heather Huffman (Romantic Suspense) A prostitute and a police detective fall in love, proving it's never too late to change your destiny and seek happiness. That is, if she can take care of herself when the mob has a different idea.

Riversong by Tess Hardwick (Contemporary Romance) Sometimes we must face our deepest fears to find hope again. A redemptive story of forgiveness and friendship.

Wolf's Rite, by Terry Persun (Adventure) _A ruthless big city ad exec is captured by mystical Native Americans who send him on a spirit walk, where he discovers love at the edges of sanity.

… and many more!

Sample our books at www.booktrope.com

Learn more about our new approach to publishing at
www.booktropepublishing.com

CPSIA information can be obtained at www.ICGtesting.com
Printed in the USA
LVOW05s2128051213

364127LV00001B/107/P